Praise for *Wings on my*

'Fascinating reading . . . Truly a "living legend ... asts, his amazing life story is quite literally "stranger than fiction". If you only buy one aviation book this year, make sure it's this one' *Today's Pilot*

'The stories beggar belief' *Guardian*

'A fascinating story . . . full of absorbing information and insight' *Times Literary Supplement*

'Copiously illustrated, filled with insights, opinion, anecdotes and observations, this is a gem of a book' *Navy News*

'A fascinating story . . . For anyone interested in aviation, this is required reading' *Aeroplane* magazine

Eric Brown is in the *Guinness Book of Records* for having flown more aircraft types (487) than any other pilot in the world. His record is unlikely ever to be broken. Now 88, Captain Brown CBE, DSC, AFC, KCVSA, became a test pilot during the Second World War and commanded the RAE Aerodynamics Flight at Farnborough. He played a key role in the design of an entire generation of aircraft. No other man alive today can claim to have interviewed the top Nazis, flown their jet aircraft or tested so many experimental machines. Today he remains a consultant for the Royal Navy's latest aircraft carrier design.

WINGS ON MY SLEEVE

CAPTAIN ERIC BROWN
CBE, DSC, AFC, MA, Hon FRAeS, RN

PHOENIX

FRONTISPIECE

'Winkle' Brown makes the world's first ever jet-landing on an aircraft carrier

A PHOENIX PAPERBACK

First published in Great Britain by Arthur Barker
Revised and updated edition published
by Weidenfeld & Nicolson in 2006
This paperback edition published in 2007
by Phoenix, an imprint of Orion Books Ltd, Orion House,
5 Upper St Martin's Lane, London WC2H 9EA

An Hachette UK company

11

A CIP catalogue record for this book
is available from the British Library.

ISBN 978-0-7538-2209-8

Designed by Blacker Design
Printed and bound by CPI Group
(UK) Ltd, Croydon, CR0 4YY

The Orion Publishing Group's policy is to use papers that
are natural, renewable and recyclable products and
made from wood grown in sustainable forests. The logging
and manufacturing processes are expected to conform to
the environmental regulations of the country of origin.

www.orionbooks.co.uk

Contents

To my wife Lynn and son Glenn
who had to endure
so many anxious years

Foreword

By the late Sir Morien Morgan CB MA FRAeS
Head of Aero Flight Section at RAE (1944–48)
President of The Royal Aeronautical Society (1967–68)
Director of RAE Farnborough (1969–78)

THIS IS THE STORY of a truly remarkable pilot. He has been called the greatest test pilot that Britain ever produced, and also the greatest naval aviator of all time. The facts do not belie these claims. He was decorated more times than any other British test pilot and Fleet Air Arm pilot, receiving the MBE, OBE, CBE, DSC, AFC, and King's Commendation for Valuable Service in the Air.

Landing a conventional military aeroplane on an aircraft carrier is generally accepted as the supreme test of piloting skill. Captain Brown has a world record of 2,407 deck landings to his credit, including many world 'firsts'. He has also recorded more catapult launches than any other pilot.

Extensive research indicates that he has flown more types of aircraft than any other pilot in the world, and certainly the most astonishing assortment, ranging through gliders, fighters, bombers, airliners, amphibians, flying boats and helicopters as well as prone and supine position aircraft, and aircraft propelled by virtually every known type of power plant.

He was Chief Naval Test Pilot at RAE Farnborough, and became the first naval officer to command the world renowned Aerodynamics Flight, which was regarded as the top post in experimental research test flying. He lived through the highly dangerous days when attempts to break the sound barrier cost many lives. He himself led a charmed life, not because of luck but by virtue of supreme flying skill, a skill which was recognized by his first Flying Instructor, who classified him as 'Exceptional' – an accolade not lightly given.

To those who have witnessed his superb aerobatic displays or flown as his test observer, there can be no gainsaying that assessment. His operational record only emphasizes the point.

This is the story of a man who has lived more fully in the air than any other pilot of his generation, and at the same time it is an important contribution to the history of the Fleet Air Arm and of test flying in Britain.

Graduation day.

Chapter 1

I WAS BORN IN EDINBURGH of parents from the Scottish Borders, and from my early days was fascinated by the portrait that hung in our lounge of my father in RFC uniform during World War I. He had been a balloon observer, spotting beyond enemy lines and also being a prime target for German fighter aircraft. Although it was also a high-risk game being a pilot in the RFC, he apparently felt that this would be his preferred option and so he found himself posted to flying training, which he barely completed before the Armistice was signed. I was born in January 1919, so was a product of the RFC, and somehow I felt flying was in my blood.

As a schoolboy I won a scholarship from my local primary school to Edinburgh's historic Royal High School, with its classical Greek temple buildings set in the heart of the Scottish capital. There I had a most happy schooling with academic honours (runner-up to Dux of School) and sporting successes in rugby (1st XV) and gymnastics (school champion).

About half-way through my school life my mother died, and I moved with my father to the Borders, so that I now had to commute by train to school every day. In 1936 my father took me to the Olympic Games in Berlin, and as an ex-RFC pilot he was invited to welcoming events by former World War I German pilots now serving in the newly-resurfaced Luftwaffe. There I met Ernst Udet, the top scoring fighter ace after Richthofen, and also the aviatrix Hanna Reitsch, who was giving a sailplane aerobatic display at a venue close to the Olympic stadium. These two very different characters were to have a considerable impact on my life. Udet was a complete extrovert, who had become a world-famous stunt pilot after World War I, and had been persuaded, rather against his will, by Goering to join the new Luftwaffe as Colonel in charge of the Technical Department of the Air Ministry. Hanna Reitsch, on the other hand, was the top female sailplane pilot in the world, an intense, strong-minded woman, filled with ambition and determination. Both were mad keen aviators, courageous and skilful, and were to play key roles in the aviation history of Hitler's Third Reich.

Bücker Jungmann trainers which were standard in the pre-World War II Luftwaffe. It was a flight in a Jungmann as a young schoolboy, with Colonel Ernst Udet, a World War I ace and famous aerobatic pilot, in Berlin that determined the author to become a fighter pilot.

Udet seemed impressed by my youthful enthusiasm for aviation and offered to take me for a flight at Halle, south of Berlin. There we drove up to a Bücker Jungmann two-seat trainer, where he put me in the front cockpit and took particular care to see I was securely strapped in – the reason for this solicitude becoming obvious to me later. It was a glorious day and Udet proceeded to put this jaunty little trainer through its aerobatic paces, and at the same time checking in his broken English that my stomach and nerves were still in good shape. After about half an hour we rejoined the airfield circuit, and on the final approach he suddenly rolled the Jungmann on to its back and we glided inverted to within what I estimated was my approaching demise – but was actually some 50ft up – when he rolled it right way up and then held off to land. I was speechless but he roared with laughter, hit me smartly between the shoulder blades with a great yell of '*Hals und Beinbruch*', the German fighter-pilots' greeting. From that moment I was unswervingly dedicated to achieving that goal.

From the Royal High School I progressed to Edinburgh University in 1937 to read for an honours degree in modern languages, with German as my primary subject. Also in 1937 I joined the University Air Unit, which was the beginning of the University Air Squadron, and flew from Turnhouse airfield, under the auspices of 603 Royal Auxiliary Air Force Squadron, whose CO was Squadron Leader 'Count' Ernie Stevens, a great friend of my father.

About this time the Foreign Office was approaching modern languages students to see if they were interested in a career in the Diplomatic Corps, and I indicated my interest at that stage. As a result such students were to be sent abroad in the penultimate year of their four-year degree course as exchange student teachers for six months in

Germany and six in France. I was allocated Salem internat (boarding school) on Lake Constance and the Lycée at Metz in northern France.

In 1938 I took the opportunity to visit Berlin again for a few days in February and called on Udet, by then a Major-General. He greeted me warmly and as a special treat took me to the Deutschlandhalle where Hanna Reitsch was to give a helicopter flying demonstration with the Fw 61. It was a weird contraption which looked like an aeroplane but instead of wings had two rotors on outriggers. All had gone well at rehearsal, but on the night in a packed stadium the helicopter could barely rise off the ground. This perplexing situation was saved when some bright spark realised that the helicopter's normally aspirated engine was being starved of fresh air by the mass breathing of the audience. The remedy was to open the large hangar-type doors leading to the arena, and this allowed Hanna to lift the helicopter to near roof-height. That evening Hanna and some of Udet's Luftwaffe friends joined us in a celebration at his apartment. Part of the celebration was Udet's favourite party game, which involved having a dartboard-like target on one wall and a mirror

Pilot Officer Eric Brown in RAF uniform after obtaining his wings in the Edinburgh University Air Squadron.

Hanna Reitsch demonstrates the weird Fw 61 helicopter at the 1938 International Automobile Exhibition inside the stadium of the Deutschlandhalle, Berlin.

on the opposite one. Each participant then faced the mirror and with a small calibre pistol shot over his shoulder at the target. Heady stuff but quite crazy and typical of the mood pervading Nazi Berlin.

While at Salem, in the summer of 1939, I had my open MG Magnette car with me and spent as much time as possible exploring the surrounding countryside. One of my favourite outings was to the popular city of Munich, and there I was staying in a small inn during that fateful first weekend of September 1939.

On that September Sunday morning I was asleep when there was a bang at the door. I stumbled over and opened it and saw two SS men standing there.

There was a woman interpreter with them. She said, 'Mr Eric Brown?'

'Yes …'

'Our countries are at war.'

I was shaken. I had been living in Germany for some months and never once felt any real likelihood of war.

'You will come with us.' I got some things together and followed them out.

A car was waiting and I was ushered into it. One of the SS men took my own MG and followed us to the SS barracks.

There I was interrogated for three days, though no threat of violence was ever made. When I was not being questioned I played chess or talked politics with the guards.

They knew everything about me, that I was twenty, that I had been teaching in Germany on an exchange scheme, that I was fresh from Edinburgh University, where I had learned to fly with a group of enthusiastic students, that I was sightseeing in Munich for the week-end.

At last I was pushed abruptly into another car and driven off, thinking that I was bound for a Gestapo cell or a firing squad, though I was puzzled to see that my MG was following along behind. To my astonishment we drove straight to the Swiss frontier. We got out and my guard said, 'There you are. You are free to go'.

I couldn't believe it. I thought that if I started to walk I would get a bullet in the back.

He said 'You can take your car with you'.

I gaped. 'Why are you letting me take that?'

'Because we have no spares.'

I got in and drove away. There was no bullet in the back. A few hours later I was racing across France for the Channel ports, afraid that the war would be over before I could get into uniform.

The RAF was not in quite the same state of flap. When I reported back to the RAFVR there was no rush for my services. But I was told that there was a very urgent demand for pilots by the Fleet Air Arm, the flying branch of the Navy.

I had no connexions whatsoever with the Navy. But I suddenly remembered a lecture at school by an Old Boy who had been a pilot in the Fleet Air Arm, flying from aircraft carriers at sea, and how exciting he had made it sound. And if it would get me into the air right away …

I took about five minutes to make up my mind. I said 'I'll join'.

I had to go to the multi-services recruiting centre at Edinburgh. I filled in some forms and waited in a long queue.

'So you can already fly?'

'Yes.' Now we were getting somewhere. 'I've got a hundred and twenty hours. I flew Gauntlets.'

'Well, you'll have to start all over again with the Navy.'

I didn't believe it. They wanted pilots badly, didn't they? When I got through to the real flying types they'd find the right niche for me.

But at HMS *St Vincent* at Gosport they confirmed that I would be

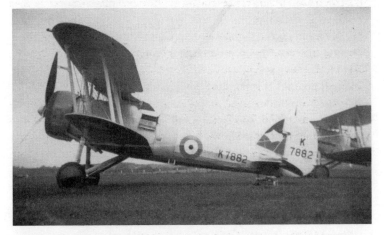

A Gloster Gauntlet. The author flew Gauntlets with the Royal Auxiliary Air Force and felt for sheer enjoyment the Gauntlet had the edge on other vintage biplanes.

Training to be a fighter pilot on a single-wing Miles Magister in Belfast.

starting the whole thing from scratch. And even before that we had to be turned into sailors. We spent a month learning naval routine before we were graded into potential fighter or torpedo-bomber pilots. We were asked our preference and given co-ordination tests. The class was a wide cross-section. The older and steadier ones went for bombers, the suicidal types like me for fighters.

It turned out to be a clever move, because we fighters went to Belfast to train, and while I was there I met my future wife. We began on Miles Magisters, and we single-wing men immediately assumed a definite air of superiority over the torpedo bombers who were puttering about in Tiger Moths down at Castle Bromwich near Birmingham. I found myself picking it up quickly and I was given extra time in advanced aerobatics while those who had not had my previous experience caught up. I came out of the course with good grades and top of the ground school. I had already found out that it was not just the actual piloting that interested me, but what went on under the bonnet as well.

It was June 1940, now. Norway was draining away air crews. The shortage in the Fleet Air Arm was desperate. We were rushed to Netheravon for advanced training.

Here we had a sobering shock. While one of our class was meandering along in a Hawker Hart a Messerschmitt Me 110 came out of the sun and ranged up alongside him. The German rear gunner swung his gun, took casual aim, and shot the Hart down in flames for us all to see. It was a terrible warning. A fighter pilot has to have a swivel neck.

Norway fell, the blitz on Europe began. The Italians declared war. The Navy sent us to Greenwich for a month to become gentlemen. We spent every night in the air-raid shelters.

We left at the end of August and I joined the new naval fighter training station at Yeovilton in Somerset on the day it opened, when it was nothing but three runways in an ocean of mud. Anyone who went off the runway went on to his nose, and there were plenty who did that. I had my first accident there. Every time we wanted to fly workmen had to be cleared off the unfinished runways. When I went off I hit a pile of rubble one of them had dumped in his haste and had to do a belly landing when I came down, with a bent undercarriage.

The Battle of Britain started and we pupils flying Gloster Gladiators always went up armed in case we met any Germans. The Gladiator was the last of the biplane fighters, an outmoded but still handy little fabric-covered plane. She had only four .303 machine guns and a top speed of about 250 miles an hour, but great things had been done with her in Norway and the Mediterranean and she could very often manoeuvre her way out of trouble.

Two of us were up in Gladiators cruising over Somerset when we spotted two Heinkel IIIs. We came up on them from behind. I was just flipping my gun button getting ready to fire when they both blew up. We were blinded by the explosion. The Gladiators bucked wildly in the blast and bits of debris rained at us like bullets. One of the Heinkels had caught an ack-ack shell in his bomb load. Two stunned pupils returned to base and for the first time poked their fingers through torn fabric. Our German instructors made our graduation as naval fighter pilots real.

I was sent to join 802 Squadron at Donibristle in Fife. No sooner had I arrived than the squadron got an SOS from 810 Squadron in the Orkneys asking for urgent replacements to make up their terrible losses. I was one of the three pilots loaned to the squadron. I did one operation with them, a raid in Skua dive bombers on oil tanks in Norway. It was a long, long haul across the sea on weak mixture at very slow speed, a flurry of blurred action over the target, and another anxious groping for home. We should have been flying from a carrier, but *Glorious* and *Courageous* had gone by then, and there were none to spare.

I went back to Donibristle and we waited for our aircraft to arrive. There was great excitement in the air, because we were going to be among the first pilots in the Fleet Air Arm to receive something very special. We were going to get some good aircraft.

Never in its history had the air branch of the Navy enjoyed planes of the quality given to the RAF. Since the war began we had been making do with the old Gladiators and the bumbling Rocs, when the RAF had Hurricanes and Spitfires. We had had to fight Me 109s and Reggianis with our old weapons, and we had lost far too many good men. But now America was sending Britain the sinews of war in Lend-Lease agreement, and we in 802 were licking our lips in anticipation of a new fighter built especially for high-performance carrier flying by the excellent firm of Grumman. She was called the Wildcat in America and the Martlet in Britain. She was a monoplane, she was fast, and she had big .5 machine guns. We just couldn't wait.

The first ones arrived and the CO, Lieutenant Commander John Wintour, rushed off to collect the first one to be assembled. We were all sitting in the squadron office, not an aeroplane amongst us, when we heard a loud whining scream in the air. The whine turned into a thunderclap overhead. We rushed to the window and saw the splendid machine screeching uphill. She was blunt-nosed, square-tipped, and looked like an angry bee.

When we came to try her for ourselves she turned out to be a tough, fiery, beautiful little aeroplane. There was a very fierce swing on take-off and landing which needed some handling. And the machines we got had been built for other European countries. Mine had a French accent and her oil pressure was in kilos. Then they were modified and given higher tail wheels, which brought the rudder into the slipstream and cured the swing.

Under John Wintour we began to get used to them and approach the very high standard he set us. The CO, tall, handsome, laconic, was a splendid leader and teacher. He kept hard discipline, he supervised each of us personally in the air until we could do a fair imitation of his own immaculate flying. With most of us raw RNVRs, with a field as small as Donibristle, and with our fierce mounts, this was quite an achievement.

We were doing well when tragedy hit us. Three of our pilots went off in the dead of winter to Abbotsinch to collect more Martlets freshly assembled there. On their way back with them they ran into a howling snowstorm. One got through. Another, with one of our most experienced flight leaders, crashed into the top of Ben Lomond. The other ditched in Loch Lomond. We had lost one pilot and two machines. Both were irreplaceable at this point. So precious were the Martlets that this loss forced us to cut the squadron down from twelve to ten. Then I had to put mine down in Burnt Island reservoir with a dead engine as a result of a massive oil leak. But the Martlet, bred to the sea, had special immersion switches which tripped in the water and operated flotation bags in the wings. My switches worked and we salvaged the plane.

Our newly grown skill was severely tested when Winston Churchill came up to see us. The CO worked up a special display for him, and I of course chose the occasion to put my Martlet into the Firth of Forth.

My party piece was to do a roll on take-off. It started well. I took off towards the sea, furiously cranked up the undercarriage, rolled, got over on my back, and there was a tremendous, frightening bang and a flash. The airscrew stopped dead. I pushed the stick hard forward and the Martlet flopped on her back into the sea. But again the flotation bags worked, swelling up so that my cockpit was clear of the water. I broke my nose on the gunsight and had a nasty crack on the arm, but I was able to swim clear. I thought it was generous of Mr Churchill to single the CO out in the mess later on and send me his condolences.

We naturally imagined that he had come to have a look at us because we were only the second Martlet squadron to form up. We could not know that we had been chosen to put one of his own very special brainwaves into action, and that we were to make history doing it.

The Martlets we were equipped with had only a lap strap and no shoulder straps as safety harness, so each pilot was instructed to fly his aircraft to Croydon for the modification to full safety harness to be fitted.

I left Donibristle on 14th May and headed south, but ran into very bad weather in Lincolnshire and was lucky to scrape into the RAF station at Cranwell. For my overnight stay I was roomed with a Flight Lieutenant Geoffrey Bone. Since there seemed to be an unusual number of civilians on the Station I asked him what was going on, but he was very evasive, and talked me into accompanying him to the Station cinema, probably to avoid further questioning.

Next day there was still bad weather and I asked the Control Tower if I could do a weather test, and reported the cloud base was below 500ft with poor visibility. I noticed as I made a landing circuit that there was considerable activity round one particular hangar, which was roped off, but I could not see what was inside.

In the late afternoon the Control Tower asked me if I would do another weather test, and this showed a slight improvement with some sign of the cloud lifting and visibility slowly improving. At about 7pm I noticed the closed hangar's doors opening and a small propellerless aeroplane with a tricycle undercarriage being pushed out. About half an hour later this weird machine started up its engine and began taxiing out to the runway, propelled by I knew not what. It took off to a screaming note of some power source unknown to me, climbed away smoothly and then seventeen minutes later returned to land. Up to that point there was nothing to indicate that this was the historic occasion of the first flight of Britain's first jet aircraft, the Gloster E.28/39, flown by Gloster Chief Test Pilot P. E. G. Sayer. My room mate, Geoffrey Bone, had been the flight engine installation engineer, but had kept this secret intact from me. Little was I to know that three years later I was to fly the E.28/39 at RAE Farnborough and that Geoffrey and I were to become firm friends.

Chapter 2

W<small>E FIRST LEARNED</small> that the Admiralty had something unusual in store for us when three of our own pilots were told off to train as batsmen[1] for our first operation. Where we were going we were not going to be able to have any fully professional ones. Nobody wanted the job, but eventually three sub-lieutenants, Patterson, Hutchison and Morris, were selected and told to get on with it.

Then we were sent to Arbroath to land into a set of arrester wires. These were only normally used to taxi into, but we apparently were going to have to miss out the usual breaking-in on a training carrier. Curiouser and curiouser. Whatever it was, it looked like something urgent.

Then came the big news. The CO said, 'You're going to a ship called the *Empire Audacity*'. We stared at him. Those who had been on carriers before racked their brains. 'What *is* she, sir?'

'She's called an *auxiliary carrier*. And now you're as wise as I am.'

It was a new one on all of us. The CO went away to be briefed on her. When he came back he called us all together right away.

'Well, I know where we're going now. This job is going to be a hard one. We're going to a carrier, but she's different from any other that ever sailed before. Those of you who have deck-landed before are in for a rude shock. Those who have never deck-landed won't know any better. It isn't going to be easy for anybody.

'I daresay you know that we're desperately short of carriers. We're so short that the few we do have must be kept with the fleet, and there aren't any left for convoy escort. As a result Focke-Wulf Kuriers have been operating from Bordeaux-Merignac against our convoys, bombing and spotting for U-boats, at ranges well outside the reach of Coastal Command and having things practically all their own way. The fighter catapult ships are one answer thought up by the PM. The escort carrier is an improvement on it – or so we hope – from the same stable. Your new ship will be the first of these to go into action. You will carry a big responsibility.

1. 'batsmen' are Deck Landing Control Officers who guide pilots in their landing approach by means of signals with two paddles (bats) to give attitude and height information.

'The ship herself used to be, ironically, a German merchantman, a banana boat. She was captured in February last year off St Domingo by the cruiser *Dunedin* and the Canadian destroyer *Assiniboine* and towed to Jamaica. Her arrival in the UK more or less coincided with the birth of this new idea, which was to cut down a merchant ship and build up a flight deck on her so she could operate a few fighters and go out as a convoy escort. As the *Hannover* – that was her German name – had already been damaged when her crew tried to set fire to her and would have to be repaired anyway, the Admiralty thought that as she was suitable otherwise she would be just the thing. So they cut her down by a couple of decks and stuck a flight deck on top of her.'

He moved to the blackboard and started to sketch with the chalk. 'It's not a very big flight deck. In fact it's only four hundred and twenty feet long and sixty in beam ...'

It was a shock, particularly for those of the squadron who had been in the *Ark Royal*. She had a flight deck just about twice as long.

'... She'll carry six Martlets. When they're all ranged aft, the first one will have about three hundred feet of deck for take-off ... For landing there are only two arrester wires. There's a barrier up for'ard, and just aft of it – about *here* – there's another wire. That's what I call the For-Christ's-Sake wire. If you miss the main two this one'll bring you up if you catch it – though you'll probably break the aircraft and quite likely your neck as well ... and there's just one more thing. There's no hangar. The aircraft will have to be parked out on the flight deck all the time. All maintenance and everything else will have to be done there.'

He finished his nonchalant speech and watched our reaction with a cynical smile. We sat speechless and aghast.

'There is one relieving feature. You will have the most wonderful quarters any warship ever had. These banana boats used to carry about a dozen passengers in luxurious accommodation. It'll be yours now.'

We tried to cheer ourselves up with that chill, small ray of comfort. Shortly after this we got a message from the newly appointed Captain of the *Empire Audacity*, an old Swordfish pilot, Commander D. W. McKendrick, who had had a big share in developing the idea of the escort carrier after Mr Churchill had produced the original inspiration, to say that the ship was going out on trials in the Western approaches and that all pilots were recommended to come out and have a good look at her.

We picked her up and circled her at about 300 feet above the ship. My main reaction, apart from her terrifying smallness, was her unfinished, naked look. Most of the big fleet carriers had the big island to starboard on the flight deck. It was a homing beacon, a lighthouse, a promise of security in the treacherous wet expanse of bare, heaving deck and cold grey sea. But the *Empire Audacity*, with a displacement of only 5,537 tons did not have an island, only two little steel matchboxes level with the flight deck, one on either side, about a quarter of the way aft from the bows. Landing on this narrow strip of runway would be like perching on a cliff ledge in a blizzard.

I thought along these lines the night before we were due to fly on board for the first time. We were at Campbeltown on the Clyde, a desolate, cheerless place to start with. The morrow was going to be a big experience in our lives. The mess was very quiet that night, and even the normal amount of drinking, never heavy, shrank to practically nothing. One by one, we all went off quietly to an early bed. I simply did not know what to expect. The whole thing was something on paper to me. I had never even set foot on a flight deck before. I weighed up what I would do if I went over the side, trying to comfort myself with the thought that I had twice been in the water in a Martlet, and knew that it floated.

We were to do six deck landings in all. Each flight of two would go out in turn, the flight leader and his wingman taking it in turns to make three landings apiece, before returning to base to refuel for the second batch.

The CO went off first alone. When he had made his three landings he came back to give us some tips and moral encouragement before he went back to watch his own number two do his landings.

He said, 'Don't worry about there being only two wires in place of the

HMS *Audacity*, Britain's first escort carrier. A terrifyingly short flight deck had been built up on this captured German banana boat and she carried six Martlets.

15

usual six. You only had two at Arbroath after all and none of you missed them. There's just one other thing. The barrier isn't rigged yet. So if you miss the wires you can open up and barge round again'.

It was a mild day towards the end of autumn. My flight leader 'Sheepy' Lamb and I were the third pair to go off. First we had to do a circuit and dummy deck landing on the airfield. I didn't want to bother about that. I was impatient. I wanted to get out there and get it over with.

It took about a quarter of an hour to pick up the ship, which was steaming up and down south of Arran. She was heading into wind all ready to receive us, affirmative and carrier flags flying. She looked like a tiny bathtub toy as she moved slowly through the solid sea, pushing her arrow of white ahead of her.

I had to circle the ship and watch Sheepy make the first approach. Worse than ever I wanted to get down and make my pass at the deck.

I saw Sheepy turn and head for the stern. He had been in the *Ark Royal*. It must have looked fearfully small to him just then. From my aery view he seemed to float in with incredible slowness, feather-light. There was no impression of his being snatched out of the air, which is what it seems like at deck level. I saw him touch, catch the second wire, and roll to a stop. The flight-deck crew pushed him back, unhooked him, he was ranged aft, and went off down the deck. It was my turn.

I always have the same experience when I do any kind of test with an aeroplane. Whatever I feel beforehand, I suddenly get filled with the calm of intense concentration. When I came to make my approach to the *Empire Audacity*'s deck that day, when I was committed, I certainly was not scared any more, though I have learned to be a lot more patient since then.

We could come in any way we chose. Some had decided to make an exploratory pass first without putting their hook down. They would watch the batsman's directions, take a wave-off, and come in again, either for their landing or for another wave-off or any number of wave-offs if they wanted. But I could not wait. I lowered my wheels and hook right away, flew round until I was between three and four hundred feet dead astern of the ship, and came straight in.

I throttled back. When we were doing seventy knots – the Martlet's deck-landing airspeed – I held her in a constant rate of descent towards the looming deck. There was Pat Patterson guiding me in with the bats, a familiar, reassuring figure. I was over the roundown. He gave me the cut. I pulled back the throttle lever. There was a bump. I was down. I had caught the first wire.

Elation surged through me. Pat jumped up on the wing. He shouted at me:

'That wasn't bad. A bit off the centre line.'

I was trundled back till my tail was right over the roundown, and the test of take-off down that tiny deck faced me. I opened up against the brakes. The signal flag fell. I let the brakes go. We surged down the deck at full power. Wheels still firmly on the deck, we were airborne over the bows without losing an inch in height.

They say that your first landing is either your best or your worst. I was lucky with mine. After that it seemed easy. As I went through my remaining six training approaches, I became more and more able to concentrate on the finer details of what I was doing, and I found myself striving to study and perfect the technique of it, to do it with some finesse. I felt the potential artistry of it.

Now we were carrier-borne. The *Empire Audacity* was certainly a most extraordinary ship, quite unlike any other warship ever built. The 'bridge' was simply a little metal tray stuck on the ship's side level with the flight deck on the starboard side about a quarter of the way back from the bows. Here the Captain, who doubled as Commander (Air), directed all take-offs and landings by direct hand signals to the pilot, acting as batsman. There was a similar position on the port side, where the Captain would sometimes station one of the pilots not on duty.

The deck below the flight deck we called the promenade deck. On this deck aft were the original passenger state rooms, lounge, and dining rooms. The latter two became the ante-room and wardroom respectively. They were adjacent and athwartships, about halfway along the ship's length. The wardroom sat about thirty-two round two tables running fore and aft. The ante-room had the inevitable small bar.

Aft of the wardroom were the state rooms, two single and six double. At the insistence of the Captain the pilots occupied these state rooms, each flight section of two being in a double room, while the CO and first lieutenant had the single rooms. Our rooms had their original furnishings, with two single beds, adjoining bathroom, and square ports, which we RNVRs shocked the RN contingent by deliberately referring to as windows. The Fighter Direction Officer and the CO's wingman, David

17

Hutchison, were in one of the remaining doubles, and two engineers in the other.

Round the state rooms ran a promenade walk, and aft of this, one deck down, was our single four-inch gun, right astern.

On the same level as the state rooms, but for'ard next to the bridge, were the business quarters. Two steps took you down from the bridge into a narrow corridor, about eight paces brought you to the crew ready room, opening off it to the left. In the crew room there was an inter-connecting door to the fighter control room, which was practically filled with its plotting table and radar screen. It was a handy arrangement, and promised swift liaison in action.

As a ship's company we were a strange assortment. To begin with, we were half Royal Navy, half Merchant Service. All the squadron person-nel were of course RN as well as the deck officers and key technicians. Most of the seamen and all the engine-room staff were Merchant Navy men. It threatened to be an impossible mixture, oil and water, for Commander McKendrick to make into a team.

What made it worse for him was the greenness of most of his pilots. I was one of those who had very little acquaintance with the sea at all, let alone of carriers. But we had a good stiffening of experienced hands. There was the CO. He was a brilliant aerobatic pilot, and he was deter-mined to shape us all in the same mould. In fact he was ruthless in keep-ing us at peak efficiency, driving us all the time to produce our best. If he caught you lounging in one of the two very popular armchairs in the tiny ready room and you were reading something other than a run-down on enemy aircraft or similar page of shop, you suffered his wrath and wished that the deck would open up and swallow you. He was forever quizzing us on the enemy machines we were likely to meet, and I got caught so many times that I prepared a special dossier on the Focke-Wulf Kurier and got it all off by heart. He was a Dartmouth man and had been a regular navy lieutenant, but had retired to go into civil aviation as an instructor. He had far more of a worldly air than most service-bound RN professionals and was considerably older than most of us. He dominated us completely.

Several of the others were regulars too. There were John Carden and Jimmy Sleigh, our two flight leaders. John was ex-Dartmouth, and had served in cruisers. Jimmy was an ex-Merchant Navy officer turned RN. A

South African, he was the only married officer in the squadron, apart from the CO, and had joined us after recuperating from a terrifying air crash in which he had fractured his skull. Hutch, a veteran of the Battle of Britain, always wore the most dissipated expression possible. Sheepy Lamb, my flight leader, was a Colonial Scot educated in Edinburgh, and like so many colonials had a particularly cheerful outlook on life. His round face and rotund figure just radiated good spirits, and he was never seen in angry mood. Sheepy was a brilliant air tactician, who had seen action operating Gladiators from the Orkneys and from the *Glorious*. Norris 'Pat' Patterson, another South African, was even taller than the CO, and his main interest in life seemed to be classical music. I clashed with him there, being a swing fan. He had the only gramophone in the squadron, and used to put up with a lot of abuse from me in his amiable way. He would put on my wild music and laugh at my jitterbugging antics.

At these times my very good friend Graham Fletcher, another VR like myself, was always required to sing 'Flat Foot Floogie', which was a show stopper because of his terrible stammer. Fletch was as English as the hop, with his fair hair, clean-cut face, and whooping horse laugh. He had come straight from St Paul's School into the Service, having spent his schoolboy savings in learning to fly. His enthusiasm for the air was refreshing.

Of the other VRs, Bertie Williams had been an office clerk in Manchester, and had given up his job at once on the outbreak of war to fly; Phil Morris was a tall, handsome Cambridge undergraduate, who acted the playboy but was a fine natural pilot, with a love of good living and a strange flair for statistics; George was an Aberdonian who had been studying for the ministry before war came, and was a fine golfer in the best Scots traditions.

Besides being broken up into two flights, the squadron was further subdivided into sections for combat purposes, each section being named after a colour. The CO and Hutch made up Blue Section, Sheepy and I – Red Section, John and Phil – Green Section, Jimmy and Bertie – Yellow Section, Pat and Fletch – Black Section, with George as spare pilot.

We were an odd assortment, but we worked and played in perfect harmony. The CO worked on us as if we were his life's mission. He knew we were boys with very little time in which to learn a man's job. When we joined convoy OG 74 on 13th September 1941, bound for Gibraltar,

Two of the flight-deck crew and four 802 Squadron pilots – Sheepy, Fletch, Bertie and Pat (in cockpit).

In the cockpit of an 802 Squadron Grumman Wildcat, renamed the Martlet in Britain.

Leading Fletch and Bertie into bad habits.

we were a good unit, though we were not fielding the full team. Yellow Section had been detached to *Argus* to act as fighter protection with two Martlets when she delivered a load of Hurricanes to the Russians, and George had dropped out after a couple of deck-landing accidents during our work-up.

Just before *Empire Audacity* sailed on its first operation, the Admiralty changed the name of this tiny escort carrier to the full-blown HMS *Audacity*.

Chapter 3

W E LEFT THE CLYDE EARLY IN SEPTEMBER, taking badly needed ammunition to Gibraltar, to be sent on to besieged Malta and the 9th Army.

On our first day out a lame duck slowed the whole convoy down to her own bumbling seven knots. The offender was an ancient collier with a huge EIRE in white letters along her rusty side. The ship was built in the eighteen-nineties, the skipper was seventy-four. On the sixth day out she suddenly foundered from sheer old age, after being nudged by a Dutch tug. With her crew safe, we gave her three hearty cheers of relief as she settled. Our speed was immediately increased to ten knots.

On that first grey, windy dawn we started flying, beginning our regular routine. We normally flew patrols in section pairs. At dawn the first pair of the day took off. Once airborne the pair split up, one flying clockwise, the other anti-clockwise round the convoy, on the lookout for U-boats or Focke-Wulfs, maintaining a height of 1,000 feet at visibility distance from the ships. We orbited in radio silence, which could only be broken if a plane sighted the enemy or the carrier had an urgent signal for us. The first patrols were lonely and dull. We sat up there like small planets in space, getting pins and needles in the bottom.

While the first pair was up a second two pilots sat in their cockpits below on the deck, at 'Immediate Readiness'. A third pair was at 'Standby' in the ready room, and had to man their machines immediately the alarm sounded. They either took off with the 'Immediate Readiness' section or remained in their cockpits as the new 'Immediate Readiness' section, according to the needs of the moment. The fourth pair was at five minutes notice, or 'Available'. After the dawn patrol landed from its one hour flight, the two pilots went to 'Stand Down', which meant that they could get their heads down. All the other three sections stayed at their respective states of readiness for another hour, and thereafter the four sections rotated on an hourly cycle. Later, when we had five sections, one of them was 'Released' every twenty-four hours.

One hour before dusk another anti-submarine patrol was flown, either by the 'Released' or 'Stand Down' pair. The dawn and dusk patrols were the most basically difficult ones of the day. Briefing for these always took at least half an hour, and both the Captain and the Navigating Officer were always present.

The latter would give us a situation report after the events of the previous twelve hours, including an account of any actions, losses, stragglers, enemy sightings, or asdic contacts, and finish by showing us the present disposition of the convoy and escorts. The meteorological rating – we were not big enough to rate an officer – gave a weather report, the Fighter Direction Officer the serviceability state of the radio and radar, allocate aircraft call signs and tell us the Very signal code colours for the period – pilots collected the cartridges from the duty armourer of the squadron as they manned their aircraft.

The Squadron CO or Duty Flight Leader reported to the Captain the serviceability state of the aircraft. Then the Captain took over for his final instructions to the pilots – what time he intended to turn into wind for take-off, the direction and height to be patrolled, with the inevitable reminder to keep radio silence except in emergency, and details of any especially dangerous sector to be reconnoitred or stragglers to be rounded up.

Finally the navigator gave us the ship's position at the estimated time of take-off and the subsequent mean line of advance of the convoy and its speed, which we had to plot on our small mercator charts. He also gave us the direction of, and distance from, the nearest friendly territory, but it was usually, of course, well out of range of our Martlets. The Captain always ended the briefing by saying to his pilots, 'Good luck and God bless you'.

For landing-on, any machines left on the deck had always to be taxied right for'ard down the deck, then the barrier and arrester wires raised into position, as there was no hangar. This was infuriating and time wasting. There seemed to be a lesson to be learned there for future escort carriers, if there were to be any.

This was our most vulnerable moment. The carrier had to leave the convoy to steam into wind, with no possibility of flying off any other planes for protection for at least ten minutes. With frantic practice and the use of every willing hand who happened to be on deck at the time we managed to cut this down to eight minutes. It still seemed like eight hours.

With all the constant patrol activity cluttering up the flight deck and nowhere else to do it, all maintenance had to be done in the hours of darkness after the dusk patrol had landed.

You can imagine the bare, open deck, rolling steadily through the darkness. Around us loom dimly our nearest neighbours in three great lines of ships, of which we are in the centre of the middle line, four ships ahead, four astern. You watch with some uneasiness the tell-tale bright phosphorescence of their bow waves.

Aft you can just make out the aircraft, hunched silent, like wing-folded gulls asleep. What you cannot see are the mechanics crouched all over them, at engines, gun ports, wheel wells, radio compartments, in cockpits. They are working with stumbling speed and urgency to bring the machines to readiness for the oncoming day, the first pale streaks of which are already lighting the eastern horizon.

All the light they are allowed to see by comes from little pocket torches hooded by bits of blue paper. These they can only show inside a compartment in the plane or shielded by a coat or by the body. The duty officer walks round to make sure of the total blackout. They are impossible conditions. But the work is done and there are never any mistakes. We owe our lives to these men.

We could hardly expect to reach Gibraltar without trouble. It came first on the 15th, when Sheepy Lamb and I were in the air.

Sheepy saw it first, the swirl of foam, but not before the U-boat had seen us. She was submerging fast.

He shouted, calling the ship, 'Tally-ho! U-boat submerging on the starboard side!'

We swung towards her. The foam was subsiding. We dived at her. We were fifty yards apart, the U-boat dead ahead of me. But she had got right under now, except for the tip of her periscope. Her shape was quite clear under the surface.

I fired 400 rounds at her. My little bullets would not dent her pressure hull, but at least we had made a sighting, we knew now that U-boats were watching us. We could prepare with certainty for attack.

The next night two torpedoes were fired at the starboard wing escort and missed. Then we were treated to a firework display as the escorts groped for the U-boat.

Again on the evening of the 20th my dusk patrol was enlivened by

The formidable Focke-Wulf Kurier; its defensive capabilities were to be treated with the greatest of respect. As Squadron Armament Officer, Eric Brown briefed pilots to attack from head on, aiming at the most vulnerable items – the pilots.

sighting another U-boat in the act of diving some twelve miles west of *Audacity*. My report put the convoy into a series of evading turns.

The alarm went shortly after dark. When we got up on deck the first U-boat victim had already gone. We saw a great flash of flame and fire slightly abaft our beam, another well astern on the port side. Two ships were lost.

We had with us the rescue ship *Walmar Castle*. Relying on her very obvious red cross identification she remained on the scene of the sinkings with the rescue tug *Thames* to pick up and care for survivors. It was a clear morning when a Focke-Wulf attacked her, straddling her with a stick of bombs and setting her on fire.

The Focke-Wulf had been sighted, we had been alerted. The two Martlets sent to intercept her arrived just after she had dropped her last bomb on *Walmar Castle*. Pat and Fletch caught her as she was heading for her next victim, the *Thames*.

25

Pat came in from the quarter raking the Kurier all the way as he slid into the astern position. He had just broken away to avoid colliding with her when Fletch let blast with a full deflection shot from dead abeam. Only thirty-five rounds were fired from each of his four guns, but the Kurier's entire tail unit fell off. The only thing picked up from her was a pair of flying overalls.

The *Walmar Castle* was ablaze everywhere. Some who had been spared drowning the night before were now to die of fire.

Pat and Fletch returned to *Audacity* with our first scalp. The squadron mechanics showed their appreciation by producing tots of grog for the pilots. This mysterious but unfailing source of liquor, which sailors always seem to have, was often to be tapped again in the *Audacity*.

At noon we were off once more. A Junkers 88 bombed *Thames* and set her on fire. Our fighters spotted the 88 just as she was going for a second ship, a straggler which *Thames* had been rounding up. The Martlets cut off the bomber's path as she was running in on her helpless target, but she turned smartly into the nearest cloud cover just before they could nail her.

This attack happened 900 miles due west of Brest, at the very limit of the Junkers 88's range. The Germans were obviously going all out to get us. They would be back.

That night three more ships in OG 74 were torpedoed. Next morning the Martlets were out again like sheep dogs searching to round up the stragglers – the usual aftermath of a night U-boat attack on a convoy.

In the afternoon *Audacity* embarked eighty-six survivors, Royal Navy and Merchant Navy officers and men, and five Army gunners from lost ships. Our two RNVR doctors had a grim evening's work on their hands. One was sent to a destroyer carrying men too badly wounded to be moved. The other operated far into the night in our small sick bay and I went down to lend a hand as an amateur anaesthetist. I was reckoned to have a strong stomach, and I needed to have. When I left the sick bay what I had seen of those surgeons' skill made my importance as a pilot seem very small.

On the 27th September four aircraft were flown off to Gibraltar just before the *Audacity* reached the Straits. We were home and dry. Five days in port were spent fraternizing with our escort corvettes and destroyers. Over glasses of gin we laid our plans to improve the ship and aircraft co-operation. We all knew the full value of team work.

On the evening of 2nd October *Audacity* sailed to pick up our new convoy next morning. HG 74 comprised seventy ships from the Mediterranean and Freetown. We soon ploughed into heavy seas and met the Bay of Biscay at its winter worst.

There were frequent scrambles against unidentified aircraft. These often blazed merrily away at our Martlets, although we could sometimes see that they were RAF as well as German before they popped into cloud. However, we could appreciate that this was no place to linger and sort out the finer points of identification. Only a handful of RAF men could have seen a Martlet before.

On one sortie like this Red Section was boring its way up to a large four-engined aircraft which was already firing. We were still well out of range. Suddenly my little side windscreen shattered and I felt a searing pain in my mouth and tasted blood. We did not have oxygen masks in the Martlet and used a hand microphone for radio work, so our faces were quite exposed.

The shock more than the pain dazed me, and as our quarry had now made into cloud we headed for home. I had to work at it to keep my wits about me on the way back to the ship, which was heaving like a mad thing in a boiling sea below.

My landing was rough. I sailed over the first two wires but caught the For-Christ's-Sake wire and was jerked violently to a standstill. My head smashed forward into the gunsight and I passed out.

I awoke and made out a little blue light in a sea of darkness. I began to panic. I put one hand up to my face and felt nothing but bandages. It seemed a long time before my old friend the doc arrived to tell me where I was.

I had collected a mouthful of Perspex splinters in the air, but this damage was lost in what the gunsight had done for my looks. I had only myself to blame for flying with my safety harness shoulder straps unfastened. These had just been added to our aircraft, as they had originally been fitted with lap straps only. I had picked up one bad American custom, but I would definitely be going British from now on.

I was out of action for the rest of that trip and bitterly annoyed lest I miss some of the show going on around me. However, the next days offered no more than fruitless bogey chases, and we reached the Clyde on 17th October without loss to the convoy.

The U-boats were having things very much their own way at this time, and the Gibraltar convoys were taking very heavy punishment. But now some of them could take their own guardian fighters along with them. On their first trip our Martlets had paid their passage. They had given the convoy warning of the U-boat pack and shot down one Focke-Wulf besides scaring off other marauders.

They used us again on another Gibraltar run starting on 29th October. This time we took eight Martlets and ten pilots. Somebody must have been looking into a very reliable crystal ball when this decision was made.

OG 76 was made up of twenty priceless ships, and soon ran into heavy weather in every sense of the words.

Our first alert was on 7th November in filthy weather. Pat and Fletch were sent off, but there was little hope of making contact in these conditions. On return for the land-on, *Audacity*'s stern was pitching sixty-five feet and the flight deck rolling sixteen degrees, and the ship was shrouded in rain.

Pat's aircraft was smacked by the after end of the flight deck as it rose and tossed clear above the arrester wires to slither over the port side. In horror we other pilots who had just taxied our Martlets for'ard of the barrier rushed to the side. The infallible flotation bags had already popped out of the wings, and the imperturbable Pat waved to us that he was all right. As his aircraft floated away astern of us we saw one of our escorts draw alongside and skilfully snatch him from the boiling seas.

Next day another blip on the radar plot sent off the CO and Hutch. They found the Kurier shadowing the convoy, probably sending our position back to Brest.

Loudspeakers at strategic points in the ship let the *Audacity*'s crew share in the combat by relaying the pilots' radio calls. We heard the CO say, 'I'm coming in astern now'. There was a pause, then an ominous cry. A moment later he was dead.

Hutch told us what had happened. The CO carried out two copy-book quarter attacks which set the aircraft on fire. Instead of skidding away so as to make himself a difficult target, he now ranged himself up alongside the Focke-Wulf, apparently convinced that he had given it the *coup de grâce*. The German dorsal gunner opened up on him. The CO banked away, but at that instant a cannon shell went right through the Martlet's cockpit and it dived into the sea.

John Wintour, the epitome of skill and airmanship, had fallen a victim to overconfidence. Hutch finished off the already stricken Kurier, but it did not make up to us for our loss. However, we carried on as he would have wanted us to, our guard a little higher.

I had little time to reflect on this disaster, as an hour and a half later Red Section was off on a chase. We had run through our stock of Martlets to such an extent that the Captain had asked me if I would fly one with a slightly bent propeller blade, caused by an over-enthusiastic group of mechanics pushing two of our machines into each other when clearing the flight deck to receive Hutch after his battle. His was a superfluous question, as we were all now in an angry mood.

Sheepy and I soon picked up our bogey, which turned out to be a civil aircraft plying between the Azores and Lisbon. Disappointed we turned back, and Sheepy had just sighted the convoy again when he suddenly called, 'Tally-ho!'

We were then at 4,000 feet. There was the Focke-Wulf below us at about 800 feet. We stuck our noses hard down in case we lost him in the scudding cloud. I heard Sheepy call, 'I see another one,' and then, 'You take the low one, I'll take this one'.

This looked like being a real party. I could just see the other Kurier about three miles off and higher than the first. I couldn't spare it more than a fleeting glance in case I lost mine as I held my dive. The second one was Sheepy's business now.

I came in on my bandit in a diving attack from the port beam, but the deflection was too much and my closing speed so high that I only got in a one-second burst before I had to break away underneath him. There was no return fire. I had caught him unawares.

As I passed under him I started to manoeuvre myself into position for a starboard-quarter attack, determined that this was going to be one from the book. It still only allowed me about a two-second burst but set his starboard inner engine alight, although he was now taking evasive action.

I came round again for another port-beam attack. Again I could only get off a one-second burst. I was being cramped in setting up my attacks by the low cloud layer and by him turning into me. On breaking away I saw the Kurier head into this covering layer as I darted after him and was soon through its 400-feet depth, but without any sign of my prey. How I swore at my luck.

I stayed on top because the cloud was broken and I hoped I might see him again. Suddenly I spotted a wingtip just poking through the cotton wool. He was turning and finding it difficult to keep his 100-odd feet of wing span tucked away in the thinning cloud. Twice I got these glimpses of him, but he eluded me.

I was in despair at the cat-and-mouse game when he appeared where I least expected him, about 500 yards dead ahead of me. I had no time to think. I just blazed away at him as we rushed on to what looked like inevitable collision.

I knew that if I missed this time I would never see him again, so I held on till the last possible second. It was close enough to see the big windscreen round the two German pilots shatter. As debris flew off its nose I took violent evading action to avoid a collision. I felt sure I must have killed both pilots.

The huge machine reared, stalled, and spiralled flatly into the sea. The port wing broke off on impact. I circled over the crash and to my surprise saw two men crawl out of an escape hatch on top of the fuselage. As the aircraft filled with water and sank they clung to the broken wing, which still floated.

Sheepy called me to say that he had lost his Focke-Wulf in cloud. By this time my engine was beginning to feel the effects of being kept at full throttle with a bent propeller attached to it, so I nursed it gently home.

It was a sad but successful *Audacity* which reached the Rock on Armistice Day. We had lost the CO, but not a ship was lost from the convoy. I think he would have called that a good score.

This immunity in the autumn of 1941 was almost a miracle for which we could not claim to be entirely responsible and which could not last.

We stayed in Gibraltar for over a month, flying from North Front airfield to keep ourselves in practice. During that time we did a lot of thinking about my head-on-attack success. I had found an Achilles' heel in the tough armour of the Kurier and we were determined to exploit it.

A new CO, Lieutenant Donald Gibson, joined us at Gib. He had been flown out in a Sunderland flying boat from England, which had been attacked by Ju 88s in the Bay of Biscay and badly shot up. It looked as if there was a jinx on our COs in 802.

During our sojourn in Gibraltar the *Ark Royal* had been sunk, and when we sailed on 14th December we carried a number of her survivors.

They did not think that they might be coming from the frying pan into the fire.

There were thirty-two ships in the convoy, disposed in nine columns, and they could expect trouble. But the escorts were in some strength this time to meet it. The commander of the 36th Escort Group was Commander F. J. Walker, and it was his first convoy as escort commander. He had with him sixteen escorts plus the *Audacity*.

Audacity had only four serviceable Martlets out of the six aircraft on board. The two aircraft lost on OG 76 had not been replaced, and the one with the bent airscrew was condemned by the engineering inspectorate at North Front as totally unserviceable until a new propeller could be fitted in Britain.

On the first night out the convoy had anti-submarine cover from Swordfish based at North Front. One of these aircraft soon got a radar contact of a U-boat steering towards the convoy and made a depth-charge attack on it. The Swordfish made another contact later but had no depth charges left to attack with.

The convoy had the benefit of shore-based air cover until the 17th, but *Audacity* started flying additional patrols at the request of the Senior Officer, Escort.

On the 17th our dawn patrol flew off as usual. Shortly after 9am, when her fuel was running low, one of the Martlets reported, 'U-boat on surface twenty-two miles on convoy's port beam,' then attacked the U-boat with machine-gun fire and forced her down.

Walker's ships raced to the scene, picked up echoes, lost them, picked up another, lost it again. Walker asked for extra patrols from the *Audacity*. Battle was joined, with *Audacity* at the heart of it.

Walker was out on the distant port bow of the convoy and about to turn and sweep across its path when his port flank escorts signalled, 'Object on horizon to starboard.' A few minutes later it was clearly identified as a U-boat.

Walker flashed the signal to all his ships to open fire when the guns bore, then called for his air patrol.

It fell to Fletch to do what he could to delay the U-boat from diving. He banked quickly on to the course for the target, spotted it, and roared across the convoy towards it, throttle wide open.

He saw the U-boat dead ahead of him, pitching and rolling on the grey water. He dived for her. She was making no attempt to dive, but had manned her gun, which was swinging towards him. The faintly glowing tracer shells began to float up at him as he pressed the gun button. His Brownings chattered out just as a cannon shell smashed into his windscreen.

The men in Walker's speeding ships saw the Martlet jolt out of her dive and fall into the sea on the end of a gushing smoke trail. She went in almost alongside the U-boat. Then *Stork*, *Blankney* and *Exmoor* commenced firing, joined soon by the destroyer *Stanley*. The U-boat lived for twenty minutes through the barrage, then the masthead lookout in the escort leader *Stork* reported, 'Enemy abandoning ship. Looks as though she's been badly hit.'

Men began leaping off the conning tower and casing into the heaving sea. Then the U-boat tilted bows-up to the sky and slid to the bottom. When Walker's ships got to the scene they picked up her panic-stricken crew. The elation aboard *Stork* abated when the whaler brought back Fletch's body. At dawn on the next day, the 18th, Walker read the burial service over him as he lay shrouded in the Union Jack. A short plunge in the dark sea, and he was gone.

Prisoners from the lost U-131 revealed that the U-boat had spent the whole of the night previous to the attack inside the convoy homing a wolf pack in to the attack in force. The heat was on.

At 0906 hours on the 18th the *Stanley* reported a U-boat six miles on the port quarter of the convoy. Thirty minutes and fifty depth charges from *Stanley* and *Blankney* later, the U-434 surfaced and the crew abandoned ship. The last of them left the conning tower as she rolled over and sank.

Audacity was reduced now to three serviceable aircraft, but at 1100 hours two Focke-Wulfs were intercepted by our new CO and Hutch. They attacked both machines but the guns on both their aircraft jammed in the first attacks and they had to break off.

On the afternoon of the 18th *Blankney* and *Exmoor* turned back to their base in Gibraltar. On the way there the U-boat prisoners they were carrying talked too freely. They signalled *Stork*, 'Have learned from prisoners that position, course, and speed of convoy are known to enemy together with name of escort carrier'.

That evening the gathering wolf pack struck. *Penstemon* sighted another

U-boat on the surface about nine miles on the convoy's port beam. Three escorts raced to hunt it, but got no results. Torpedoes were fired at the *Convolvulus*. A little after the end of the middle watch in the darkness of the early morning the escorts rejoined the convoy. As she took station *Stanley* reported a U-boat in sight. Almost simultaneously she herself was hit and blew up in a sheet of flame.

The two other remaining escorts were narrowly missed by torpedoes, and *Stork* steered for the wreck of the *Stanley* and dropped fifteen depth charges over a contact. They brought U-574 to the surface 200 yards dead ahead, and *Stork* tried to ram her. The U-boat turned continuously inside her at a speed of two to three knots less than the *Stork*. *Stork*'s four-inch guns could not be depressed far enough to bear on the German and the British gun crews were reduced to shaking their fists and roaring oaths

Crews of 1 Gruppe of Kampfgeschwader 40 parading in front of their Fw 200C-3 Kuriers. This Gruppe was the only exponent of the Kurier over the Atlantic during its heyday and between 1 August 1940 and 9 February 1941 accounted for 85 Allied vessels, totalling 363,000 tons. The debut of *Audacity* and the other escort carriers marked the beginning of the decline in effectiveness of the Kurier.

interspersed with an occasional burst of .5 machine-gun fire when these guns would bear.

But *Stork*'s first lieutenant hung over the top of the bridge screen firing a stripped Lewis gun and raked the conning tower to good effect. Eventually, after three full circles, *Stork* rammed U-574 just for'ard of the conning tower. The sloop scraped over her, then blew her to pieces with depth charges. She was now the third U-boat victim. Then *Stork* raced to pick up survivors from *Stanley*. There were twenty-five in all. *Samphire* picked up the German survivors.

An hour later *Audacity*, inside the convoy, was narrowly missed astern by a torpedo, and the leading ship in the port wing column was hit by another. She was abandoned and sunk by *Samphire*'s gunfire.

On the morning of the 19th two more Kuriers appeared and I quickly despatched one of them with the head-on attack technique which I had inadvertently learned. Sheepy got a short burst in at the other one in a similar attack but found that by the time he had manoeuvred round for his next run-in the Kurier had reached the safety of the cloud layer. She was certainly damaged, as he had seen bits fly off her in his first attack.

Soon after our return to the carrier our third and last serviceable aircraft sighted a U-boat on the port beam of the convoy. It dived and managed to avoid the escorts.

In the afternoon we had another Kurier visit. This one was sighted by *Stork*, who called up *Audacity*. Yellow Section took off at once and was directed towards the Focke-Wulf by bearings passed from *Stork* to *Audacity*. *Stork* also fired an occasional four-inch round in the direction of the enemy aircraft.

Our Martlets made a number of astern attacks without any visible effect on the heavily armoured German aircraft. Then Jimmy Sleigh got impatient and tried a head-on attack, with impressive results. The Kurier fell and as Jimmy pulled away to avoid it he hit its port wing tip, and landed back on *Audacity* with the Focke-Wulf's aileron hanging on his tail wheel. Shortly afterwards we sailed past the wreckage of my FW of the morning.

The night was unexpectedly quiet, but next morning at 1030 hours we had our routine visit from a Kurier. Red Section was off again, but we had to play a most exasperating game of hide and seek in the heavy cloud layer. This pilot was taking no chances of joining the long casualty list of his squadron, Kampfgeschwader 40.

At 1500 hours the Martlets reported two U-boats nearly ahead of the convoy. Commander Walker altered the convoy course but did not send a striking force as it was too late in the afternoon.

Again the night was uneventful. It was the calm before the next storm.

At 0910 hours on the morning of the 21st I was on my dawn patrol stint when I saw something I could hardly believe. Two U-boats were lying side by side on the surface some twenty-five miles astern of the convoy. There was a plank between them, and men were moving from one to the other.

As I approached they opened up on me with Oerlikon-type guns. Remembering Fletch's fate I circled round and climbed. I soon noticed that the guns did not seem capable of being elevated above about sixty degrees, so I got right overhead. By this time I had seen that one of the U-boats had a hole in the port bow. These were probably our two friends of the previous afternoon. This explained why they had not attacked us last night, I thought. From my position overhead I rolled over into a screeching dive and blazed away in the general direction of the two conning towers. Three men were shot off the plank, while the others vanished into the bowels of their submarines. Then slowly both U-boats made off on the surface away from the convoy.

Commander Walker got my radio report and deduced that the two U-boats had collided during the night and were transferring the whole of one crew, or perhaps only a working party, from one to the other. He detached four escorts to hunt them down, and I was ordered not to attack further but merely to keep the U-boats in sight until *Audacity* could get relief aircraft to the scene.

By 1126 hours I could see the striking force of four escorts some twelve miles from the U-boats, and then had to start back to the *Audacity* as I was getting low on petrol.

At 1130 hours I heard the other Martlet which had started the dawn patrol with me call that he could see two U-boats on the convoy's port quarter. These were probably the ones I had just left, as by now I was coming in from the port quarter also to join *Audacity*.

There was trouble getting a third Martlet serviceable to go out and keep an eye on these two U-boats, and when it did eventually get off it reported that the submarines had dived. They had probably sighted the approaching hunter force and decided to duck out of sight. Diving must have involved a grave risk for the damaged boat. It is possible that this was the U-567, a boat whose signals faded that day and were never heard again.

At 1300 hours *Stork* sighted another U-boat ten miles on the port bow, and at 1510 hours yet another, twelve miles away. Walker decided that no matter where the convoy turned it was for it, so adopted a direct course for home in the daylight, then a drastic alteration after dark.

Every pilot on *Audacity* had flown a long sortie that day, and it came the turn of Sheepy and I to do the dusk anti-submarine patrol again. This was to be a double sweep at ten miles and twenty miles range, and it took us longer than usual. But by the time we got back to the ship it was getting quite dark. We had seen no U-boats. All heads were down for action.

Sheepy came in for his landing. The ship was rolling in a steady cross swell. I could see that they were using two hand torches to bat him in. He made it, and I came in hard on his heels. The ship fired two Very lights, a warning for me to go round again, as she was rolling too violently. She altered course slightly and steadied up. I watched those two twinkling eyes of light with grim concentration as Pat guided me in. I didn't want another wave-off, as it was getting darker every minute, and we had no deck lighting.

Finally, at 1920 hours, I was aboard, and the whole convoy wheeled into a turn to alter course. *Audacity* normally stayed in the middle of the convoy at night, but now she went off alone on the starboard side, zigzagging at her full speed of fourteen knots. The Captain was afraid that if the U-boats made a dead set at the *Audacity*, snug in the centre of the convoy, they would be very likely to hit the merchant ships around us. He did not have Walker's approval for this move, but as he was actually senior to the escort commander he could do as he liked with his ship.

Walker ordered four detached escorts to stage a mock battle astern of the convoy with depth charges and starshell to draw the U-boats away from the real position of the convoy. The plan failed because some of our merchant ships, believing it was the genuine thing, fired snowflake and lit us up.

At 2033 hours the balloon went up. The rear ship of the centre column was torpedoed and another shower of snowflake was fired. This illumination revealed to Oberleutnant Bigalk on the conning tower of U-751 a sight that made his heart leap. An aircraft carrier was passing him within torpedo range.

At 2037 hours I was sitting in the wardroom finishing my after-dinner coffee when a torpedo hit us aft right under the point where our mechanics were still working on the Martlets. The tremendous explosion and shock from aft spilled my coffee on my lap. We all rushed on deck.

The ship was down by the stern with half the gun platform awash and the gun useless. We were still under way, but the rudder was damaged and we could not steer. The Captain was afraid of ramming a merchantman or escort, so he ordered the engines stopped. There we lay, dead in the water, hoping that we would last till morning, then get a tow. We were about ten miles from the convoy.

Meanwhile U-751 was closing in on us. She stopped some little distance from us, and the Germans, for whom this was just too good to be true, worked frantically to reload their torpedo tubes.

Some twenty-five minutes after the first hit we saw the U-boat about 200 yards away from the ship on our port beam. She was covered in phosphorescence, glowing eerily.

For about five minutes nothing happened. We simply regarded each other across the water. Then one of our seamen leapt for an Oerlikon and began firing at the U-boat.

It must have been at about the same time that Bigalk's tubes were finally brought to the ready. Our lone gunner had only got off about two rounds when we all saw plainly the white bubbling tracks of two more torpedoes coming at us. Everyone rushed for the starboard side of the flight deck.

Then they struck, both in the bows. There was a tremendous explosion, probably of aviation petrol, and the whole of the for'ard quarter of the ship disappeared. The rest reared up in split seconds so steeply that we could not keep our feet. We were all scrambling about amongst the aircraft lashed down aft. Above the other noises I heard the frightening sound of the wire lashings whining under the impossible strain ...

They seemed to part together with a great twang. The Martlets plunged down the wildly tilting deck as if in formation. There was a jarring, broken crash as they hit each other, then splayed out over the deck. The cries and screams of men being mowed down by the monsters mingled with warning shouts. Many leapt off the flight deck into the sea, a long jump from the high-angled deck, and were badly hurt on impact.

I jumped down the ladder on to the catwalk which surrounded the flight deck, then down on to the promenade deck outside our cabins. From there the only step was overboard.

It was about twenty feet to the sea. Going over I was frightened of landing on someone in the water – the sea seemed thick with heads. When I landed I was scared of someone else jumping down on me.

I had on my leather Irvine flying jacket and my flying boots over my full uniform. Stuck into the opening of the jacket were the two things I had given priority in the scramble to salvage something before the second torpedo had hit – my log book and a pair of silk pyjamas I was bringing back for my fiancée. I tried to blow up my Mae West and found my flying boots dragging me down. I kicked them off. I tried to swim away but found the log book restricting my movements. Reluctantly I let it go. Then I struck out away from the ship, frightened of being jumped on or sucked under by the ship.

At a safe distance I turned round. The ship was tilted up now at a terrifying angle, her single propeller right out of the water. Suddenly she lurched farther up until she was almost vertical, then very quickly was gone. There was no suction, but a great series of explosions cracked through the water like depth charges.

I swam off, wondering if the U-boat was going to search for prisoners. The familiar voice of Leading Seaman Budge called out, 'Sir, we've got a dinghy here. We can't get into it but we can hang on.' I swam over and joined him and three other ratings clinging to the rubber dinghy. The water did not strike me as very cold, and we were all in that high-spirited mood of escape from death.

Then I heard Sheepy Lamb's cheerful voice call out from somewhere, 'Hi! You all right, Winkle?'

'Yes, I am.'

'Is your Mae West working?'

'Yes, fine.'

'Well, come on with me. We'll make much better progress.'

So I left the dinghy and the two of us struck purposefully out as if we had somewhere to go. We did manage to get well clear of the wreckage, in case the U-boat came round looking for likely evidence of success.

Presently we watched a corvette steam up and begin to pick up survivors out of the water. We struck out towards her and were within hailing distance when she suddenly turned about and made off again. She must have picked up an Asdic ping and gone off on a hunt.

To the best of my knowledge it was about three hours before she came back – it seemed more like twenty-three. There had been about twenty of us around in the sea earlier in the night, but only the two of us had survived the three hours, probably because of our pilot-type life jackets.

We yelled, and this time they took us aboard. She came as close as she could to us and lifebelts on the ends of heaving lines came plopping down from her decks. We were supposed to climb that wet heaving cliff. My legs were too weak and I got badly skinned going up.

We were taken below to the ship's tiny wardroom, where there were already some of our men lying about asleep. They had all been massaged and dosed with rum, and there was a terrible stench of the stuff everywhere. They poured a lot of it down us as well, and we began to come to life a little. The CO was there, awake, waiting to see which of his boys would come in. He managed a weary, 'Glad you're okay, Winkle'. Leading Seaman Budge was there as well. He said, 'You should have stayed with me, sir. You'd have got here earlier'. I thumbed at Sheepy. 'I may have to follow him in the air still, but this is the last time I let him lead me in the water.'

Next morning our ship, the *Convolvulus*, transferred us to the *Deptford*. Here we learned something of the aftermath of the *Audacity* sinking. Three corvettes had rushed to assist the carrier. Half an hour later a U-boat was sighted by *Deptford*. In the resulting confusion of the chase *Deptford* rammed *Stork*, her bows cutting into *Stork*'s quarterdeck and killing two of the five German U-boat prisoners in *Stork*. The collision reduced both ships to a maximum speed of ten knots and disabled their asdic sets. The three corvettes sent to help *Audacity* now had to take over the asdic hunt for the contact and leave her.

Next morning a Liberator appeared and gave anti-submarine cover to the convoy for two and a half hours. This did not deter our usual morning Kurier, which came on the scene at 1115 hours. Then the relief Liberator spotted two U-boats on the surface at 1600 hours, both of which at once submerged.

That night Walker ordered a mock battle by *Deptford* and *Jonquil*, and altered the convoy course. I was aboard *Deptford* with the other *Audacity* pilots by then. We did not enjoy this invitation to lurking U-boats to have a go at us.

NAVY LOSES FOUR SHIPS

Convoy Escort Hits Back

Three U-Boats Sunk ; Bombers Destroyed

TWO ADMIRALTY COMMUNIQUES ISSUED TO-DAY ANNOUNCE THE LOSS OF A BRITISH CRUISER, TWO DESTROYERS, AND AN AUXILIARY VESSEL.

THE CRUISER (H.M.S. NEPTUNE) AND THE DESTROYER KANDAHAR WERE VICTIMS OF ENEMY MINES IN THE MEDITERRANEAN.

THE OTHER TWO VESSELS WERE LOST DURING AN ATTACK BY U-BOATS ON AN ATLANTIC CONVOY WHICH LASTED FIVE DAYS.

THE HUNS PAID DEARLY FOR THIS ATTACK, HOWEVER, AS THREE U-BOATS AT LEAST WERE SUNK, WHILE TWO NAZI LONG-RANGE BOMBERS WERE SENT HEADLONG INTO THE SEA AND A THIRD WAS SEVERELY DAMAGED.

ONLY TWO MERCHANT SHIPS FROM A CONVOY OF 30 WERE SUNK.

Here is the full story of the attack on the convoy, as told in an Admiralty communique issued this afternoon:

"Week after week our convoys continue to arrive, bringing vital supplies to our shores. Among those which arrived recently was one which was subjected to an exceptionally determined and sustained attack both by U-boats and long-range aircraft.

"Over 90 per cent. of the merchant shipping tonnage in that convoy arrived safely, and serious losses were inflicted upon the enemy by the convoy escorts.

"It is known that at least three of the attacking U-boats were sunk, since prisoners of war from three U-boats were taken.

"Two of the German long-range Focke-Wulfe aircraft were shot down into the sea, and a third was severely damaged and may not have regained its base.

LEADERS HONOURED

"The successful passage of the convoy and the losses inflicted upon the enemy were not, however, achieved without loss to the convoy escorts, and the Board of Admiralty regrets to announce that the ex-American destroyer Stanley (Lieut.-Commander D. B. Shaw, O.B.E., R.N.) and the auxiliary vessel H.M.S. Audacity (Cvmmander D. W. Mackendrick, R.N.) were sunk.

"The next-of-kin of casualties in these ships' companies have been informed.

"The convoy consisted of more than 30 merchant ships with Vice-Admiral Raymond Fitzmaurice, D.S.O., as Commodore. Vice-Admiral Fitzmaurice has seen much service as a commodore of convoys during the present war, and he was appointed K.B.E. in the New Year honours for this work.

"The senior officer of the convoy escorts was Commander F. J. Walker, R.N., in H.M.S. Stork. Commander Walker has been awarded the D.S.O. for his service with this convoy.

DEPTH CHARGES DID IT

"The attack on the convoy developed on December 17, and before noon on that day the first U-boat was sunk. The U-boat was sighted on the surface and was sunk by gunfire from ships of the escort. The prisoners taken from this U-boat stated that it had been forced to the surface by damage inflicted in depth charge attacks earlier in the day.

"That afternoon two Focke-Wulfe aircraft approached the convoy. They were engaged and driven off by naval aircraft from H.M.S. Audacity.

"Next day the attack by U-boats was continued, the escorts counter-attacked strongly and successfully, and another U-boat was forced to the surface by depth charges and then sank. Some of the crew of this U-boat have survived as prisoners of war.

"Some hours later the ex-American destroyer H.M.S. Stanley, which had taken part in the destruction of this second U-boat, was herself torpedoed and sank. The other escorts countered with heavy depth-charge attacks, and yet another U-boat was forced to the surface. It was rammed and sunk by H.M.S. Stork, some prisoners being taken.

BOMBERS' FATE

"On December 19 three Focke Wulfe aircraft approached the convoy and endeavoured to attack it. They were at once engaged by naval aircraft from H.M.S. Audacity. Two of the Focke Wulfe were shot down into the sea, and the third was badly damaged and driven off.

"For the next few days the enemy continued to attack the convoy with U-boats. During this time H.M.S. Audacity, one of the auxiliary vessels provided for the defence of convoys against German long-range aircraft, was torpedoed and sunk.

"Throughout these two days the remaining U-boats were relentlessly hunted and heavily depth-charged by convoy escorts.

"On December 21 the attack was finally broken off.

"American-built Liberator aircraft of Coastal Command of the R.A.F. joined the convoy at this stage and played a conspicuous part in the final series of counter-attacks, which eventually freed the convoy from further pursuit."

The *Deptford* made Liverpool, however, with no further trouble. I was to be married when we got home, and I reflected sadly that my first chosen best man, poor Fletch, was dead, and my second, Pat, missing.

Later we heard that the Captain was dead. The *Penstemon* had sighted him swimming exhaustedly in the gathering sea. Her first lieutenant dived in from the whaler which was going to pick him up and managed to get a lifebuoy on his limp body. He was being hauled in when a big sea jerked the lifeline into the water and Commander McKendrick drifted away out of reach. He was a great loss, a man of very high principles and deep understanding, who had managed to turn the strange hybrid *Empire Audacity* into a brave and useful little ship, a pattern and example for many new ships of her type which were to come.

Her epitaph was written by Grand-Admiral Doenitz himself. 'In HG 76,' he said, 'the worst feature from our point of view was the presence of the aircraft carrier *Audacity*. The year 1941 came to an end in an atmosphere of worry and anxiety for U-boat Command.'

HMS *Audacity* was the world's first operational escort carrier, and she proved her worth in providing vital air protection for convoys in the early days of the crucial Battle of the Atlantic. There is little doubt that such ships were very demanding of their crews, because their construction gave little protection against torpedo attack, they were unstable platforms in heavy seas for deck landings, and they were basically too small for the operation of fighter aircraft. However, they came into their own when operating slower aircraft in the anti-submarine role. In spite of these limitations, large numbers of escort carriers were built and gave sterling service on the seven seas for the Royal Navy and the US Navy.

A page from the author's scrapbook – the newspaper report of the attack on convoy OG 76.

Chapter 4

W E HAD A MONTH'S SURVIVOR'S LEAVE, during which I got married, then five of the seven surviving *Audacity* pilots re-formed 802 Squadron with Hurricanes at Yeovilton on 1st February 1942. In March four of us, Jimmy Sleigh, Bertie Williams, Hutch, and I, received the DSC for our work in the ship. John Wintour and Fletch were given posthumous mention in despatches. Our excellent fighter direction officer, ex-Cambridge don John Parry, got the MBE.

The pattern of my flying life in 1942 began to look like a prognosis of what the future had in store for me. The first assignment I was given after *Audacity* was to be sent by the Admiralty to RAE Farnborough to fly the Miles M.20 fighter and assess it as a possible prospective naval combat aircraft. At Farnborough I was briefed by the CO of Aero Flight on this innovative machine, which looked somewhat of a cross between the Hurricane and Spitfire, but with a smaller wingspan. Its eye-catching features were the fixed undercarriage, the bubble-type cockpit hood, and its wooden construction.

On 1st February 1942 five of the seven surviving *Audacity* pilots helped to reform 802 Squadron at Yeovilton. The squadron was equipped with Hurricanes.

The cleverly conceived Miles M.20 which the author was sent to Farnborough in January 1942 to assess as a prospective naval combat aircraft. He reported that the plane, although surprisingly nippy in performance, could not match the Martlet, Hurricane or Spitfire for manoeuvrability.

It was a surprisingly nippy aircraft, but not as manoeuvrable as the Martlet, nor had it the excellent deck landing characteristics of the latter. The M.20 had virtually double the firepower and endurance of the Hurricane and Spitfire, so it would have, as intended, made a most capable stopgap if reinforcements had been needed in the Battle of Britain.

We were working in the normal way when suddenly, in May, I was taken out of the squadron, and my whole life changed abruptly. Unknown to me Commander McKendrick had told the Admiralty that I had a natural flair for deck landing which should be exploited. I was posted to 768 Deck Landing Training Squadron at Arbroath to carry out the first attempt at getting a Hurricane aboard an escort carrier. Hurricanes had been operating successfully from the big fleet carriers. I had to find out whether the same thing could be done on a deck half the length, with six arrester wires instead of ten. My first reaction was to be hopping mad at having to leave my old *Audacity* pals when we seemed on the verge of another spell of action together.

The Martlets from America were in limited supply and there were no specially designed single-seat deck-landing fighters in Britain, so necessity demanded that the RAF high-performance Hurricanes and Spitfires

43

be adapted for the deck. Their design, their performance at low speeds, and their strength all left much to be desired for deck landing. Their long noses gave the pilot a very poor view of the deck, and their undercarriages were brittle things lacking the generous shock-absorbing characteristics of the Martlet's. But we had to have them. They were fast, with terrific fire power. The Navy simply stuck an arrester hook on them and played it by ear.

The Hurricane's hook was halfway up the fuselage, whereas the Martlet had hers right in the tail, where it had the best opportunity of snagging a wire. You had to make a perfect three-point landing in a Hurricane, or you missed the wires, or the hook bounced clear of them.

I did the trials from the first of the 'Woolworth carriers', the adapted merchantmen which we were to get from America, the *Avenger*. To my delight I found that with reasonable care the Hurricane could be operated from these little flat-tops quite successfully. They were not ideal, but they were better than the slow and stately Skuas and Fulmars. Pilots would be able to catch Focke-Wulfs with them and on the Russian convoys do battle confidently with the nippy Junkers 88s.

After the deck-landing trials I was retained as a deck-landing instructor and sent to the old *Argus*, the Deck Landing Training Ship. I joined my CO and two torpedo bomber pilots in the highly nerve-testing job of teaching newcomers to the deck. We demonstrated the technique first and then had to clamber into the back seats of our Fulmars and Swordfish, which had no dual controls fitted. Sitting imprisoned in the observer's seat of a Fulmar, from which you can see nothing dead ahead, while your trembling pupil gropes for the deck must be one of the most hair-raising experiences on record. Dangling over the side on one's hook from a grossly overloaded arrester wire, with the propeller scratching the ocean, is only the worst that happened to me. I spent almost the entire period speechless with horror, when I should have been exhorting my pupils down the inter-communicating voice-pipe. I was delirious with delight when our Fulmars were replaced by Hurricanes. They had no back seat, thank God.

Early in July 802 went off in their Hurricanes to the *Avenger* for another battle against the wolf packs and the FWs. I was posted to a front-line squadron for a time, joining 897 at Stretton in Cheshire as senior pilot, but it was only for flying practice. We had Hurricanes to start with, then took delivery of Seafires. When I had put in a few hours familiarization on them I was sent to the Service Trials Unit at Arbroath. From there I was to do with the Seafire what I had previously done with the Hurricane.

The Woolworth carriers were beginning to come over from the States in increasing numbers, and almost everything about them was new. As I seemed to be turning into some sort of escort carrier pilot specialist I came in for test after test to find out how the new techniques of flying from them were going to work out.

Biter was the next on my list. In her I was to do the Seafire trials. But there was another job to do first. The American-type catapults in all these Woolworth carriers were quite different to the British ones, and had to be proof tested. My first launch from *Biter* was the beginning of a very long series.

I had been shot off once or twice before from British catapults, but there was a difference between the two. The British method involved hoisting the machine up on to a trolley where four claws connected up with four spools on the belly of the plane. When the trigger was pulled trolley and aircraft shot down the deck, the trolley fetched up against a stop near the bows, its front legs collapsed forwards, and the machine was airborne.

The American system was very different. With this, a shuttle ran along a slot in the deck for'ard. At the after end of the slot was a hold-back hook. The plane was simply taxied over the slot, its belly fixed loosely to the shuttle by a strop, its tail to the hold-back which incorporated a breaking ring in it fixed to break at a certain pressure. With the aircraft in this position the shuttle was then tensioned till the strop and hold-back hook were taut.

Readying the machine certainly took much less time than with the British catapult. I settled myself in my Martlet, head braced well back against the pad, right hand holding the stick central with the elbow tucked into the stomach so that the shock of release would not jerk my arm and the stick abruptly back and stall the aircraft at the beginning of its run.

I opened the throttle. The engine roared as I brought it to full power, the whole machine shook and vibrated violently. When the throttle was wide open I screwed up the friction nut which held it fast in that position.

45

I raised my left hand clear above my head to show the flight-deck officer over to starboard that I was ready. He raised his flag. Over in the catwalk to port the catapult officer's assistant repeated his signal with his own flag for the benefit of the catapult officer, who was at his trigger below, out of sight of the flight deck.

Time to go. I dropped my hand according to drill to a position behind the throttle – in case the friction nut should give under the strain. The flight-deck officer dropped his flag. There was a two-second pause to allow for any last-minute hitch to be spotted, then the catapult officer made his switch.

No sudden, dramatic lunge forward. The aircraft strains mightily forward under full power and sinks squatting down on its oleo legs. The shuttle moves forward slightly as the hold-back takes the weight.

The breaking ring reaches its pre-set maximum, parts, and releases the straining machine. I feel the instantaneous jerk and the great 'g' force against me – much more than in a British-type launch. Then I am airborne. I relax, ease the throttle back, raise my wheels and flaps.

The launch had had a double purpose. I had been deliberately sent off with the ship thirty degrees out of wind to see how the Martlet would take that amount of cross-wind. I was pleased to find that she behaved impeccably. We gave full marks to the American Tail Down Catapult for its simplicity and greater speed of operation.

Now came the day for my first deck landing in the Seafire. This threatened to be a greater hazard than the first Hurricane landing. The view for'ard from the cockpit of the Seafire was even worse than from the Hurricane and called for a special technique of approach. The normal straight approach from dead astern was not advisable. Then the possibility of ever putting the machine down on a pitching, rolling flight deck had definitely not occurred to the designer, and the Spitfire undercarriage was delicate for naval usage. These snags had been very evident on the first deck-landing trials on HMS *Illustrious*. This second trial of mine was to find out if the small size of the Woolworth carrier would aggravate the faults so that they became unacceptable to a pilot who had to operate from this kind of ship.

There were two ways of tackling the approach to the deck. My CO in the Service Trials Unit, Commander Peter Bramwell, had been the first pilot to deck land a Spitfire, and he used the curving, sharply banked approach. He had also tried another method, in which the pilot made a crab approach. He personally disliked this method, but it was the one I decided to use. He did not discourage me in this, but reminded me that my margin for error must be much less on *Biter* than his had been on *Illustrious*.

The date was 11th September 1942. The ship was in the Clyde. I took off from Macrihanish just before lunch and headed for the *Biter*'s position.

I picked her up and started to think about my approach. I flew round the ship, turned on to my approach path, and came in. As I closed the stern I swung the nose to starboard with the rudder, and counteracted the swing by putting on slight opposite bank. In this way I made the Seafire crab in sideways, so that I had a view of the deck over the leading edge of the wing.

I sank towards the stern. I was over the roundown at a speed very close to the stall. Quickly I took off the bank and kicked off the rudder as she sank on the deck. She made a good three-point touchdown and caught a wire.

At this time familiarity had made me very casual in my use of the batsman. In my approach I had not even questioned why there was no batsman on the deck. And that was not all. There was, I now noticed with wonder, no one at all on deck. I thought, *My God, this is a switched-off ship!* An awful thought occurred to me. I shot a glance over the side. The wire which my hook had miraculously caught was flat on the deck. I still did not quite catch on. Then I saw a senior officer advancing on me down the deck, the brass glaring from his cap.

He stepped up to the cockpit. It was the Captain. He said, 'I say, old boy, there's nobody here. They're all at lunch'. It was only then that I saw there was a G flag flying, meaning 'Go home'. The carrier was actually twenty-five degrees out of wind. I felt very small, very stupid, inexcusably careless – and stupendously lucky.

Fortunately the Captain took my wild adventure in quite another way. He reasoned that I had successfully landed a Seafire under just about the most adverse conditions possible – in a cross-wind, with no batsman, and the arrester wires down. He made the signal, 'Trials completely successful'.

I did make one more landing first, however, in more usual conditions. This time the strain which I had put on my undeserving aircraft showed

The highly manoeuvrable Fiat CR.42 in which the Italian Air Force made a disastrous operation against Britain. It was the first enemy aircraft flown by Eric Brown.

up dramatically. I crabbed in successfully again, my hook picked up a wire – and tore off. By all normal standards this should have happened before, when I had come in at a dangerously high entry speed.

I knew that even with brakes full on I should go off the bows. I did the only thing I could do and swung towards the island. I screeched along the deck, men running madly out of my path, and my wingtip crumpled with a rending crunch on the island's steel plates.

As an aftermath of these trials I was posted to the Service Trials Unit (STU) at Arbroath, where my flying began to have even more variety than before. For example I was afforded the opportunity to fly my first enemy aircraft – the Italian Fiat CR.42, which was on a par with the Gloster Gladiator, both being beautiful aerobatic machines. I also had a go at a Heinkel 115A-2 floatplane on the River Tay at Dundee, where I had been getting acquainted with STU's Walrus amphibian.

Ten days later I was in London preparing for my investiture with the DSC which I had got in the *Audacity*. That night, the night before I was due at the Palace, I was recalled to go up to Scapa Flow for urgent trials on board the fleet carrier *Victorious*. I rushed to the Admiralty and persuaded them to let me attend the investiture, then, that night, left for the north. There was no time to book a sleeper. I did not even have a seat. I reached Donibristle after a nightmare journey, picked up a Martlet and flew to Hatston in the Orkneys.

From here I flew off to *Victorious* to do the same accelerator and side-wind trials which I had already done in escort carriers, only from a British-type catapult. I used two different machines, a Martlet and a standard Seafire 2c. I had no prangs this time, and some sound results. I did launches and landings in both machines in various conditions of wind, while a team of scientists from the Admiralty and Farnborough photographed, measured, and analysed the performance each time.

We pushed the Seafire to its limit, which was the amount of stress the frail undercarriage would take. The Martlet's sea legs were far stronger and more resilient than the Seafire's. If the Seafire was landed on its main wheels instead of being three-pointed, it would bounce like a spring lamb, whereas the Martlet's bandy legs would just give a bit more at the joints and harmlessly absorb the heavy shock. This was an important characteristic because landing bounce meant missed wires and a ticket into the crash barrier.

Now followed for me a long and varied series of these trials in all sorts and types of carriers. I had to do arrester gear and catapult tests in every escort carrier as she came into service. Part of this kind of test consisted in landing into each wire on the deck at least twice, and using at least two different types of torpedo bomber and two different types of fighter. My life was one long stint of launching and landing, in one type after the other.

For some time at the beginning of the flow of escort carriers into service I was entirely alone, owing to the general shortage of pilots, particularly those who had landed on Woolworth carriers. This meant that I had to take all four aircraft through the performance on each ship. There were six or eight wires on each flight deck, and there was usually a tight, two-day time limit for the job, as the carriers were wanted urgently at sea. Seldom did I have the use of a batsman. Either the ship did not have one at all at that stage, or the one on board had had no experience at all with the type of machine I was using and was of no practical use.

In twelve months of this I piled up a staggering number of deck landings – in one case I did 112 in a row on one ship – as well as an astonishing degree of accuracy, so that I could literally almost pick my wire.

Most of my ships were the American-built escorts, though every type of carrier in use was included.

On *Activity* I had a narrow escape. I flew out to her first in a Swordfish to discuss the trials programme. The wind when I took off again was so high – 52mph over the deck – that I was 600 feet up in the air before I had crossed the ship's bows, but trials were always a matter of urgency and had to go on.

I took my first three aircraft through the programme without too much trouble, then landed on in my last one, a Hurricane. By now the weather had blanketed Macrihanish. I decided to finish the trials after lunch, then go back with the ship to Greenock.

I did not know that the lift, which was normally supposed to tilt slightly, so that the after end was just below flight-deck level, had somehow risen a fraction *above* the flight deck. On landing, this protruding edge caught my trailing hook and tore the claw of it right off. The weather round the ship did not encourage me to try landing on again without a hook. I *had* to make Macrihanish.

I went down to sea level and probed the coast of Arran to see if I could find a clear path across the Mull of Kintyre. But there was none, and I dared not risk climbing into cloud, for the mountains surrounding Macrihanish discouraged a blind let-down to within a few hundred feet of the runway even if the radio – unreliable in those days – worked. I had to fumble my way all round the edge of the Mull before I wandered back to the fold.

The constant pressure of time forced me again and again to take risks. For this reason I did a whole series of tests with *Dasher* while the ship was at anchor. All we could do was to let the ship swing into wind from her stationary berth. There was sixteen knots of it, just enough to operate with. The *Dasher*, a tragic ship, blew up at sea shortly after this with heavy loss of life.

Between deck landings I got the chance of flying a splendid assortment of machines. I continued to fly the Walrus, the Navy's old faithful amphibian, and learned to fly an Oxford, my first twin-engined machine. Both these adventures were to have startling sequels for me. We flew some interesting aircraft as well as some freaks. There was the Swordfish with the lethal-looking torpedo slung under the fuselage – which was actually full of batteries for the huge Leigh Light searchlight under one wing. Under the other wing of this horrible monster hung eight 100lb anti-submarine bombs. She was supposed to sink U-boats, but the poor old Stringbag could barely fly in this delicate condition. Cruising speed was about five knots higher than stalling speed.

Early in 1943 I had an interesting and far-reaching escape from routine when four new types arrived from the experimental centres at Farnborough and Boscombe Down for tests at sea. There was a Seafire fitted with new Rocket Assisted Take Off Gear, an improved Barracuda, and two brand-new prototype fighters, the Blackburn Firebrand and the Fairey Firefly, both British designed and built. They went to Arbroath for preliminary deck-landing practice into the wires there, and I was allocated to them to act as batsman. We did endless landings, then I was told to go out with them to *Illustrious* and bat them on.

I was no professional batsman, and I was not looking forward to coping with these very fast aircraft. However, the *Illustrious*'s own Deck Landing Control Officer felt so keenly slighted by my appointment that he persuaded his Captain to stop me from batting. Nothing could have pleased me more, especially as I was allowed to fly the rocket Seafire as a consolation prize.

The trials went off without mishap. The Firefly looked like a useful machine, but the cumbersome Firebrand was one of those machines

Rocket assisted take-off trials at RAE Farnborough using a Seafire.

which make test pilots shake their heads in disgust. Here was a machine supposedly designed from scratch specially for deck landing. Yet, with all the experience of landing the long-nosed Spitfires and Hurricanes which we now had, she had been given an even longer nose. The for'ard view was nothing short of terrible, and the angular view for deck landing not much better.

April brought me a temporary but violent change of scene. I was whisked off down to Kenley near London and attached to 411 and 416 Squadrons of the Royal Canadian Air Force to teach them how to land their Spitfires on a deck. I had my own Seafire with me.

The Canadians showed lukewarm interest in the idea. To begin with they were heavily engaged on fighter sweeps over France, and to make matters more unsatisfactory neither they nor I had the remotest notion why we were doing what we were doing.

The Wing Leader, Johnny Johnson, was sympathetic to my problem, but pointed out to me that the Canadians were already driving him grey-haired with their high spirits. He gave me a free hand to tackle them as I thought best.

In the end they blackmailed me into a kind of exchange. For every deck-landing session I had to do a fighter sweep with them.

This kind of flying was a revelation to me, an incomparably satisfying business, in which a pilot lived on his wits and reflexes all the time.

On one outing we scrambled and picked up ninety-four Fortresses at Beachy Head. We went with them as far as Rouen, then they went on to bomb the Renault Works at Billancourt, while we orbited up sun east of Rouen at 28,000 feet.

I saw a tremendous column of smoke rising to 10,000 feet over Paris. Then the Fortresses appeared, bringing with them shoals of Me 109s and Fw 190s. The next thing I knew was that there was a wild dogfight all round me, with Spitfires and 190s everywhere and the Americans firing at everybody. I fired at a 190 but broke away before I could see the result, as someone was firing at me from behind.

I saw a Fortress go down in flames, another fall spinning. The ball-turret gunner baled out and floated down. Two FWs and a Spitfire went down trailing smoke. Never a dull moment!

On my way back to the Service Trials Unit from Kenley I had to call in at Digby in Lincolnshire to teach another Canadian squadron deck-landing technique. I was still wondering what this extra-curricular activity was for. Later we knew it had been to prepare the Canadians, who were all destined to support the Salerno landings, for emergency landings on the supporting carriers in the event of the beachhead being pushed back.

In May I had an unusual experience while flying an Avenger, a Lease-Lend machine which we called the Tarpon, from the Rolls-Royce airfield at Hucknall near Derby northwards along the coast. Near Middlesbrough low cloud forced us down on the sea. The cloud turned to fog and trapped us. Aboard us was fitted a new device called a radio altimeter, which gave extra sensitive readings of height, and I thought that this was the time for a practical demonstration to help us find a piece of beach to land on. I turned out to sea, switched on, and came back in low on the water at right angles to the shore with the radio-altimeter needle showing fifty feet. I got a good response from the beach and caught a glimpse of it as we flashed over it. It was far too narrow for a landing. Dead ahead of me was a towering slag heap and, tucked away below under its side, a very small grass field. We had to come down somewhere and soon. Calling on my deck-landing experience I dropped the Tarpon into it. We stopped and stared up at the slag heap right in front of our nose.

I added a Mac-ship to my deck-landing list. These Merchant Aircraft Carriers, as they were properly called, were an emergency measure thought up first by the Admiralty, who hit on the idea of fitting a flight deck to a grain ship, which did not have to work cargo vertically through her hatches, so that she could carry three or four aircraft for the protection of her convoy and continue to carry her normal cargo as well.

Then Mr John Lamb of the Shell Company went even further. Sickened by the terrible losses to his friends at sea in the Company's tankers, he put up the idea of doing the same thing with them. It took him a long time to convince the Admiralty that there was no real extra fire hazard in operating aircraft from a tanker with a full cargo, but he won his point in the end and many tanker Mac-ships were converted.

I put a Martlet aboard one of the first of them, the *Amastra*. Normally the Mac-ships were to carry three or four Swordfish on their flight decks, but in these early days of the experiment I had to find out if fighters could be used. The *Amastra* was an unsophisticated little carrier, larger than the *Audacity*, but with only four wires and no catapult. The trial was successful, but by the time the Mac-ship experiment was in full swing the Focke-Wulfs had disappeared from the ocean and anti-submarine work could be done just as well by the old Swordfishes – which were going spare by then – and fighters were never used in Mac-ships.

It was now that I had my first deck-landing crash. I had gone to the trials ship *Pretoria Castle* to do tests with the new Firefly.

I was making a good approach, as I thought. Wheels and flaps were down and, I thought, the hook. At least the green light had come on when I moved the release lever, so as far as I was concerned everything was in order. But the hook had not in fact come down at all, and the batsman had not noticed. I set her down. But where she should have caught a wire she did not. Nor did she catch any of the others, but shot along the deck, and I found myself, very surprised, staring the barrier in the face. The Firefly's nose cleared the top of the barrier, which sliced the undercarriage clean off. The rest of the machine slid on and came to a stop right in the bows of the ship, sitting askew on the catapult.

In September came the Salerno landings and in their wake a new job for me. The pilots of Admiral Vian's close support force of four Woolworth carriers, most of whom were inexperienced to start with, had the bad luck to strike absolutely windless weather for the operation. The little flat-tops could only make about seventeen knots for themselves, and this lack of a good wind, added to the pilot's relative inexperience, resulted in a startling number of flight-deck accidents to their Seafires. Planes came roaring in at dangerously high speeds, tore their hooks out, bounced over the side, turned over, crashed into the deck park for'ard, or hit the island.

In November I was given the task, as a matter of urgency, of investigating the low windspeed characteristics of the Seafire. I was given three aeroplanes for the job and told, literally, to go on until I broke something.

I made an electrifying start. I picked up the first machine at Abbotsinch and took off for Ayr, where the other two were to be delivered for me. I had only just got airborne when the throttle jammed open at full power. I did not think it would do the machine too much damage so I went screeching down to Ayr, which I reached in under four minutes. I switched off and made a dead stick landing, and that afternoon flew out to *Ravager* to do the tests. There I found a whole team of boffins waiting to conduct them.

I did a first batch of ten landings, each one at a lower wind-speed until the deceleration rate soared to 2.05'g'. At that point I pitched forward on my nose and fractured the props on the deck. Now there were two. I flew ashore in a Barracuda to pick up my second aircraft.

For the second batch the settings of the arrester wires were altered each time round. Now I ran into trouble with the batsman. A temperamental man to begin with, he could not quite cope with my crab approaches, and the accident to my first mount was worrying him. He kept waving me off. Eventually I ignored him and came in. As I flashed past him he threw his bats at me in rage. After that it was only fair to both sides to retire him from the scene. I then functioned without a batsman and felt very much happier. This was how I was used to doing it.

Early in December I rang down the curtain on my Woolworth show. It had been a long run. I carried out the same kind of trials as before, this time with a Firefly. Once again we pushed up the rate of deceleration until the machine tipped on to her nose and clipped the prop tips.

By this time there were four of us conducting escort-carrier trials – one for each type of machine. But for the first few months I had to do all the work alone. Since I had begun this intensive stint I had really got acquainted with the flat-tops. They had come in all sizes. I had tried all the wires – twice over – on every new escort carrier as she came into service. There were the American-built ones, *Avenger, Biter, Dasher, Archer, Attacker, Hunter, Stalker, Fencer, Tracker, Striker, Chaser, Pursuer,* and *Ravager*. Mingled with these had been the British-built escorts, *Activity, Nairana* and *Vindex*. I had also had brief encounters with the big fleet carriers *Victorious, Illustrious* and *Indomitable,* as well as the *Pretoria Castle, Unicorn* and the *Argus,* where I had had such an uncomfortable time. In all these ships I had now collected a total of some 1,500 deck landings.

Chapter 5

AT THE END OF 1943 I took another big step into the blue, I moved out of service-trials flying altogether into the experimental world of aviation proper. It was my promotion from the provinces to the big city. I was sent first to Boscombe Down, originally for two years.

I went to see Group Captain Purvis as soon as I arrived. He said:

'What have you been flying up to now?'

'Single-engined fighters, sir.'

'Well, you'd better make a start right away on twin-engined stuff. By the end of the month I want you to be on four-engined aircraft.'

Four-engined aircraft. I thought he was joking. I had had only the very sketchiest experience on twin-engined machines, let alone any idea how to master the huge Stirling I saw on the airfield.

I was on Christmas leave at my wife's home in Belfast when I received a call on 5th January from Boscombe Down, saying I was to report to Prestwick for transit to Italy by Beaufighter. I would receive my instructions in an envelope from the pilot, who would accompany me until our scheduled return to Boscombe on 9th January. The envelope was duly handed over and contained instructions from Wing Commander Sammy

The Italian Macchi C.202 was a beautiful fighter. Designed by Mario Castoldi, it stemmed from a Schneider Trophy heritage and was powered by a Daimler-Benz 601A engine.

Wroath of 'A' Squadron at Boscombe, for me to get as much flying as I could on captured Italian twin- and three-engined aircraft, and if possible on the Macchi C.202 fighter, and write up an assessment report on the latter when I returned. I was not over-surprised by this event as I reckoned I was being offered the chance of building up some much-needed multi-engine experience as well as giving the boss some idea of my test reporting ability.

We visited four airfields in southern Italy and I flew two three-engined aircraft, two twins and two single-engine fighters, including the Macchi C.202. The latter was a beautiful-looking aeroplane and, like the Spitfire, showed its Schneider Trophy lineage, having been designed by the famed Mario Castoldi, and combining his aerodynamic flair with the power of the German Daimler-Benz 601A engine.

On my return to Boscombe Down I was greeted warmly by Sammy Wroath, who was possibly surprised to see me alive, and intimated he had a surprise for me. He then drove me out to the Short S.29 and said now I could graduate to four engines.

So they started me off on the Short S29, a half-scale Stirling, and to my delight I found her fully aerobatic and not too difficult to fly. I graduated to the full-scale bomber quite quickly. It was a rude shock all the same after you've been sitting so long in a Seafire with your bottom close to the deck to be perched right up in that big glasshouse with four mighty engines roaring about you. Nobody seemed at all disturbed that this was my first experience ever of a machine anywhere near this size. There was no dual instruction. Another pilot showed me the taps on the ground, and that was all. This was the real professional world. Here you just got on with the job.

I had been at Boscombe Down just a month when I took a phone call from the Admiralty …

'How would you fancy landing a Mosquito on a carrier if you were asked to do it?'

It was my second big shock in a month. So this was test flying! I thought swiftly of my barely double figures in twin-engined aircraft and quailed. Then I found myself murmuring, 'I should think it would be a fairly straight-forward proposition, sir'.

'Right, you've got the job. You're off to Farnborough. Report there on the 17th January. The naval test pilot there has just been killed on the rocket Seafire.' It was too late to have second thoughts.

So I went down to Farnborough and joined the famous Aerodynamics Flight. I was first interviewed by the Chief Test Pilot, Roly Falk. He did not seem in the least concerned that my time at Boscombe had been so short, and passed me on to Group Captain Wheeler, the OC Experimental Flying, who was relieved very soon afterwards by Group Captain Alan Hards. Hards had been in Coastal Command, and had had no previous experience of experimental flying at all. He made himself very popular with me by saying, 'Well, we're both new boys starting at the same time. Let's go up and fly together'.

He took me up in a Wellington, and after he had flown her for a quarter of an hour he handed over the controls to me. For a rather lost and bewildered junior lieutenant, RNVR, it was an encouraging start.

At Farnborough I entered the rarified, dangerous atmosphere of pure experimental flying. In my first month there I flew thirteen types of aircraft, seven of them entirely new prototypes. This seemed phenomenal to me, though later I was to take up twenty-four new types in a month. It was wartime, and machines came pouring into us to test, real quaint aircraft, many of them.

I flew my first captured German machine that first month, a Focke-Wulf 190. I am rather short in stature, so they cut out a special cushion for me to sit on in this machine. It was of green leather with a piece cut

Farnborough: the test pilots of the Experimental Flying Department, 1944.

out in the front to allow for the backward movement of the stick and it was made for me by the son of Samuel Cody in Beta Shed, where his famous pioneer father had worked on his early experimental machines. I found the Fw 190 a very fast and manoeuvrable machine for that time, with a performance equal, if not superior to that of the current Spitfire 9, her very high rate of roll making her a formidable aerobatic aircraft. But she was difficult to land, and had some very nasty stalling characteristics.

A short time afterwards I very nearly handed the Germans a brand new Typhoon in exchange. I was up in the machine doing a test at 20,000 feet, above some very dense cloud which was growing rapidly worse. Twice during the first fifteen minutes I had to call up Farnborough for a bearing to keep a check on my position. I asked for a third time and was told that my transmission was distorted. They gave me a third-class bearing of 236 degrees. To confirm it I gave a long tuning transmission and asked for another bearing.

The girl operator answered, 'Hello Brownjar 54. This is Attest. I am afraid conditions are not favourable to pass QDM at the moment. Will call later.'

Immediately after this a girl's voice called, 'Hello Brownjar 54. Am handing you over to Lynx.'

I allowed a short pause for the change-over, then a man's voice broke in with my call sign, Brownjar 54, said he was 'Lynx', and gave me a course of 136. This seemed fairly reasonable, as the last third-class bearing had been 236. I steered this course for about five minutes and called Lynx for another bearing. Again I was given 136. I flew for another five minutes, asked again, and was again given 136. By now I was getting uneasy about these bearings, as I had been flying at 20,000 feet towards the south-east. I decided to go down and take a look.

When I broke cloud I found that I was over the sea, with a coastline ahead. 'Lynx' had been homing me into Occupied France. I turned round at once and twenty-five minutes later picked up Selsey Bill.

It was a clever attempt by a German VHF station operating from the French coast somewhere near Pointe Haut Banc to cut me out. Whether it was a deliberate attempt to capture a Farnborough test pilot by careful monitoring of our frequency or whether a routine watch had brought them this windfall we never knew.

Very early in my time at Farnborough I began to enjoy the experience

A B-25 Mitchell medium bomber of the US Army Air Force ready for take-off on the USS *Hornet* for the raid on Tokyo led by Lt. Col. Jimmy Doolittle.

of living as one of a large, happy family, as the test-flying community there really was. Everyone helped everyone else, there were no distinctions of rank whatsoever, service pilots and civilians mixed together as equals, whatever their experience or seniority. On top of this you had the never-ending excitement of flying new and interesting aircraft, and being part of a really constructive step in advancing aviation. It was happy hey-day for me all the time on that score, though it was to be darkened by many shadows, by close brushes with death, and by the death of friends.

My first major project was, of course, to carry out deck landing trials on an aircraft carrier with the high-performance Mosquito fighter-bomber. I had not been made aware of the purpose behind these trials, but had an instinctive feeling it was something influenced by the famous Doolittle raid on 18th April 1942 against the Japanese mainland by sixteen B-25 Mitchell medium bombers of the US Army Air Force taking off from the aircraft carrier USS *Hornet*. Led by the ubiquitous Lt. Col. Jimmy Doolittle the force flew some 600 miles to Japan and dropped their token bomb loads on enemy territory, but had no capability of landing back on the aircraft carrier so had to carry on to seek refuge in China or Russia. All sixteen aircraft were lost (none from enemy action) although only nine of the eighty aircrew lost their lives, but the propaganda value of this operation was considered inestimable in offsetting the debacle of Pearl Harbour to American morale.

On reviewing in my mind what lay ahead, I had to face some stark facts about what concerns were involved about the Mosquito, and these were speed, weight, strength and size. The Pilot's Notes quoted a recommended approach speed of 125 mph using about –4lb boost on each engine. The stalling speed with undercarriage and flaps lowered was 110 mph. However the boffins calculated that on the fleet carrier proposed for the trials the maximum indicated airspeed on entry into the ship's type of arrester gear would have to be no greater than 83 mph. On the face of it this seemed an impossible requirement. In addition, the weight of the Mosquito Mark 6 was to attain 20,000 lb, which was twice the weight of any aircraft which had hitherto been landed on a British aircraft carrier.

The weight and speed problems were exacerbated by the fact that the Mosquito was of wood construction and would be subjected to heavy vertical velocities on landing and severe horizontal 'g' forces on being arrested. Some pessimists predicted it would come apart at the seams. Also the wingspan of the Mosquito was 54 ft, and this meant it would be in close proximity to the island, which intruded on the flight deck of the carrier.

It was obvious that the only way I could get the landing speed down to that required for the trials was by approaching with a considerable amount of power on the engines and literally hanging on the propellers until within a foot or two above the deck before cutting the power. With this in mind my two navalised Mosquito Mark 6 aircraft were fitted with Merlin 25 engines capable of operating at +18 lb boost instead of the standard +12, and to absorb this increase in power they drove experimental (non-feathering) four-bladed de Havilland metal propellers cropped to 12 ft 6 in diameter to avoid any possibility of them striking the deck when they pitched forward on being arrested. In such a deck landing approach configuration, it was certain than any power loss on one engine would result in a fatal accident. We were playing for high stakes.

At this early stage I was only of limited use to the firm. As yet I was trying to learn the language of test flying, with not much more than my chauffeuring to offer. But I now began to work with a scientist in close co-operation and mature a little.

My boffin for the Mosquito tests was Bill Stewart, a young Glasgow University graduate, a fellow Scot, and about as new to the Royal Aircraft Establishment as I was. Bill's utter absorption in the work and bland acceptance of the risks of flying with a comparative novice I found challenging.

We went up to investigate the Mosquito's stalling characteristics. Bill, sitting alongside me up front, lowered 100 feet of rubber tubing through a hole in the fuselage, on the end of which was a thing called a trailing static bomb. This device would give Bill a reading of the true airspeed of the plane when she stalled, which he could plot on his graph ...

'Right. Slow her down to 140 ... Okay, now I'll put the bomb out. Okay, bomb's down. I've got a reading. We're all set. I want a stall at landing conditions – plus two boost, flaps down, wheels down.'

Gradually I brought down the speed. Suddenly the stick cracked over into the corner, the ailerons locked, and she stalled with a bang, turning almost completely upside down. I was shaken. I had never been in such a vicious stall. There would be no margin for mishandling. Out of the corner of my eye I saw Bill, apparently quite unmoved, still reading his precious dial.

We went on with this, stepping up the power each time until we reached conditions of really frightening violence. We finally called it a day when we came out of a stall with Bill's rubber tubing wrapped all round the tail of the machine.

We were finding out, too, that the normally accepted landing speed of 120mph could be reduced considerably by the use of high engine power on the approach, but this power had to be kept on till within a few feet of the ground. If the throttles were cut too early when the speed was low the Mosquito would snap into her sharp stall.

I was not particularly scared in these tests. As a result largely of Bill's imperturbable behaviour under stress I found that my main worry was how to fly and produce accurate results, to make my own competence match his. On the ground I was always worrying about this. I kept on thinking, 'Is my flying going to be good enough?' A test pilot's concern is that all the points on his boffin's graph should be on the curve. When

Bill said after a flight, 'Okay, Winkle, that's a good day's work,' I was happy.

I practised take-off technique on a strip of runway marked out with the dimensions of a flight deck, with Bill taking photographs of the performance and afterwards taking measurements of my course along the strip. For take-off I held the Mosquito on the brakes with as much power as I dared use, and pushed the throttle open. Then I had to put on full starboard rudder to counteract the strong swing to port. The thrust produced from the engines on these Mark 6 Mosquitoes we were using was about twice that of the Merlin 21 of the standard Mark 4 in RAF squadron service, and in the real thing could easily send the machine pitching into the sea.

We had to bear in mind that the wingspan of the Mosquito was too great for her to be able to take off in the normal way with her nose over the centre line of the deck. Instead I would have to keep her starboard wheel on the centre line. This did not matter quite so much in landing as it was optimistically taken for granted that the machine would be arrested before she was abreast of the island.

The plane's bouncy undercarriage would have to be allowed for too. Every landing would have to be a perfect three-pointer or she might bounce over all the wires. With this hot machine a pilot would have to wait until he had actually touched the deck before he cut the throttle or she would drop her nose sharply and land on her main wheels only. The rubber-block type shock absorbers in the undercarriage legs reacted violently to this sort of treatment.

A Barracuda-type arrester hook had been fitted to the rear end of the fuselage, which had been specially strengthened internally to take the heavy strains likely to be inflicted on the plywood structure. This did not give me any trouble when I flew up to Arbroath and made a few landings into the wires there. RN Air Station Arbroath had a short runway, fitted with four arrester wires. It was used for tests on equipment fitted to naval aircraft involved in decklanding trials.

While I was there I met the batsman detailed to accompany me on the trials at sea, and we carried out two days of aerodrome dummy deck landings together at nearby East Haven airfield. They were not very satisfactory as the batsman disappeared from view under the port wing and engine much earlier than I had anticipated.

63

The world's first deck landing of a high-performance twin-engined aircraft, a Mosquito, on HMS *Indefatigable*.

As I travelled up and down the country in my Mosquito I had another pilot following me round in a Seafire 15, which I was testing at the same time. This double bill put a certain amount of extra strain on me, of course, but it was quite normal for the Flight.

March the 25th was given as the date for the first Mosquito landing at sea. This would be my first big test as an experimental pilot. I had got some sort of reputation as a deck-landing pilot, but now for the first time I was being asked to do something for which there was absolutely no precedent.

My worry was not my flying, but the reliability of the machinery, which I knew the scientists connected with the project all shared. Would the arrester gear cope? Would the hook stand the strain of a real carrier landing? And there was the structure of the Mosquito. I had seen the entire back end pulled off a metal aircraft on the deck. Here we had a wooden machine ... all my RAF friends at Farnborough, although they never said anything openly to discourage me, were obviously sceptical of putting such a fast, heavy plane on to a carrier's deck without any trouble.

What would I do if one engine suddenly failed on take-off? And always there was the nagging thought, 'If I ditch, how the hell am I going to get out?' This was a very real worry for a Mosquito pilot. The escape hatch

With the Mosquito's long wingspan it was essential to take off with the starboard wheel on the centre line of the deck to miss the island. The aircraft would thus be displaced even more to the side where the engine swing would carry it.

consisted of a knock-out panel above the heads of the crew. The pilot had to let the observer escape first lest they should both get jammed in the narrow roof hole, so his chances of escape were cut down considerably.

The trial was set for the afternoon. I had lunch at Macrihanish and prepared to fly out to the *Indefatigable* and give all the brass and boffins who had embarked in her their money's worth. For this reason I did not do the usual preliminary aerodrome dummy deck landings first, in case I broke something and put off the trials. There were some Very Important People on board who could only spare this one day.

The ship signalled to say she was ready. I took off and steered to pick her up. There she was, steaming between the bottom tip of Arran and Ailsa Craig. It was a beautiful blue-and-gold day over the sea, the wind-speed good, the water smooth, and I was on my old stamping ground, where I had made so many carrier landings before.

I arrived fast and low down to give them a real taste of the Mosquito's style, then went into my circuit of the ship. Flying past the starboard side I could see the island packed with goofers. As I went past the island I lowered my hook.

I banked ahead of the bows and came down on the port side. Opposite the island downwind I lowered the undercarriage and put the flaps down to the take-off position, the propeller pitch levers to fully fine. This is always the moment when I tense up and begin to concentrate hard, in tune with the rising hum of the airscrew moving into fine pitch.

About a mile and a half astern of the ship now, I turned in on to my approach path, putting my flaps fully down, checking my airspeed very carefully, and switching on the special accelerometer which would record the deceleration 'g' of my arrested landing.

In front of me was the most wonderful view of the deck I had ever had. For the first time I could really see everything. From about 400 feet I settled down, expecting to land on the ship at about 85mph.

She was as steady as a rock coming down. I did not for once have to turn and twist to get a look at the deck. Then we were very near the roundown. I could see the batsman, Lieutenant Commander Bob Everett, very clearly standing out near the centre line of the deck. He was giving me a good steady signal all the way, with only a small correction to level up my wings as the machine caught the inevitable funnel gases over the stern. I felt the lurch quite distinctly. The Mosquito was slow to straighten out. Her aileron control at these low speeds was not good.

I watched Bob Everett, worrying that if he did not get out of the way smartly he would be chewed to bits by my port propeller.

As I crossed the roundown he slashed his paddles across in his inimitable brisk cut signal. Then I saw him dart across the deck into the nets on the port side.

I did not cut the throttles right back, just eased them back, in case too sudden a loss of power dropped her abruptly to the deck and she bounced.

She sank. I judged her about a foot or two from the deck and cut the engines completely. She touched the deck in a perfect three-point attitude and ran forward. Astonished, I felt a very gentle pull as we decelerated. We had caught the second wire. We ran very quietly to a stop. I reached behind my head and switched off the accelerometer, then the engines.

I climbed out. First to arrive on the scene were the boffins, all swaddled in their Sidcot suits against the fierce wind which tore down the deck. A few quiet words of congratulation from one or two of them – you never get more than that from a boffin – then Flag Officer Air (Home), Rear-Admiral Portal, and Commodore Slattery, Chief Naval Representative at the Ministry of Supply, appeared. Commodore Slattery was his usual unruffled self. He had had confidence in the trial and showed no surprise at its successful outcome. At least, that was the impression he always gave.

The Mosquito was struck down into the hangar for a thorough check of instruments and airframe. The film of the landing was developed and it was found that I had landed at only 78mph, much slower than I had anticipated. In fact this is usually the case when you come to put an aircraft down on the deck of a carrier at sea after trials on land only. The sea is kind, the airflow is smoother, with no trees, houses, haystacks to ruffle it, and you are not worried by obstructions in your path. The accelerometer recorded an astonishingly mild declaration in spite of the high aircraft weight. My Seafires had weighed about 6,000lb. The Mosquito had carried much more than twice that load, at 16,000lb.

After the machine had been checked over I took off for a further four landings. I was much more concerned about the take-off than the landing. With the Mosquito's long wingspan I would have to take off with my starboard wheel on the centre line of the deck so as to be sure of missing the island. Thus I would be displaced even more towards the side where the engine swing would carry me. When I released the brakes I would have nearly full power on. Unless I picked it up very rapidly on the rudder I could go over the side.

As soon as we started to move forward I put on starboard rudder to counteract the swing. With the forty knots of wind I was getting, the rudder bit much more quickly than normally and we got off very smoothly. I still had to be very quick with the rudder. I had an almost overpowering urge to look to starboard to see if the wingtip was clearing the island.

That night on board everyone had their own special party. At a very late hour I made enquiries about a place to lay my weary head. In the end it had to be the wardroom couch, after the last of the celebrating horde had gone. They had forgotten to give me a cabin. I felt a little hard done by, particularly when I was turned out in the cold grey dawn by a steward who wanted to sweep out. And I had to be off the deck again at 8.45.

I had been alone so far. Now Bill Stewart was to fly with me to supervise a further three landings at steadily increased weights. We did two landings without incident, the first at a total weight of 16,800lb, the second at 17,000.

We came in for the third, for which the weight had been put up to

18,000lb, and touched down. The extra weight made us decelerate hard. I knew that we had picked up a wire. Suddenly there was a lurch, the tail kicked, and the deceleration stopped abruptly. We careered on up the deck.

I had a fraction of a second to make up my mind. What had broken? Had the hook gone? Had the rear end been torn off? In that case to open up and try to take off again was suicide. Had the arrester wire parted? If so, there was a danger of snagging another wire and tearing hook or tail right off if I was to accelerate again by opening up the engines.

I had had some experience of these things by now, and I thought it was most likely the hook which had parted. I opened up instantly to full power, slamming the throttles wide open far more harshly than I would ever have dared to do normally. I had to pick up power quickly. We had used up a good third of the deck already and been slowed down to start with.

I had opened up so quickly I could not check the swing, which took us off to port. We rushed towards the side. But I did not want to check the swing entirely as we were dangerously near the island. I saw that the port wheel was about to go over the edge of the deck. I pulled back gently on the stick and lifted the machine fractionally off the deck – enough to miss the excrescences that cluttered the side.

We cleared the edge by our momentum, but we were so near stalling speed that we at once sank low towards the water. I was prepared for us to go in. But we pulled out with the wheels ten feet off the sea.

Bill and I flew back to Macrihanish in shaken silence. All he said when we got out was, 'Well, you can't blame *my* calculations for *that*'. We found that the claw at the end of the hook had sheered. The Mosquito was returned to the makers at Hatfield to have the hook strengthened.

When tests started again on 9th May I had my old CO of Service Trials Unit days with me as second Trials pilot, Commander 'Tubby' Lane. For this series our machines were fully loaded, with all operational gear aboard, including bombs. As a special treat we were allowed to drop the bombs near the ship. This got the aircraft down to landing weight more quickly than stooging around burning up petrol. The trials went smoothly, except for one landing when Commander Lane missed all the wires, narrowly missed the island, and screeched to a stop inches from the bows with his brakes completely burnt out.

We had proved the thesis. It was decided to build Sea Mosquitoes.

Chapter 6

THERE WERE FOUR OF US PILOTS in Aerodynamics Flight. Our job was supposed to be pure experimental flying for Aerodynamics Department rather than the service-acceptance type of flying I had done at Boscombe Down. But we had many other things on our plate.

We did the flying for the Structural and Mechanical Engineering Department. This called for flying which would help investigate vibration and structural stress or the performance of experimental equipment fitted to the aircraft. Any machine that we flew for SME was loaded with vibrograph recorders, strain gauges, or some other piece of ironmongery, the delight of a dedicated boffin.

The four pilots of the Aerodynamics Flight. From left to right: Sqn/Ldr Tony Martindale, Sqn/Ldr Jimmy Nelson, the author and Sqn/Ldr Doug Weightman.

The Air Physiological Laboratory used us too, usually to take up some courageous doctor and push him – or her – to the physical limits of a man in an aeroplane. Resolutely they suffered very high 'g' to find human red-out and black-out thresholds, deliberately induced anoxia, chronic air sickness.

In my case I was also the only naval pilot at Farnborough, so I came in for all the research flying for the Catapult Section of Designs Department – soon to become the Naval Aircraft Department – which was responsible for catapult and arrester gear design, and the testing of any new type of aircraft on this equipment, with the trials culminating aboard a carrier.

For good measure all the test pilots also had to do a regular stint of fighter defence patrol duty. Two Spitfires were kept at armed readiness day and night to take off if an air-raid alarm was sounded. RAE had already been bombed once, and was obviously a choice target.

So I had an over-full programme. The speed with which I had to switch from one type of machine to another, with scores of new ones flowing in all the time, forced me to invent a special system of memorizing the layouts of the various cockpits, fuel systems, hydraulic systems, engine settings, landing speeds, and other vital data. I enjoyed this mad leapfrogging but I wanted to stay alive.

The fatal accident rate during the war years was very high among test pilots, and I felt sure that much of it was through bad cockpit drill. So I started a simple quick-reference memory refresher in a loose-leaf pad which I carried on every flight and studied continuously in my spare time. It gave the essential actions for take-off and landing, as well as the critical actions for emergencies such as fire in the air, undercarriage lowering malfunction, engine failure in multi-engined types, and any unusual drill associated with the type.

The big job in Aerodynamics Department when I arrived was the exploration of high-speed flight problems. It was the first full-scale research in the country on the compressibility of airflow causing loss of control at transonic speeds – the first probing of the sound barrier. Chasing higher and higher Mach number[1] decimals we dived our machines from high altitude until they began to go out of control.

[1] Mach 1 is the speed of sound at any height, and percentages of that speed are Mach numbers as indicated to the pilot on a Machmeter in the cockpit.

Early in 1944 Lt.Gen. Jimmy Doolittle, who had recently taken over command of the 8th USAAF visited the RAE to ask for a series of hands-on tests on the three USAAF escort fighters, the P-38H Lightning, P-47C Thunderbolt and the P-51B Mustang. He was worried about the heavy losses suffered by the fighters on high cover over Flying Fortresses. Tests were required into the handling behaviour of the aircraft at high speeds up to their tactical (manoeuvring) and critical (loss of control) Mach numbers. The tests revealed that the Lightning and Thunderbolt fell well short of the tactical Mach numbers of the Me 109 and the Fw 190. As a result of the RAE report Doolittle asked to be supplied solely with P-51s which proved to be the finest fighters in the European war theatre.

This transonic flight testing took on a new emphasis after a visit to RAE early in 1944 by Lt. Gen. Jimmy Doolittle, who had just taken over command of the 8th USAAF. This American air force had started to suffer worrying escort fighter losses when the fighters on high cover over the Flying Fortresses dived down to intercept German fighters attacking the bombers and lost control before they could engage the enemy in combat.

The Americans needed urgent help, and the RAE was the world leader in transonic flight testing. There was no time to set up a normal instrumented research programme, but what was wanted was a hands-on series of tests on three USAAF escort fighters – the P-38H Lightning, P-47C Thunderbolt and P-51B Mustang. The requirement was for a detailed description of the handling behaviour of these aircraft at high speeds up to their tactical (manoeuvring) and critical (loss of control) Mach numbers, so that the operational pilots could recognise they were near these limits without reference to instruments in the cockpit. These tests were initiated in late January 1944 and continued through to early March.

It must be remembered that in the Second World War, Machmeters were not fitted to any Allied or enemy operational aircraft, but only to a few research aircraft. We knew from tests at RAE on captured German fighters that the Me 109 and Fw 190 both had a tactical Mach number of 0.75, so that figure was the name of the combat game at 30,000 feet. The tests we conducted on the American fighters revealed that the Lightning and Thunderbolt fell well short of that figure, with tactical Mach numbers of 0.68 and 0.71 respectively. However, the Mustang with its laminar-flow wing achieved 0.78 tactically, and soon after receiving these results Doolittle asked that his Force be supplied with only P-51s. Subsequently the Merlin-engined Mustang proved to be the finest escort fighter in the European war theatre.

Our own research programme had progressed through the Hurricane to the Spitfire, which could fly higher and faster. We took a Spitfire XI, a photo-reconnaissance type, and stripped it of all operational equipment, so that even with the boffins' recording gear aboard it was well below its normal weight.

Our Spitfire would go to 40,000 feet. Up there we would fly it flat-out before pushing it over into a steep dive. You would hold on in this screaming plunge until the Machmeter read 0.83. Then a gentle shaking started

Spitfire PR11 which achieved a Mach number of 0.92 – the highest speed ever reached by a piston-engined aircraft.

on the tail, and the machine started to nose down into a steeper dive without any pushing by the pilot. The dive angle steepened rapidly and the Spitfire started shaking really badly and rolling from side to side. At 0.86 the pilot had to pull the equivalent of 60lb to stop the dive steepening any further. Closing the throttle (if the pilot dared to take one hand off the control column) made little difference to the dive speed as this was almost totally due to gravity effect.

This was my physical limit. Even with both hands I could not pull more than that on the Spitfire's stick. Our flight commander, Squadron Leader Tony Martindale, was a big, powerful six-footer. One day he dived to 0.92, at which point he was pulling about 100lb on the control column to recover, when the over-speeding propeller became detached, together with its reduction gear.

The resultant loss of weight at the front end made the Spitfire tail-heavy and it zoomed almost vertically upwards, blacking out the pilot under a force of 11'g'. When he recovered his sight again Marty found himself back up at about 40,000 feet with his straight-winged aeroplane now having acquired a very slightly swept-back look. It speaks volumes both for the pilot and the Spitfire that Marty somehow managed to land it back at Farnborough on its wheels, with the valuable camera records intact. The speed he reached in that dive is still the highest ever registered by a piston-engined aircraft.

Our other job for Aerodynamics was to find the cause of any disaster epidemic on one type of aircraft. We had to find out why the Navy's Barracuda began to dive into the sea during practice torpedo runs, taking the crew with it. This was a tough problem as there were no survivors to give us a lead. It involved the flight observer, Mrs Gwen Alston, whose husband had been killed in a flying accident when he had been a scientist in the Department, in some very dangerous, nerve-racking flying before the main sources of trouble were located in the inter-action of the dive brakes and the rudder when operated simultaneously in post-attack evasive action.

In a torpedo attack the pilot is required to dive to a low altitude using the dive flaps, level out, launch the torpedo, retract the flaps and make a rapid and evasive breakaway to one side. Now from previous experience of flying the Barracuda I knew it had a tendency to rudder overbalance, and when that actually happened the nose dropped quite sharply. I also checked the change of trim when the dive brakes were retracted at the bottom of a high-speed dive, and this was markedly nose down.

The next stage was to try out the combination manoeuvre at altitude. I made the simulated torpedo attack and when the speed had dropped below the limit for retracting the dive flaps I raised them to the cruise position and kicked on rudder as I pulled away to starboard. In a flash the aircraft was in an inverted dive that would inevitably have had fatal consequences at low altitude.

The RAF started losing an abnormal number of Halifaxes during evasive manoeuvres on night operations over Germany and in operational training in England. We had to throw this big bomber round the sky at night in a corkscrew pattern, cut one of its outboard engines, and measure how long it took to get out of control. We could not exactly reproduce those grim moments over the target, but we did our best, even performing in searchlights to simulate the glare which the pilot had to suffer. To find the fault became very urgent, and Wing Commander Leonard Cheshire came to Farnborough to drive us to a quick answer. He stood behind me impassively as I risked his life and mine on the limit of disaster.

There were the 'rogue' aircraft. These were examples of normally well-tried and trusted machines which had suddenly developed dangerous habits, apparently inexplicably. We usually found the answer fairly soon, but there were exceptions. When the magnificent Lancaster was put into production in Canada the entire first batch of deliveries to Bomber Command came to us as rogues suffering from an aileron defect, until we discovered that the ailerons were being badly assembled in Canada by unskilled labour.

The doctors of the Physiology Department used to go on operational flights over Germany in their study of human reactions to inhuman conditions. But I most admired our young Miss Worthington, an attractive medical assistant, who often flew with me in the back of a bomber while I threw it round the sky in corkscrew evasive action until she was so sick that she considered she would no longer have been a useful air-crew member.

In these initial six months at Farnborough I flew many 'firsts'. The first tail-down launchings of British aircraft from a catapult were followed by the first rocket-assisted take-offs. In fact accelerated take-offs became as

TOP: The rocket catapult launch which went wrong at Farnborough. The Seafire accelerated along the catapult but the trolley remained attached to the aircraft when it took off. Fortunately Eric was able to shake it off before landing.
ABOVE: The right way to do it.

much a part of my flying life as normal ones. In the Naval Aircraft Department we had two catapults, one worked by cordite, the other, of the type used on the Catapult Armed Merchant Ships which operated one fighter in defence of their convoys, using rockets. I also broke many aeroplanes testing them in very harsh conditions on our mock-up of a flight deck which was fitted with every type of arrester gear to be fitted to our carriers.

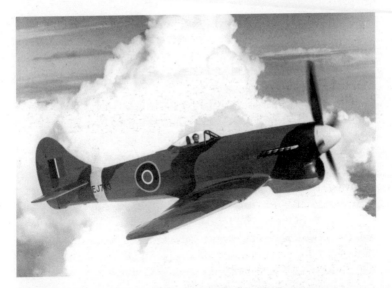

The Tempest V became the top killer of the V1 flying bombs. It was from a Tempest V that the author had to bale out at 1,300 feet when the engine caught fire.

This summer of 1944 was the time of the frightening buzz bombs. One of the first to come over fell on my house in Aldershot, fortunately leaving my wife unhurt, so I had a special interest in the attempts which we made to improve the performance of RAF front-line fighters so that they might have a chance of catching the fast-speeding, low-flying V1s. We first investigated the possibilities of polishing the wings and smoothing off all external excrescences, but the gain was very small, so we took very drastic measures and developed the engines of the Spitfire 14, the Tempest 5, and the Mustang 3 to give abnormally high power, to be used for strictly short bursts, otherwise the engines would crack up.

Using a 150-grade aromatic fuel specially developed for us we made an exhilarating series of low-level trials, in which we got the Spitfire to 365mph, the Tempest to 405, and the Mustang to the very high speed of 420mph. As part of the job we visited the actual squadrons fighting the V1s to tell them about the improvements they could expect and warn them of the limitations. Leading one of the Tempest squadrons and piling up a good score of V1 kills was Roland Beamont, later to become a test pilot himself for English Electric.

One pleasant July day I was flying one of these high performance runs in a Tempest when I smelled burning coming from the floor of the cockpit. I checked the dials. Oil pressure zero. Oil temperature zero. The engine had never faltered and I suspected oil-gauge failures, but I asked for an emergency homing on the R/T.

When I thought I was near base I started to come down. I had to descend through nearly 4,000 feet of thick cloud. As I put the nose into it I saw the whole top cowling between the exhausts glowing hot in the gloom. Before I got out of the cloud the engine was misfiring badly, the propeller starting to overspeed. The revs mounted higher and higher until there was a loud bang in the engine and a spray of oil, which covered the windscreen.

To see out of the cockpit I had to undo my safety harness, which was a new type with no spring release to give a limited degree of freedom of movement, and peer out round the obscured windscreen. The propeller had seized solid, the fire under the cowling had burst into intense white flames which were creeping into the cockpit through the floor near the rudder pedals, so that the belly must have been well alight. When I had to take my feet off the rudder pedals because of the fierce heat I thought it was time to bale out.

I took off my helmet, which was attached to the R/T plug, and tried to reduce speed by pulling up the nose. But this only brought the tips of the flames near the cockpit, so I trimmed for level flight at 1,600 feet and 170mph and, standing up on the bucket seat, put my left leg over the port side of the cockpit, only to find myself jammed there against the open hood by the tremendous air pressure. I struggled for a second or two in vain, then reached back into the cockpit and pulled the stick hard over towards me. I noticed that the altimeter read 1,300 feet now. The machine banked sharply over and threw me clear. I pulled the ripcord at once and, almost instantaneously it seemed to me, I hit the ground. Two hundred yards away from me the Tempest smashed into the ground and exploded.

In fact I hadn't hit the ground, but landed in a duck pond with rather slimy water up to my waist. I discarded my parachute and carried it to the nearest grassy edge, but there I was confronted by a very aggressive black bull with a steel ring in its nose, head lowered and emitting clouds of steam from its nostrils as it pawed the ground. This was not a Spanish fighting bull but was giving a realistic impression of being so. I therefore did an about-turn to the opposite side of the pond, but this bull was smart and was awaiting me with all the Spanish body language. There I was stuck in limbo while the emergency services of fire brigade, ambulance, police and Home Guard all arrived, but remained firmly behind the nearby hedge while assessing the situation. Eventually someone alerted the local farmer who arrived, put a short rope through the bull's nose ring and resignedly led it away with the words, 'Come on, Ferdinand'. I could swear that bull winked at me as he departed.

But all this was mere routine compared with something else which happened to me at this time. On the far side of the airfield from the main buildings was a small hangar very heavily guarded by RAF military police and their fierce dogs. Inside this hangar were the first jet aircraft to be seen in this country.

Commanding the jet flight was Group Captain H. J. Wilson, who had at one time commanded Aerodynamics Flight and often came in to see how we were getting along.

· One day he strolled in and said to me, 'Isn't it high time the Navy was taking an interest in jets?'

I said, 'Of course it is. But you won't let us get near the damn' things'.

'Well, as a matter of fact I've come over now with an invitation to you to come and fly them, and help us with some of the work. We're getting a bit short-handed.'

I went over and flew the Meteor. It was a revelation. Here was everything a naval pilot wanted – tremendous speed and performance, perfect view, a tricycle undercarriage, freedom from noise and vibration. There was only one snag that I could see, and that was its poor take-off performance, involving a run far too long for any carrier.

As soon as I landed from that first flight I wrote to Commodore Slattery at the Ministry of Supply urging deck-landing trials on jets right away. As usual when he agreed with something he was quick to move. Back came an order to fly all the jet aircraft at Farnborough to select the one best suited for naval use.

It was while I was doing this that I met Frank Whittle. He was interested that a naval pilot should be in the first half-dozen men in this country to fly jets and we had a discussion on their potentialities for naval use, which he had never foreseen. But anything which remotely involved his great invention was of absorbing, possessive interest to him, and he obviously felt a personal responsibility towards everyone in the jet field. He listened intently to what I said about the jet engine's slowness in accelerating to maximum power, which, I said, made it far from ideal for a deck-landing pilot who wanted to open up quickly and go round again. He promised that he would take up the possibility of development in this field with Rolls-Royce.

I went on enthusiastically testing the jets we had. I quickly ruled out the Bell Airacomet, a terribly ponderous aeroplane, and the little original Gloster E.28/39 – the latter because it was purely a research aircraft, and the only one of its kind left. The Meteor had too long a take-off run, but I found that this had been much improved upon in the little De Havilland Spider Crab, as it was then called. This seemed to be the one for us.

The author with Sir Frank Whittle. Whittle was interested that a naval pilot should be in the first half-dozen pilots in Britain to fly jets.

Chapter 7

THE ACCENT WAS NOW HEAVILY ON JET FLYING. We were on a steep learning curve, for this was a new form of propulsion with a new type of fuel, and operating primarily at high altitude. We had to find out how jet aircraft would behave in aerobatic manoeuvres, formation flying, simulated combat, in rain and icing conditions, and the reaction of the engine to high 'g' acceleration (catapulting) and deceleration (arresting). We would also have to find out the power plant's sensitivity to surface water ingestion on take-off and the effects of bird strikes. Altogether it looked as if a whole new ball game was ahead of us.

In our jets we went higher and higher, faster and faster. Now we were able to reach the high speeds in level flight which the piston-engined planes could only do in almost perpendicular dives. Mach 1, the door of the sound barrier, drew closer. In the rarified air of the high altitudes the mixture in the engine became poor, the combustions subsequently became unstable and unreliable, and inevitably we had engine failures. If this happened I tried to make Farnborough if I could, but more often than not had to glide into some little airfield.

Britain's first jet aircraft, the Gloster/Whittle E.28/39. It undertook a comprehensive test programme at RAE Farnborough and between March 1944 and its last flight on 20th February 1945 the author was the main test pilot.

The He 177 heavy bomber snatched out of Vichy France by RAE pilots in September 1944. It arrived at Farnborough sporting French roundels and the legend 'Prise de Guerre'. After putting in many hours on the plane the author described the He 177 as 'one of the very few German aircraft of the period that I tested that I did not enjoy flying'.

My sudden materialization, inevitably in shirtsleeves, in a plane without a propeller, asking for fuel which they had never heard of, professing to be a naval officer flying an RAF machine from a civilian establishment, was a shock. I was often virtually arrested.

When I was eventually allowed to telephone Farnborough they sent over the jet-mother plane, a Lancaster with a huge fuel tank in its bomb bay carrying our special fuel. For this early high-altitude work we used the original little Gloster E.28/39, Whittle's first real jet aeroplane. We had already lost one of these flying test-beds in a high-altitude accident and, as more new types of jet aircraft came into being, it was decided to preserve this historic aircraft, and the survivor was sent to the Science Museum at South Kensington.

But jets were only part of my crowded programme. Work of all kinds poured in.

At RAE in wartime we had very little time off from our flying duties, but Saturday lunchtime usually meant a convivial get-together of pilots in the Mess before a much-welcomed free afternoon. Such a session had just got under way on 2nd September when the CO Experimental Flying (COEF) was handed a signal advising that an operation could be carried out in Vichy France by combined groups of French Maquis and Allied support units, who could isolate a Heinkel 177, Germany's latest four-engined bomber, at Blagnac airfield near Toulouse, where Heinkel had

Three rare views
of the Gloster
E.28/39 being
flown by
Eric Brown on
its last flight on
20th February
1945.

a repair centre. The RAE was to organise delivery of a snatch crew for the collection of that Heinkel. Instantly at Farnborough it was all hands to the pumps and COEF decided he would fly the Chief Test Pilot and a flight engineer to pick up this unexpected war prize, and take two Beaufighters from Wireless and Electrical Flight as fighter-escort. My job was to make a list of the likely German cockpit markings they would find and append their English translations.

After about one and a half hours the three aircraft were on their way with the Hudson, taking five hours fifty minutes to locate Blagnac airfield in poor visibility. There it left the pirate crew and took off at once, having seen them in contact with the Allied commando force. En route to Blagnac the Beaufighters became separated from the Hudson in bad weather, and after being airborne for seven hours both ran out of fuel; one pilot baled out over the French coast and was rescued by the Maquis, the other pilot crash landed in France and was picked up by the Maquis, who looked after him. Both were eventually repatriated.

Meanwhile at Blagnac the pirate crew were taken under the wing of the Allied commando group until the time was right for a snatch operation. The latter took place on 10th September and this valuable war prize was flown back to Farnborough in two hours forty-five minutes without further incident.

Shortly after its arrival I flew the He 177 and was singularly unimpressed. Outwardly it looked twin-engined but in fact its two power plants each housed two DB 605 units mounted side-by-side with a single gear-casing connecting the two crankcases and the two crankshaft pinions driving a single airscrew shaft gear. The two huge four-bladed propellers were rotated in opposite directions to eliminate take-off swing. In the event of an engine failure the dead engine automatically disengaged itself from the airscrew shaft.

The German Air Ministry called for the 177 to have dive bombing capability and be fitted with the automatic dive recovery system, but this was plainly absurd since its controls were far too light and its structural strength far too weak. Indeed my feeling with it was that of flying a glass aeroplane.

In October I was sent to Beccles airfield near Lowestoft to instruct 618 RAF Mosquito squadron in the art of deck landing. I was slightly puzzled by this mission, but was given no clue as to what lay behind it.

A wartime secret of Beccles airfield

In October, 1944, a secret operation was rehearsed on a specially marked area of one of the main runways on Beccles airfield. Here is the story behind the operation.

ON MAY 18th, in this year of the 50th anniversary of the foundation of the R.A.F., the 25th anniversary of No. 617 Squadron's, the "Dam Busters," first spectacular operation — the breaching of the German dams on the night of May 16th-17th, 1943 — is to be commemorated in London with a reunion dinner.

The story of this epic attack, which was made by 19 Lancasters led by the late Wing Commander Guy P. Gibson, V.C., D.S.O., D.F.C., is too well known to mention here. Suffice to say that Paul Brickhill, in his book, *The Dam Busters,* noted: "The haze of Norfolk passed a few miles to port . . . and a minute later they were low over Southwold, the shingle was beneath them, and then they were over the water, flat and grey in the evening light. England faded behind . . . ."

❊ ❊ ❊

Barnes Wallis, the scientist who designed the spinning mine which was used for the attack, was at Beccles airfield in 1944 to supervise the fitting of the Highball spherical bomb, as it was called, to the Mosquitos of No. 618 Squadron for special operations in the Far East. Each equipped to carry two Highballs, the Mosquitos were to be used against the Japanese Navy in 1945.

What exactly took place at Beccles airfield, now more or less derelict?

In October, 1944, Fleet Air Arm pilot Lt. Cmdr. Eric M. "Winkle" Brown (later Commander Brown, O.B.E., D.S.C., A.F.C.) was sent there to instruct the Mosquito squadron "in the art of deck landing."

The commander was puzzled by his mission. He was given no clue as to what lay behind the deck landings which were carried out on a specially marked area on one of the main runways.

After the war, Commander Brown related how, during a visit to a hangar at Beccles, he saw a Mosquito with "a strange object peeping out of the bomb bay." Near by — and this gave Commander Brown his first clue — stood Barnes Wallis, the scientist, who, in addition to designing the dam-busting weapon of 1943, was the man responsible for the geodetic method of construction used in the famous wartime Vickers Wellington bomber.

The Beccles-based 618 Squadron — it will be seen that this squadron was formed immediately following the number given to the dam-busting squadron — went on to land on an aircraft carrier in preparation for operations in the Far East. However, a few days before the Mosquitos were due to take off — that was in August, 1945 — the first American atomic bomb was dropped on Japan and, on August 14th, Japan accepted the Allied demand for unconditional surrender.

Records kept by the De Havilland company, who made the famous Mosquito, state that "one of the most interesting projects for the Mosquito was its adaptation to take the Highball spherical bomb, to be bowled along the surface of the sea at enemy ships and targets."

In 1945, when the De Havilland company made a film about the Mosquito, the Highball project was the only aspect which for security reasons could not be depicted.

I remember watching the Mosquitos of 618 Squadron on many Saturday mornings from the Mutford side of Beccles airfield. But we schoolboys, who seldom missed a new feature on any aircraft, were never given a glimpse of the Highball hitched under a Mosquito. The secret was too well guarded.

Christopher R. Elliott

Barnes Wallis

A newspaper report about the secret operation at Beccles – from the author's scrapbook.

However, I began to hazard a good guess when I saw one of the squadron aircraft in the hangar with a strange object peeping out of the bomb bay, while nearby stood Barnes Wallis, the inventor of the spinning bomb used by Guy Gibson's Lancasters to breach the Mohne Dam.

The type of bomb used in the Mosquito was a spherical shape rather than the oil-drum cylindrical type used in the Dambuster Lancasters. The activity at Beccles was all in preparation for Operation High Ball to be made against Japanese capital ships in harbour.

I learned later that the 618 pilots had eventually been given actual deck landing practice in Barracuda aircraft on HMS *Rajah*, and obviously found it difficult as they pranged five Barras. After this costly initiation into the black art of deck landing they embarked in the two escort carriers *Rajah* and *Striker*, already carrying twenty-seven Sea Mosquitoes, which sailed from the Clyde on 31st October 1944. The squadron had been working up ashore in Australia for the operation and was almost ready to go when the American atomic bombs on Hiroshima and Nagasaki ended the war. To the best of my knowledge, the 618 pilots were never required to land their Mosquitoes on an aircraft carrier.

I went on throwing planes into the wires on our dummy flight deck. Slamming a machine into the wires deliberately off-centre was a regular thing, done to test the strength of the hook under the appalling side loads it had to take then. When I put the new Firebrand 3 twenty-five feet off the centre the entire back end tore off.

This sort of thing happened far less often when we fitted the American-type sting hook right in the tail of our fast deck landers instead of sticking it under the fuselage. The strain was taken through a stronger point and, because the sting hook hung lower, there was a better chance of catching a wire as well. I had not abandoned ship work during my testing, and I tried out the sting-hooked Seafire on the *Pretoria Castle*.

We were using the Seafire 15 with the bigger new Griffon engine now, and there was a later one still, the Seafire 45, a version with a new and different wing altogether and a special five-bladed airscrew. One day I had just touched down in a Mark 15 on the deck of the *Pretoria Castle* when I was told to hop straight over into the cockpit of the new Mark 45, which I had never even seen before. Jeff Quill, Supermarine's chief test pilot, had delivered the 45 on board, having taken a deck-landing course with the Navy to understand the customer's problems.

The prototype of the British Miles Libellula, showing the tail plane in front and the wing behind. During his six years at the RAE the author saw many weird and wonderful aircraft, but few stranger than the Libellula.

We began to get many American machines to test and with them new ideas and experiments. With the new American power-boosted ailerons you could roll a big plane with one finger instead of having to heave on the stick with all your might. We also got our first experience of the tricycle undercarriage, so valuable for deck landing. And there were the freaks …

The British Miles Libellula was an attempt to give a naval pilot a perfect view forward for deck landing by having the tail plane in front of him and the wing behind. It was a delightful, bird-like aeroplane to fly, but the canard layout had unfortunately too high a drag to give promise of good fighter performance.

The same idea inspired the Supermarine S.24/37. When a pilot was sinking towards the deck he had to tilt the nose of his machine upwards in the three-point attitude in order to maintain lift, and thus seriously obscure his view. The S.24/37 tried to overcome this by incorporating a variable-incidence wing. When it came in to touch down the wing only tilted upwards, rotating itself under pilot-controlled electric power, while the fuselage stayed level. The snag here was that the extra mechanism involved made the machine too heavy, and she had some nasty stalling characteristics at the higher wing-incidence settings.

The Vickers Windsor was a big, high-altitude bomber, in which the pilot perched on top of the nose in a little glasshouse. A sensible, if amusing, feature of the Windsor was its four separate landing wheels, one

87

The Vickers Windsor – a high-altitude experimental bomber.

under each engine. The big advantage of this was proved when an outer wheel refused to come down and the big aircraft was still able to land smoothly on the other three.

She had one frightening aspect. The wings flapped in flight. At full load on take-off the wingtips flexed as much as six feet. She went along looking like a huge, gentle seagull. The flexing of the geodetically-constructed wings had an adverse effect on performance, but I enjoyed flying this aircraft. It really arrived too late on the war scene to be adopted for service.

On 4th August 1944 I had received a handwritten memo from Mr W. S. Farren, Director of the RAE, saying 'I would like you to start taking a close interest in the supersonic research project being conducted by RAE in conjunction with Miles Aircraft Company. To this end you should liaise with Morien Morgan'. The latter was Head of Aero Dept. Flight Section.

By now we were knocking on the wall of the sound barrier in our jets. What would happen when we had an aircraft which was fast enough to smash the wall no one knew. The Miles M.52 was designed to cross the threshold of the unknown and find out.

This supersonic jet was designed to be a very hot ship. Everything about her was new. There was her special razor-edged, bi-convex wing, with a section like an elongated diamond. The engine was to be a Whittle jet incorporating a special new ducted fan. The fan blades of this 'augmentor' were extensions of the turbine blades mounted on rotors in the exhaust stream of the engine. It was a kind of sophisticated form of reheating.

The fuselage was cylindrical, shaped like an 0.5in bullet, with a cockpit diameter of 4ft, so the pilot had to be no taller than 5ft 8in and this probably helped my selection. The pressurised cockpit was a conical nose capsule, located in the annular air intake for the jet engine. The capsule could be detached with cordite charges to project it forward in an emergency, and its drogue parachute would slow it down sufficiently for the pilot to bale out with his own parachute. The Gillette wings, as the bi-convex aerofoils were known, only spanned 25ft and were extremely thin and to all intents solid in structure, so were unable to house fuel or an undercarriage. The latter folded up into the fuselage, with the nose wheel housed in a well between the pilot's legs as he lay in a semi-reclining position.

Farnborough Fantasy. An artist's impression of the Miles M.52 in flight over the RAE. That the aircraft could have gone supersonic – if the project had not been cancelled – was proven in effect when one of the models launched from a Mosquito at 36,400ft, achieved a speed of Mach 1.38 in level flight on 10th October 1948.

The aim of this research aircraft was to reach Mach 1.07 in a dive from 50,000ft to 36,000ft, and with the lead we knew we had on the Americans – and suspected we had on the Germans – in the region of transonic flight testing, our hopes were high that the M.52 would be the first aircraft in the world to break the sound barrier and fly at supersonic speed.

Perhaps the most magical feature of the M.52 was its 'flying tail', which is a single-piece combined tailplane and elevator, giving a more powerful horizontal movement than the standard fixed tailplane with moving elevator attached to its trailing edge. This tail was, together with a full-scale wooden mock-up of the M.52 bi-convex wing, fitted to an M.3B Falcon Six light aircraft which I flew at RAE in April 1945. The 'flying tail' was intended to give the M.52 a smoother ride through the compressibility region's strong longitudinal trim changes of transonic flight.

In the early spring of 1945 the British government instructed the Miles company to hand over every detail and drawing of the M.52 to a visiting American delegation, and in return a British delegation was to visit the USA and receive information on American high speed research. The latter visit was cancelled by the Americans, which raises doubts as to whether they had any reciprocal information of substance to offer.

When the M.52 was 82 per cent complete towards the first flight, the project was – without warning to either Miles or RAE – cancelled by the Ministry of Supply in February 1946. No satisfactory reason for this decision was ever given, and to this day it remains shrouded in mystery.

Certainly the Americans were the beneficiaries from all this, as our fifteen-month lead over the Bell X-1 supersonic contender disappeared, and when that aircraft ran into compressibility problems in 1947 it was rescued by fitment of the 'flying tail'. The consequences of the fateful cancellation of the M.52 are reflected in the Conservative Government White Paper issued in February 1955 in which it was stated that 'the cancellation of the M.52 seriously delayed the progress of aeronautical research in the UK'.

I was anticipating a few days off at Christmas, but that hope evaporated when I was informed I was required to go to Italy to assess the latest Italian fighters our forces had captured there. This was to be something of a repeat of my New Year jaunt to Italy. I arrived this time just before Christmas and completed my task in time to have Christmas at home.

I found three of the Regia Aeronautica's best fighters at two airfields in northern Italy, and each got progressively more impressive than the last. It was really like having a Maserati, Lamborghini and Ferrari lined up for test drives. There was firstly the stubby Reggiane 2000, whose radial-engined design had been influenced by one of its designers having spent two years in the USA. Although it handled nicely it was basically under-powered. This shortcoming was addressed in its successor the Re 2001 with a German Daimler-Benz DB 601A in-line engine, but was not up to the performance of the Macchi 202 powered by the same engine. However, the supreme Italian fighter I flew was the Macchi 205V powered by a DB 605A, which was on a par with the Mustang and Fw 190 in that time scale.

Nineteen forty-four came to an end. Looking back I thought I could not possibly have another period of such exciting, such varied flying. But the new year made it seem tame.

It started off quite literally with a bang on New Year's Day of 1945. In jet engine development the method of increasing thrust by injecting fuel into the exhaust outlet was being pioneered mainly at Whittle's Power Jets company by suspending a jet engine under a four-piston-engine Lancaster and experimenting with what in turn has been variously called 'thrust augmentation', 'afterburning' and 'reheat'. This was thus being tested in comparative safety, and had reached the stage where its reli-ability justified it being done on a pure jet aircraft at RAE. A Meteor I was chosen and an aperture was cut out behind the pilot's cockpit so that a flight observer and some test apparatus could be housed in this coal hole. I made this flight with a young observer of about my own age and he controlled the injection of fuel into the jet pipe and when the tempera-tures got too high for comfort he would call out, 'I'm cutting fuel injec-tion now because we're cooking'. In general the experiment went very well and I certainly admired my unseen passenger's nonchalance.

On 11th January I attended a meeting at Farnborough to discuss the possibilities of operating planes without undercarriages from carriers. The reinforced undercarriage of a naval aircraft not only accounted for a serious proportion of its total weight, but often forced a designer to make a wing thicker than he would like for performance in order to house the landing wheels. The meeting went into the advantages of using fighters without permanent undercarriages, and we heard what the Aero and Designs Departments had thought up to replace them.

They suggested soft ground or sand, a sprung floor, a flexible surface floating on water, a pair of longitudinal wires suspended from towers, a wire net, a trolley running on a railway, a steerable trolley on a runway, and a 'pick-a-back' or carrier aircraft.

None of these looked very practicable in the cold light of experience, but the Chairman introduced Major F. M. Green, the veteran aero-engine inventor, who had been working on another idea.

Major Green described a scheme in which jet fighters landed on a large carpet which was suspended along both sides and one end by shock absorbers. The landing, he said, would be safe and easy, as the deflection of the carpet could be made practically dead-beat and the absence of an undercarriage gave a very much better chance of picking up the arrester wire at the rear end of the carpet.

Both the arrester wire and the action of the carpet would tend to keep the aircraft central. Once stopped, the aircraft could be pulled backwards by the arrester wire to a hinged flap in the deck. This would tilt down and the aircraft would slide on to a trolley on the top hangar deck. The flap would close up again, ready for the next landing.

Landings would probably be possible every thirty seconds. The carpet would be 40 feet wide by 150 feet long for an aircraft of about 8,000 lb normal weight. It would be made of similar fabric to that used for tyres, the cords running from end to end of the carpet and transversely across it. The wear on the surface would be small – considerably less than on a tyre – especially if the surface was kept damp.

Major Green pointed out that petrol, oil, and varying climatic conditions would have no more effect on the carpet than on ordinary tyres, that storms would not blow the carpet away, that the deck could be built level with the carpet, and that by building in a kind of bead wire and suitably shaping the edges the transverse tension in the carpet could be quite uniform although the shock absorbers were placed at intervals of three feet. By suitably arranging the high lift flaps to bear on the carpet the aircraft could be made stable sideways, and a mean retardation from all causes of 2'g' could be expected on landing.

We discussed his scheme. It was suggested that there might be trouble with the rise and fall of the ship. I said that I thought this would not prevent the aircraft from picking up a single wire fairly easily, and if it was positioned near the fulcrum point of pitch on the flight deck would help the pilot's judgement enormously, and the view from the aircraft would be excellent.

Major Green added that the high rate of accidents due to side pressure on the undercarriage would be removed, and both the Chairman, Mr W. G. A. Perring, and I agreed that the whole method seemed safer than the present one. He thought that the extra strengthening needed in the fuselage would not offset the advantage of no undercarriage.

It was agreed that the scheme should be carried further by work with models and calculations. If these were successful we could go on to live testing. This looked like another job for me, and I looked forward to it.

In February we heard that three new helicopters were to be allocated to us in Aero Flight, a present from America. I had never seen a tail-rotor type

The author flying the Sikorsky R-4B helicopter 'hands-off'.

helicopter, and I was all agog. Early in March I saw one for the first time when it paid a short visit to Farnborough. I had a short twenty-minute flight in it as a passenger. On the very next flight the pilot crashed it.

Within days Squadron Leader Martindale and I were off to Speke Airport at Liverpool to collect two new Sikorsky R-4B helicopters.

When we got there we found the American mechanics finishing assembling the machines out of crates. In charge was a huge technical master-sergeant. I said to him, 'Right. When are you going to teach us to fly these things?'

He said, 'Whaddya mean, bud? Here's your instructor,' and handed me a large orange-coloured booklet.

Alarmed, we went back to the mess and read the book. It must have been written by an optimist.

We managed to get the first machine started with the help of the building crew, and I got in to try and make the horribly unfamiliar thing fly.

I fiddled with the controls, and within a few seconds I was charging all over the airfield. The brute just wouldn't obey me. You had a stick and rudder pedals, as usual, but these had to be used in careful co-ordination with a thing called a collective pitch lever down on the left-hand side. This lever was the main control for the vertical movement of the machine, and it also had at the tip a twist-grip, motor-bike-type throttle. All these controls had to be handled skilfully in conjunction. I tried to make it hover, but it was all I could do to set the thing down again without damaging it, me, or the other aircraft on the field.

Speechless, we both had a stiff drink, then tried again. Eventually we thought we had better try and make Farnborough and after a touching and ominous last farewell from the Americans, who were as shaken as we were, we lurched into the air.

I don't know how we made it. Our formation all the way down was quite the loosest ever flown. At times we were as much as two or three miles apart.

We were now supposed to test the machines, but this was obviously quite out of the question until we had learned to fly them. So whenever we could spare the time we went over to the new RAF Rotary Wing Training School at Andover for instruction. By the end of March we were fully trained, and could get on with the real job.

I found myself assigned to do all the helicopter testing, with Bill

One of Eric Brown's 'firsts' in aviation was the landing of a tricycle aircraft, the Airacobra, on the flight deck of the Pretoria Castle.

Stewart once again my boffin. We made some useful discoveries in the course of experimenting. It was supposed to be impossible to stall a helicopter, but we discovered a stage when control was lost as completely as in a normal machine in a stall. We also investigated the flow pattern of air past the rotors by having them photographed as they passed through a coloured smoke screen laid down by another plane. It was the first fundamental research on helicopters done in this country, and Igor Sikorsky, the inventor of the helicopter, was keenly interested in our results when he visited Farnborough during a trip over from America.

April came with a promise of spring for everybody. The war in Europe was folding fast. I went to sea again on the 3rd to do the first British tail-down catapult launch in a Barracuda. The next day I was going to make some approaches to the deck to find out how it would have to be done for the carpet-deck scheme. I was going to use an American Bell Airacobra which had been given to me to use as a private hack after its honourable retirement from test work, and which was the only Airacobra in the world to have had a deck-landing hook fitted to it. This had been fitted to test the behaviour of its tricycle undercarriage in runs into arrester wires.

I had already collected a few 'firsts' in aviation, and I rather wanted to be the first pilot ever to put a tricycle aircraft down on a flight deck. The Airacobra was not officially cleared for such a landing, but the boffins had told me privately that it would probably take the strain.

This was not on the official programme at all, but I hoped that I could persuade Captain Caspar John of the *Pretoria Castle* to turn a blind eye to what I had in mind. I wrote to him beforehand and asked him if he would be prepared to take me aboard in the event of sudden engine trouble. He saw at once what I was after, of course, and was good sport enough to go along with it. He suggested that it might be a good idea if my engine trouble occurred on my last approach.

Strangely enough it did. I began my approach, then, just for the record, called up the ship and complained that my engine was running rough. Would they accept me? Back came Captain John's instant 'affirmative'. I put my hook down, touched down, and caught a wire with no trouble at all.

The trouble came when I tried to get off again. To take off from a carrier's deck was of all things far from the designer's thoughts, and the Airacobra had a dangerously long run. With the ship steaming at absolutely full bore I just managed to stagger off the deck.

Chapter 8

NOW CAME A STRANGE INTERLUDE. At the beginning of the year the Director found out that I had once taught in Germany and asked me to organize classes in German for selected scientists who would be flown into Germany as soon as the war ended to investigate certain valuable items of German research before the Russians could get them or the Allied soldiers destroy them by mistake. He said I would probably be going myself to help. We were thoroughly briefed on the different establishments to be visited, and the personalities to be captured and interviewed. My list ran like this:

Dr Werner von Braun
Dr Heinkel
Willy Messerschmitt
Kurt Tank (The Focke-Wulf designer)
Hanna Reitsch (The famous woman chief test pilot at
    Peenemünde, the equivalent of our Farnborough)
The Horten Brothers (The leading glider designers).

I was then designated CO Enemy Aircraft Flight at RAE. In mid-April we were alerted to stand by to go. Then came the great day. We were on our way to Germany.

I landed with the first team at Fassberg, the nearest airfield to Luneberg Heath, because it was not very far from one of our most important objectives, the Göttingen Aeronautical Research Centre.

Also near at hand was Belsen. When I had seen my scientists dispersed over Germany to their various objectives, I went there to see for myself what we had only read in what sounded like the worst horror fiction.

There I saw for myself the piled dead, the still open graves. I tried to speak to some of the silent, shuffling ghosts of men, in their striped rags. They would listen, staring dully at the ground, then step aside and move on. I had known the Germans, I had been happy in Germany. In the war

I had made excuses for them, blamed the Nazis. There could be no excuse for this.

The 2nd Army medical Brigadier Glynn Hughes who was the senior officer at Belsen was surprised to find a naval officer visiting the camp, but when he saw my high-profile pass and found I was German-speaking, he asked me to interrogate the camp commandant Josef Kramer and his female assistant Irma Griese in his presence. Two more loathsome creatures it is hard to imagine, especially the woman who had arrived at Belsen from Auschwitz armed with an already fierce reputation for cruelty.

We followed our advancing troops up into Schleswig-Holstein and I headed for my main objective at Husum airfield where a Group of JG 400's operational Me 163Bs were based. The aircraft were intact, and after spending a couple of days there I made up my mind that I was going to fly a Komet under power, although I realised this would require some preparative training and co-operation from the pilots and ground crews, who were now all prisoners-of-war. Most of the pilots were reluctant to impart technical information but the 'black men' (ground crews) seemed less recalcitrant, and after some interrogation I felt three could be particularly relied on to give responsible help, so I had them segregated from the other POWs.

The Germans had retreated back to Scandinavia, taking many of their latest types of aircraft with them. It was my immediate job to go up to the big night-fighter station at Grove in Denmark and pick up there a very new jet reconnaissance bomber called the Arado 234B.

I learned from the Army when they expected to have units in Denmark, so I decided to fly up to Grove. However, I was unaware that the Army's advance had been slowed by running into an enclave of German resistance at Flensburg, where Grand Admiral Doenitz, Hitler's successor after the Führer's suicide in his Berlin Bunker, had established his headquarters, protected by a crack regiment of the SS.

When I climbed out of my Anson there I was met by a major of the Luftwaffe, who handed me his sword, thus surrendering this vast airfield and its 2,000 men to me. I had flown far ahead of our advancing forces. I was not equipped to handle such an occasion. I made the best job of it I could before I got on with my real task. We saw the Arados, as well as some interesting new types of radar-equipped night fighters, and arranged quickly to return and collect them in a few days' time.

A sinister beauty. This Me 262A-1 was one of the captured aircraft tested at Farnborough. The author was convinced that this was unquestionably the foremost warplane of its day, although accident fatalities in the Luftwaffe had been appalling, particularly among night-fighter pilots flying the heavier model. The Me 262 was not equipped with an ejector seat.

After an uneasy night at Grove, our Army advance forces arrived next morning so I decided to return to Schleswig-Holstein, where I had selected Schleswig airfield as my destination since I had a report that some jet aircraft were there. I left my co-pilot with the Anson and to look after the boffins while I appropriated a serviceable German Fw 190 and headed south. En route I flew over Flensburg and noted much activity in the area, so decided to land and report to our Army about the situation at Grove. As I approached Flensburg airfield I thought my aircraft would be taken for a Luftwaffe pilot surrendering but as I touched down I attracted some sporadic small arms fire and so opened up at once and took off for Schleswig, little realising the Doenitz drama taking place at Flensburg.

At Schleswig, where our Army was in control, I found some intact Messerschmitt 262 twin-jet fighters, most of which were single-seaters, but there was one two-seat night fighter. With the help of the Luftwaffe POWs who were still not 'caged' on the airfield, I decided to have a go

99

at this machine, since it was a rarity and too unusual to miss, but the single-seat fighters were my real targets.

This was, in fact, my first experience of a German jet aircraft and I was immediately struck by the complexity of starting up its axial-flow engines, and by their sensitivity to throttle movement in flight – to move the throttles at all quickly invited a flame-out of the jets.

Then I had to break off from Germany and hurry back to Farnborough to carry out the first test for deck-landing potentialities on the new De Havilland Vampire jet fighter, which the little Spider Crab had now been renamed.

I did the test at Hatfield on 19th May. The machine I used was a Vampire 1 modified to the extent of having its flaps and dive brakes enlarged, but with no deck hook fitted as yet. That stage was some way off. This was just the most basic of trials.

The little Vampire was a very pretty thing, with its small cockpit nacelle, slender twin booms, and streamlined shape. She was a classic little aeroplane, and looked airworthy from the start.

I took off with no trouble, enjoying the feel of the machine at once. The engine had to be opened up slowly, unlike a piston engine, and the aircraft just began to creep against the brakes as full power was reached, so that acceleration was good and a very good take-off run was possible, with the right flap setting.

There was, of course, no take-off swing, my old bogey in the Mosquito, and the view was absolutely perfect; when I put her through her paces she performed excellently. There were some points which would need modification, of course. The jet engine was still rather too sluggish in picking up in a sudden emergency, the sort which would occur when the wires had been missed and the pilot had to open up and go round again. This was a prototype aircraft, so the cockpit layout was the usual piece-meal maze of instruments, but this could be put right without too much trouble.

This version of the Vampire was entirely suitable for deck-landing trials, subject to a satisfactory hook mechanism being fitted. I put in my report, 'In spite of the difficulties facing a pure jet aircraft for deck land-ings, this "Vampire" represents an extremely apt aerodynamic attack on the problem ...' A test pilot's report is never lyrical.

I was due back in Germany for the serious part of my mission there, but things were happening fast now, and another special assignment got in the way.

We got a signal from the Air Attaché in Dublin to say that about two weeks previously a Junkers 88 carrying the latest German radar gear had force-landed in a field north of Dublin at five o'clock in the morning. The Irish were prepared to let us collect this plane, provided we arrived in an aircraft carrying civilian markings, and wore civilian clothes. I was to lead the party to go.

The first condition was impossible, as there was not a single aeroplane in all Britain with civilian markings after six years of total war. The second was flouted by our Group Captain, who insisted that for prestige value we went over in uniform, carrying our civvies in suitcases. On 2nd June 1945 we landed at the Eire Air Corps field of Gormanston, a little grass field where the men lived in tents, and where the Junkers had put down. There it was, standing forlornly on the field.

In our martial glory we got a very cold reception from the Irish. Icily we were told to go at once into the CO's office and change. But no sooner had we done this, than the same unfriendly characters were all over us, slapping us on the back, pumping our hands, filling us up with Guinness.

The night fighter Junkers 88, carrying the latest German radar gear, which force landed in a field north of Dublin.

We spent a hilarious night in Dublin, before interrogating the German crew next morning.

They had a strange story to tell. The pilot was a German South African, who had had, he said, no interest whatsoever in the war, being very comfortably settled with his family in South Africa, but had been forced to return to Germany to fight after threats to the safety of his children if he did not. This was the way the Gestapo operated in the ex-German colonies.

As the war was drawing to its close and the Germans were retreating, their CO had got all his pilots together and said to them, 'Look, it's all over, we're finished. We might as well get out of here. Every pilot can have his aircraft and full petrol tanks. He can take anybody else he chooses aboard, and clear out wherever he wants. Personally, I'm off to Sweden'.

Four of the pilots decided to make for Eire, some for Sweden, others for Spain. The four for Eire set off in formation. Over Manchester flak split them up and one of them was shot down. Our man did not see the other two planes again, and they were almost certainly lost in the Irish Sea in the foul weather then prevailing.

He flew above the filthy weather and picked up the coast of Ireland on his radar, broke cloud at 400 feet in the pouring rain, flew south down the coast until he saw the field at Gormanston, and landed with great skill in the half-light of five in the morning on the wet grass of a landing strip only 900 yards long. Now he was longing to go back to South Africa and become a man of peace again.

We examined his radar, ran up the engines, and just managed to squeeze out of the little field. We headed for Anglesey, and there a flight of Spitfires picked us up and escorted us to Farnborough, just in case there were any suspicious gunners about.

The immediate months following the German capitulation were a period of frantic activity as captured enemy aircraft were examined and flight tested, and their design engineers and test pilots were interrogated by the Allies. As the CO of the Enemy Aircraft Flight at RAE Farnborough I was heavily involved in all this activity, and I was advantaged by the fact I was German-speaking.

The defeat of the Germans in 1945 revealed the extent of their technological advances in aerodynamics, rocketry, engines and weaponry as well as ancillary equipment.

AERODYNAMICS: The German scientists were greatly aided in their work by their advanced wind tunnels, especially by their unique supersonic model, and this gave them the opportunity to test sweptback and forward-swept wings, all-wing and delta shapes, which were translated into hardware in such aircraft as the Me 262 (sweptback), Me 163 (all-wing/vertical tail), Ju 287 (swept-forward), Horten IX (all-wing), and Lippisch DM-1 (delta).

Professor Busemann, the leading authority on sweepback, gave an open lecture in Rome in 1935, describing its advantages in delaying the effects of compressibility at transonic speeds, and although attended by international scientists, the idea went virtually unheeded by them, leaving the Germans to enjoy sole benefits.

In the key area of stability and control the Germans concentrated on giving to their fighter aircraft a high rate of roll, and excellent examples of this were the Fw 190 and the He 162, the latter having the lightest and most effective aerodynamically balanced controls I have ever encountered. On the larger tandem layout Do 335 fighter they introduced powered ailerons, and in the huge Bv 222 flying boat they used servo-tab controls on all three axes, which in my opinion made them almost dangerously light for that particular aircraft.

ROCKETRY: The Germans had experimented with solid fuel rockets for propulsion in aircraft as early as the 1920s, and liquid fuel rockets in unmanned vehicles, but the breakthrough came in the early 1940s with the use of liquid fuel rockets which were throttleable and so gave the pilot a much needed degree of flexibility, whilst doing nothing to remove the highly dangerous volatility of the fuels used.

The liquid fuel A4 (V2) rocket, the brainchild of Wernher von Braun, was a potent weapon in the later stages of World War II, and eventually led the way to space travel.

ENGINES: The whole range of German supercharged piston engines could have power boosting systems installed, providing either methanol/water injection (MW) or nitrous oxide injection (GM1) into the supercharger. These systems gave speed increases of some 20 to 30 mph.

Compression ignition (diesel) engines were developed for long endurance operations, and were fitted mainly to flying boats with

103

successful results. I flew such engines on the twin Do 18, the three-engined Bv 138, the four-engined Do 26 and the six-engined Bv 222 and found them very quiet but dirty and smelly – not by any stretch eco-friendly.

Although Britain had an initial lead in jet propulsion technology, this was dissipated by bureaucratic inertia, allowing Germany to overtake us and build the world's first single- and twin-turbojet-engined aircraft. Initially both nations favoured the centrifugal-flow jet engine layout for simplicity and reliability, but Germany rapidly changed to the axial-flow layout because of the reduced aerodynamic drag of the nacelle shape and superior specific fuel consumption offered for a given amount of thrust. However, the complexity of the axial-flow engine caused production problems for the Germans, and the lack of the strategic metals to withstand the inherent heat stresses meant that their early operational turbo-jets had a scrap life of only 25 hours. Nevertheless the first two jet aircraft to become operational in 1944 were the twin-axial-flow-engined Ar 234B unarmed photo-reconnaissance bomber, which depended on its speed for survival, and the twin-axial-flow-engined Me 262 fighter-bomber, which was the most formidable aircraft of World War II, being at least 100 mph faster than any contemporary aircraft. Finally the nippy little single-axial-flow-engined He 162 appeared in some numbers at the end of the war, but too late to get operationally involved. It was remarkable, however, in being produced in less than three full months from issue of specification to first flight.

A variation on the turbojet was the pulse-jet engine of the pilotless V1 'flying bomb' which harassed the south of England in the summer of 1944. The device was ramp launched, using hydrogen peroxide and calcium permanganate for initial acceleration until it left under its own power.

WEAPONRY: The Germans used a wide range of varying calibre weapons as both fixed and free aircraft guns throughout World War II, but in the later stages introduced 30 mm cannon on their jet and rocket fighters as a low velocity, high capacity weapon. They also used heavy calibre (50 and 55 mm) anti-tank guns in some of their aircraft specialising in ground attack.

The most devastating air weapon to be used by the Me 262 in the final stages of the war was the R4M air-to-air rocket missile carried under the wings in racks of 12 or extended racks of 24. A strike on an enemy aircraft meant its total annihilation.

Another successful development was that of the Schräge Musik (inclined organ pipes) fitted to night fighters, and consisting of 2 × 30mm cannon slanted forward at 60 degrees and located between the tandem cockpits. These were fired into the underside of a bomber once the crew had identified it in silhouette as an enemy target. On the first operational sortie of an He 219 using the system, it shot down six Lancasters.

ANCILLARY EQUIPMENT: (i) Ejection seats were in use by the Germans at the outset of World War II, and indeed the first ejection in anger was made in January 1943 from an He 280 twin-jet which got into icing difficulties. Their seats were propelled by compressed air, and besides being fired by pulling the seat face blind, they had a secondary trigger fitted to the side of the seat at thigh level to deal with high 'g' emergencies. The first production aircraft fitted with ejection seats was the He 219 two-seat night fighter.

(ii) Piloting prone position in the cockpit had been tried out by the Germans before World War II in the Berlin B.2 research aircraft and in the Ho IV high aspect ratio sailplane. The former had a completely prone layout, but the latter had the less tiring 'praying mantis' position.

(iii) Auto dive recovery was fitted in the German Ju 87, Ju 88 and He 177 bombers. It was activated by opening the dive brakes, and initiated the pull-out when the bombs were dropped at a preset release height. It was an effective and reliable system on the Ju 87 and Ju 88, but never used on the four-engined He 177.

(iv) Electronics were widely used in German aircraft in place of hydraulics, which were considered more vulnerable to combat damage. One of the more interesting applications of electronics was the Kommando-gerät, which was intended to free fighter pilots in combat from the demands of controlling engine boost, propeller pitch and engine rpm by having these automatically controlled through a single throttle lever.

(v) Propeller reverse thrust was fitted to the Bv 222 flying boat's middle engine on each wing of this six-engined giant to facilitate water manoeuvring during taxying. It was also fitted to the very aerodynamically clean tricycle-undercarriaged Do 335, which had a very long landing run. Use of reverse thrust on the front tractor propeller reduced the landing run by 25 per cent.

(vi) A skid undercarriage was fitted experimentally to the Ar 234, and as standard to the Me 163B. The advantage of such a layout is reduced weight and drag, because it is easier to house than a wheeled arrangement. However, a skid can only be landed on a grass surface, and after landing retrieval of the aircraft is slow.

Mention should be made of the considerable progress made in Germany in rotary-wing development, and some types reached the production stage and then operational status, though in very small numbers because of Allied bombing of their manufacturing facilities.

The advance state of German aviation technology reflected their lengthy preparation for war by building up a large number of technical high schools, aeronautical departments in key universities such as Brunswick and Göttingen, and particularly well equipped research establishments such as Völkenrode, Darmstadt and the LFA Vienna.

The skid undercarriage, which was fitted as standard to the Me 163B.

The proliferation of new aviation projects which abounded in Germany from the late 1930s up to virtually the last days of the war in Europe can be seen as a weakness in controlling the conduct of its war, for it was draining resources away from the vital necessity to concentrate on development and mass production of only key elements such as the Fw 190 and Me 262 for daylight defence, and the He 219 and upgrading of the Me 110 night fighter in defence of the hard pressed Third Reich. Of course much of this argument only holds good if those measures would have largely prevented intruder interference with pilot training, the bombing of oil refineries and aircraft and engine manufacturing plants – a very big IF indeed.

In the final analysis the Germans had undoubtedly made significant advances in aeronautical technology, which in turn made a huge impact on the post-war aviation world and heavily influenced the new design philosophies in Britain (DH 108), the United States (F-86 Sabre) and the Soviet Union (MIG-15).

Chapter 9

I WAS POISED to go back to Germany when along came two absolutely new naval aircraft to test. The Sea Hornet, a twin-engined deck-lander developed from the Mosquito, followed on the heels of the single-seat Hawker Sea Fury.

Neither was yet fit for the deck. The Fury had the big Centaurus engine driving a five-bladed airscrew, and its rudder would not control sufficiently the vicious swing to starboard this engine gave it. But it was a splendid aircraft, and this problem just had to be solved.

The Sea Hornet was free of this trouble. Its 'handed' engines – one turning one way, one the other – eliminated all swing. But its aileron control, excellent at high speeds, was poor in the low register. I had to work very closely with Bill Humble of Hawker's and Geoffrey Pike of De Havilland's on these fast machines.

I started to do all the deck-proofing work on the two and fit in whirlwind visits to Germany as well. It was a very hectic programme, but I enjoyed it. Then I was landed with the Seafire 46 as well.

The Me 163B flown in towed and gliding flight by the author, the Walter rocket motor having been removed and an auto-observer installed in its place to record test data.

I wouldn't have complained. But I was relieved, nevertheless, when the Establishment asked for help on my behalf. Commander Robertson from Boscombe Down took over the Sea Fury. I still averaged four or five flights a day, each about forty minutes, and often seven or eight. In the month of June I flew thirty different types of aircraft. My more hectic days would run something like this one:

Take-off time	Aircraft	Flight duration	Test
0810	Bell Kingcobra	30 min.	Boundary Layer Investigation
0905	Meteor 1	40 min.	Directional Snaking
1015	Supermarine S.24/37	45 min.	Stalls
1120	Sea Hornet	40 min.	Dummy Deck Landings
1335	Junkers 188	55 min.	Single-engine Performance
1500	Lancaster 3	1 hour	Stick Forces per 'g'
1620	Sikorsky Gadfly	40 min.	Trim Curves in Auto-rotation
2010	Tempest 5	30 min.	Speed Course

Speed-course flying runs were usually done in the flat calm of evening at very low level along the straight fourteen-mile stretch of railway track between Farnborough and Basingstoke.

Despite all that we knew about the latest German prototypes, I was completely fascinated by what I knew about one fighter, their tiny – and lethally dangerous – rocket fighter, the Me 163, and had an overwhelming desire to fly it as soon as possible. It was obvious that I could not just hop into a 163 and take off, as I had done so many times before with a minimum of briefing. The approach speed was 145–150mph, the touchdown speed 125. Landing was done on a skid. Then there was the, to us, still unknown quantity of the volatile fuel mixture.

I went over to Kiel with a team of scientists to the Walter works, where Dr Walter, inventor of the rocket motor used in the 163, put on a demonstration for us. It was a frightening display, weird and futuristic.

109

Immured behind a glass panel nine inches thick we watched the motor run out on the bench for two minutes. The roar of noise was shattering, the whole place quaked and trembled. All the men taking part in the demonstration were swathed in rubber aprons, gumboots, and hats, and looked very Wellsian.

But the simple performance which followed was even more sobering. Dr Walter took two glass rods, on one of which was a droplet of concentrated hydrogen peroxide, called T-Stoff and on the other the same quantity of a solution of hydrazene hydrate in methanol, called C-Stoff. He slowly inclined first one, then the other. A droplet from one rod fell on the floor. A teardrop from the other fell on top of it. There was a violent explosion which blew both rods out of the doctor's hands. After this Faustian exhibition we fully appreciated how dangerous those volatile rocket fuels were.

I next flew to the airfield at Bad Zwischenahn where the remnants of the 163 training unit were located. I had already familiarised myself with the training programme, which I started by making five flights in a Stummel Habicht, a special clipped-wing version of the well-known Habicht (Hawk) glider. I had located a sole Me 163A and had it flown by a German instructor under tow by a Me 110 to Fassberg by another German pilot while I flew alongside in company. There I made three flights under tow to 20,000 feet and found the 163A a very easy and pleasant aircraft to fly as a glider.

While at Fassberg I heard that, because of a rash of accidents caused by RAF pilots attempting to fly captured German aircraft, the C-in-C Germany had issued orders to British Forces banning any use of German rocket fuels. Only RAE accredited pilots were exempt but this position was likely to change shortly. So it was virtually now or never if I was to experience power flight in the Komet. My desire to do so now became an obsession, which I realised would not be requited except by a clandestine operation, so I set about making plans to achieve my objective while the immediate post-war chaotic conditions in Germany still made it possible. I reckoned I had quite a few factors in my favour – a remote airfield at Husum, pre-selected German ground crew, and plenty of aircraft to choose from, although action would shortly be under way to send 25 Komets to Britain for evaluation, and rocket fuels would soon be disposed of. I had also done my training stint in the 163A, interrogated JG 400 aircrew and ground crew, and had a set of 163B Pilot's Notes in my possession. My trump card, however, was my very official looking letter from RAE to all Allied Forces requesting full co-operation in providing access to captured enemy aircraft and associated personnel, stressing that I was fluent in speaking the German language. Indeed I was brim full of confidence, whether misplaced or not, about flying the Komet.

Two things remained to be done – to alert my selected German ground crew, and to ensure they were retained at Husum, then to arrange a ground run of the rocket engine on the Komet the day before I intended to fly it. I, therefore, rapidly returned to Husum, but my crew were apprehensive about what might happen to them if things went wrong. I reassured them by giving them a note saying they had been selected to work with me and were temporarily under my command, but instructed them to remain discreet about their duties.

By the time I was ready to return to Husum for the big event, RAE was establishing a staging base at Schleswig airfield, so I got air traffic control to alert Husum of my intended arrival date in early June. On arrival there I made a thorough check of the Komet I was to use, and did an engine run for familiarisation of the rocket system. It was a thunderous, but reassuring, experience, and after that we prepared the machine for the next day, and in particular preset the cockpit torsion seat at the height I required.

I had decided to make the take-off at about 6 o'clock in the morning to be as discreet as possible. This was aided by a good weather forecast, which would enable me to take-off directly over the North Sea into the prevailing wind. Clad in an appropriated non-organic flight suit, I was in the cockpit at 0600, and after cockpit checks I moved the throttle to IDLE and pressed the start button till the engine was firing. After checking all the instruments were in the green, I gave the ground crew the signal to disconnect the auxiliary power unit. I then moved the throttle through the 1st stage and 2nd stage to the 3rd stage which produced enough thrust for the aircraft to jump the shallow inclined chocks and I was away on the take-off run.

There was heavy bumping on this run due to the non-resilient nature of the supporting trolley until unstick at 280kmh (175mph). After jettisoning the trolley and retracting the skid, the Komet accelerated very rapidly to 725kmh (450mph) to set up a 45° climb – all of this felt like being in charge of a runaway train. The steep angle of climb required the aircraft to be flown on instruments as I could not see the horizon, and I reached 32,000 feet in 2¾ minutes. As I levelled out I had to ease the throttle back at once otherwise compressibility effects were likely to be encountered in a matter of seconds.

After catching my breath I simulated an attack on an imaginary bomber at 30,000 feet and was surprised again to find how fast the Komet accelerated in a dive with the rocket shut down. It would require considerable skill to down a bomber, and I did not see combat with a fighter as an option, but the Komet should certainly be able to escape enemy fighters.

With all rocket fuel expended, I started the glide back to Husum, which was easy to pick out even in the slight morning haze. I had no trouble at all with the landing drill, although the inadequate view because of the very flat glide angle necessitated a rather wide circuit. I made the final approach at 215kmh (135mph) before pumping down the flaps to reduce speed to 200kmh (125mph) for landing.

After recovery of the aircraft by a very relieved ground crew, we had a celebratory drink together and then they were given their clearance passes to make their own way home. So ended my first exhilarating flight, which was the first of a series I was to make with the Me 163B, stretching over some two and a half years.

It was now some ten days after Germany's capitulation, and although *de facto* no political zones of occupation had been agreed amongst the Allies, these did in fact exist. I found no trouble in entering the American or French military territory, but I was keen to try out the Russians. I therefore flew to Schleswig where I had made arrangements to take over a German Siebel 204D light twin transport for my personal use. I had its swastikas obliterated and replaced with RAF roundels – just in case.

My destination was Tarnewitz airfield in East Germany which was occupied by the Russians. I was not at all sure what my reception would be, but ran into a stroke of luck when I found the commandant was a pilot who had formerly flown Hurricanes gifted to the Russians by the British in the early stages of the war. We conversed in German and he offered me the compliment of flying some of his aircraft, which in the case of the Yak-9 single-seat fighter and PE-2 twin tactical bomber were pretty well up with the state of the art except in the matter of cockpit instrumentation. Also it must be said I am not too keen on the Russian design philosophy that military aero-engines should not be built for longevity; but they could certainly sound old.

My new-found friend passed me on to another Russian occupied airfield near Meissen, where I found the hospitality a bit thin and amounted to letting me try out a rather sick German Bv 141 which was due for destruction and they probably hoped I would save them that bother. So it was back to Schleswig and a look around the area as I was already of the opinion that this airfield would make an ideal collection base for the RAE's acquired German aircraft, where they could be checked out before onward transit to Farnborough.

In checking out the area I had two pleasant surprises. Firstly, at the neighbouring airfield of Leck was virtually a new fighter wing of Heinkel He 162 single-jet engine interceptors, and secondly at Husum, a mere twenty miles away on the west coast, were three squadrons of JG 400's Messerschmitt 163B rocket fighters. There was no doubt that Schleswig must be the RAE's choice of base.

The Blohm and Voss Bv 141 was probably the most extraordinary looking plane flown by Eric Brown. The Russians allowed him to fly a 'sick' Bv 141 which they had found near Grossenhain and which they had marked for destruction.

113

The search for Hanna Reitsch, the famous German woman test pilot was now getting my attention, as I picked up some rumour of her possible location from loose talk in a German pub in Lübeck. This was the fabulous creature who was reputed to have flown her Fieseler Storch on and off the roof of the German Air Ministry in the last days of the Third Reich, acting as a courier to the Hitler bunker. On her last trip she had found the roof gone, and had landed amongst the rubble in the streets. I had met her in Berlin before the war when she gave her helicopter flying display, and I had a good idea what she looked like. But her whereabouts were completely unknown.

We started to probe for information. Our first lead took us to Bavaria on the trail of both Hanna and the Horten brothers, the German glider experts.

I took the opportunity of visiting the Messerschmitt test airfield at Augsburg. Here, in one corner of a damaged hangar I found, of all things, an Me 109 fitted with an arrester hook. This machine had been specially adapted for deck-landing trials on the Germans' one and only carrier *Graf Zeppelin*. But the machine was considered impossible for deck landing because of its poor forward view and weak undercarriage, the very same faults which had very nearly ruled out our own Spitfire. In any case the *Graf Zeppelin* was never used, which was maybe fortuitous as it was also planned to use the Ju 87 Stuka dive-bomber as a shipboard aircraft, but it proved to have a weak undercarriage in land operations.

About this time I made contact again with Colonel Watson of the USAAF, who like us had set up an enemy aircraft collecting base at Lagerfeld near Augsburg and had a team of pilots, who became known as 'Watson's Whizzers'. Similarly, too, he roped in a few German pilots and ground crew to aid and hasten the collection process. His ultimate objective was to round up his targeted aircraft at the collection base and then ferry them to Cherbourg for embarkation in the escort carrier HMS *Reaper* and onward transit to the USA.

We in northern Europe had a near monopoly on Arado jet bombers so these proved a good horse-trading item with the Colonel. I really didn't require any aircraft from south Germany, but I did need access to certain key German aviation figures and interrogation rights, and Watson was most co-operative in that respect. He was very well respected at high level in the American forces and had a pass endorsed by General Eisenhower,

Reichsmarschal Herman Goering shortly before his interrogation by the author.

which like mine was an open sesame to many otherwise closed doors. My association with Watson could not have been better; we were both test pilots and kindred spirits.

One of the best deals I brokered with Colonel Watson arose out of the unusual situation that he failed to find any airworthy Arado 234 jets in his southern zone of operations. On the other hand we had discovered a considerable number located at Sola-Stavanger in Norway and Grove in Denmark.

We willingly gave two of those aircraft to the Americans, but Watson came back with a special request for a further two. We agreed to this provided he would use his influence to try and get me interrogation rights to the Reichsmarschal Hermann Goering. The gallant colonel was as good as his word, and to my surprise was successful.

The meeting was arranged after Goering had been moved from Augsburg to the Palace Hotel at Bad Mondorf, some twelve miles from Luxembourg. From there he was eventually to be moved to stand trial at Nuremberg.

I was flown to Luxembourg on the evening of 16th June to overnight prior to a one hour session with Goering next morning. On arrival at the Palace Hotel I was introduced to my Invigilating Officer, who briefed me that he would be present throughout the interrogation and that I was to restrict this to aviation matters and neither touch on political matters nor on the invasion of Russia.

When Goering entered the interrogation room, walking between two guards, he looked pale and drawn, with dark semi-circles under his eyes, and his uniform, stripped of all insignia, hanging rather loosely on his once bulky frame. At first he looked disinterested until he realised I was a pilot talking only aviation to him, and he then came to life. He listened very intently, thought a while before answering, but was co-operative and polite in his replies. He even smiled quite a lot and I began to feel a likeable charisma about this rogue.

The main questions I asked him were, firstly, how he felt about the outcome of the Battle of Britain, which he proclaimed had been an indecisive draw, as he had had to withdraw his forces in preparation for Operation Barbarossa, the invasion of the Soviet Union.

Secondly I asked why he had never supported the formation of a heavy bomber force – as favoured by the new Luftwaffe's Chief of Staff – to attack Russia's armament-producing industrial centres in the Urals. He said it would have been unnecessary because Hitler's blitzkrieg policy was intended to bring about a short all-out war and not a prolonged conflict.

I also asked him if he had supported Hitler's decision initially to use the jet Me 262 as a fighter-bomber rather than as a pure defensive fighter. To my surprise he loyally backed the Führer, who had decided that opposing the invasion forces must take priority over home defence against Allied bombing.

Finally I turned to his personal opposition to General Galland, who in the later stages of the war rebelled against the misuse of the formidable Me 262 jet fighter. Goering bridled somewhat at this, and said he had wanted to court martial Galland for insubordination, but Hitler would have none of it, although displeased with the fighter ace. Goering then went on to say that fate had struck him a severe blow when General Mölders was killed as a passenger in an air accident, because he was a superb fighter pilot and a brilliant air tactician, whom Galland had succeeded but was never of the same calibre.

Throughout the interrogation I was struck by two aspects of Goering's behaviour – his unswerving loyalty to Hitler, and his readiness to admit responsibility for his own actions. Indeed, for a man who was almost certain to be facing the death penalty as a war criminal, he gave a kamikaze performance. It gave me an uneasy feeling he was certain in his own mind he was going to cheat the hangman's noose, one way or another – as, of course he did. Condemned for guilt 'unique in its enormity' he committed suicide on 15th October 1946.

In an American hospital near Kitzbühl was a woman thought to be Hanna. We started for the place but were diverted by a reliable tip that a key member of the Horten brothers' team was living in a village in a remote part of Bavaria.

Here we asked questions all round the village, starting with the

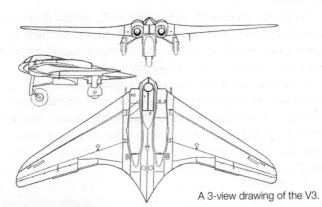

A 3-view drawing of the V3.

The totally revolutionary Horton IX V3 at Wright Patterson Air Force Base, Dayton, Ohio 1945, and below the Horton IX V3 as it was found by the Americans.

burgomaster, and eventually knocked on`a certain door, which was answered by the man we sought. He tried to hide his identity at first, but when we convinced him that we were merely after information and not his executioners he told us that the brothers had remained at Göttingen to await capture, but had urged their workers to leave.

He also told us of an amazing plane which the Hortens had been developing at the end of the war. The Horten IX was completely revolutionary in design. It was an all-wing, swept-back, twin-engined, single-seat jet fighter of high performance. Three of these aircraft were found by the Americans in varying stages of assembly at the Gotha works in Friedrichroda.

Hanna Reitsch, fanatical aviator, fervent German nationalist and ardent Nazi, with Colonel Ernst Udet, Head of the Technical Branch of the Ministry of Aviation.

The Americans decided to ship the Ho IX V3 back to the USA and en route let it have a short stopover at Farnborough, where we had the idea of fitting it with two British jet engines, but these proved incompatible with the engine mountings in the wings meant for the German Jumo 004 engines.

Meanwhile we rushed back to Kitzbühl and the suspected Hanna Reitsch. By now the Americans had established that she was Hanna beyond any doubt, and had taken her into proper custody. I was allowed to interrogate her eventually in early July.

This fanatical aviator, fervent German nationalist and ardent Nazi, was surprisingly feminine. She was smallish, fair, petite, a woman in her mid-thirties. At first she was very suspicious, but I reminded her of our former meeting and convinced her that I only wanted to talk flying, and she began to talk freely.

Hanna Reitsch had flown a wide variety of German civil and military aircraft, largely thanks to the patronage of Ernst Udet, for she was not an accredited test pilot. These aircraft included the V1 flying bomb, which she advocated should be used in a manned version for suicide missions, but this idea did not have Hitler's support.

I was interested too in her helicopter experience, but my real aim was to get her impressions of flying the remarkable Messerschmitt 163 rocket fighter. However, in this I was somewhat disappointed, as I found out that she had never been allowed to fly the aircraft under power, but only make production test flights from towed glides.

Although she was reluctant to admit this, she gave graphic descriptions of the inherent dangers of powered flight in the 163 – the unstable and highly volatile rocket fuels which caused violent explosions if mixed in uncontrolled conditions. She herself had had a near fatal accident on landing after failing to jettison the wheeled take-off trolley properly.

In some respects I was fortunate to catch Hanna in an emotional state, still stressed out after hearing of her doctor father's slaying of all the females in his household to prevent them falling into Russian hands, and then killing himself. She spoke of Udet dispassionately without any sign of loyalty, but the fanaticism she displayed in her attitude to Hitler made my blood run cold. ...

I was keen to get the truth out of her of how she flew to Hitler's bunker in Berlin, and it was a saga of pure courage all round. Luftwaffe General

Ritter von Greim had been summoned to the bunker by Hitler and asked Hanna to fly him by helicopter from Rechlin test centre some 70 miles north of the capital. Their intended helicopter had been destroyed in an air attack, so the only way was in a special two-seater Fw 190 fighter flown by a sergeant who had previous experience of the flight into Gatow airport. Remarkably Hanna went along as an impromptu passenger, wedged into the small empty space in the rear section of the fuselage. With a fighter escort they reached Gatow, where they boarded a Fieseler Storch flown by the General with Hanna as a passenger. En route across Berlin they were hit by Russian ground fire, with von Greim receiving an armour-piercing bullet in his fight foot. Hanna leant over the inert General's shoulder and managed to reach the throttle and stick with enough control to reach the Brandenburg Gate and land in the road nearby, where they were picked up by a military lorry and driven to the bunker.

As a postscript to my relationship with Hanna, it had a somewhat bizarre finale. At the beginning of August 1979 to my utter surprise I received a letter from Hanna, in which she said we had a common bond in our love of flying and of danger, but neither I nor anyone outside Germany really understood her passionate love of the Fatherland. The letter was short and finished with the words, 'It began in the bunker, and there it shall end'.

These words (in German) puzzled me, and only the news of her death in Frankfurt on 22nd August 1979 gave me a possible key to this mystery. It was well known that Hitler had given her and von Greim each a cyanide pill before dismissing them from the bunker on 28th April 1945. Hanna always considered that she and von Greim had made a binding pact to commit suicide, one after the other, but with an intervening period to prevent rumour of a love affair. Von Greim swallowed his pill on 24th May while under arrest in hospital at Salzburg. Had Hanna finally honoured her pact some twenty-four years after von Greim's death? It is known that Hanna had managed to retain her cyanide pill throughout these years, and then again news of her death was not made public until a fortnight after her demise. Also there appears to have been no post mortem made on her body, or at least no such report is available. Anyway I sent her letter to her brother Kurt, whom I knew in the post-war German Navy, but received no acknowledgement. To the bitter end Hanna Reitsch managed to surround herself with controversy.

In June also it was decided that the time had come for some more carpet-deck-landing approaches on the *Pretoria Castle*. This time I used a Hellcat which was going spare, leaving it behind afterwards for the Service Trials Unit pilots in the ship to try out in the new technique which we were attempting to build up. Our main object at this stage was to determine how accurately the pilots could judge their height when flying at low speeds just above the flight deck. Their estimates were checked against camera recordings of their approach runs.

That month a bunch of RAE ferry pilots were sent out to Schleswig to run the staging base for captured German aircraft which we had previously selected there. When a scientist found an aircraft of interest one of us from Aero Flight was to go and pick it up, bring it to Schleswig, and stage it back to Farnborough. The more familiar types of enemy aircraft would be left to the ferry pilots to bring back.

We Aero Flight pilots used these ordinary machines as a taxi service to get us around Germany on our searches for new aircraft. Any separate pieces of equipment which were of interest were ferried in the big German transport aircraft.

The pride of this fleet was Himmler's own personal Focke-Wulf Condor, a machine which I got to know well. I was very interested in these machines to start with, as they were roughly the same as the ones I had operated against from *Audacity*. And Himmler's toy gave me a particular thrill to fly. It was most luxuriously appointed, with a very up-to-date kitchen. Prize exhibit was Himmler's special throne. The whole high-backed seat was armour-plated, and two big armoured flaps protected him from the sides as well. At his feet was a round jettisonable door. Himmler himself had control of the lever which operated this, and in desperate circumstances could get rid of the door and bale out.

I was tasked with taking a senior boffin to Rechlin, the main German experimental flight research centre located some seventy miles north of Berlin, where he had to inspect the facilities there, which had suffered considerable bombing. I used a Firefly for this trip, but with intent, because I planned to visit my anglophile Russian at nearby Tarnewitz, and I felt he would not offer me any more aircraft to fly except on a swap basis. In that surmise I was dead right, and he was delighted to swap a MIG-3 and then a Lavochkin 7 for two hops in the Firefly.

The MIG-3 was old hat stuff and not very impressive, but the La-7 was

121

The Russian Lavochkin 7; its wooden construction and poor equipment made it very vulnerable.

a different proposition. Its handling and performance were quite superb, and it had the qualities necessary for a fine combat fighter, but not the equipment. Its firepower and sighting arrangements were below par, its wooden construction would have withstood little combat punishment, the pilot was poorly protected and the blind flying and navigations instrumentation were appallingly basic. Strangely, all Russian aircraft I flew had that distinctive wood and resin smell, just as the German machines had their distinctive paint smell.

I already had the feeling that Soviet Union co-operation – even with their favoured British friends – was beginning to wear thin, and left Tarnewitz with my Firefly thankfully still intact, and glad to have experienced some Russian aircraft, albeit not over-impressed.

We had a standing date to go back to Grove and pick up the first of the Arado 234B twin jets, and later that month Marty and I went there to fly two of them back to Farnborough. In these very fast jets we were faced with an unknown quantity. The axial-flow type jet engines which powered them had a life like that of a fierce firework. During their brief span they gave tremendous power, but each engine required a complete overhaul after ten hours and had a total life of only twenty-five hours altogether. This in itself would have caused us headaches – if the Germans had not destroyed all the log books of the engines. Now we had no idea how many hours each one had done. We would taxi the first two Arados out on to the runway not knowing whether our revving engines had done nine hours and were due for an overhaul, or twenty-three hours and were very near the end of their life. It would be too bad if we found out when we were over the sea.

We decided to make one handling flight first. Mine was ready first, so I taxied out and opened up to full power. I was on the very point of releasing the brakes when there was an almighty explosion and the starboard engine blew itself to pieces and took a huge chunk of the wing with it. I shut the other engine off and climbed shakily out.

Had the engine failed near overhaul or was it sabotage? We got our team together and inspected the wreckage. It seemed possible that it had been tampered with.

We got the permission of the RAF Regiment Squadron Leader now in charge of Grove to interrogate the prisoners who had serviced the defunct

An Arado 234B being refuelled by Luftwaffe POWs at Grove before being flown to the RAE at Farnborough.

One of the nine Arado 234Bs which was flown to Farnborough for evaluation. With its slender shoulder-mounted wing, slim underslung engine nacelles and smooth fuselage profile it exemplified careful aerodynamic design.

The biggest operational flying boat in the world, the six-engined Blohm and Voss 222. It was a remarkable aircraft, not only by virtue of its size, but because of its unusual control system which seemed dangerously light for such a huge machine.

engine. I questioned them all but could get nothing out of them. We promised them that if the culprit would give himself up we would take no action other than removing him from the team. That failed too. The Squadron Leader drew his revolver, pointed it at them, and looked fierce. They all instantly pointed at one man. He was taken off the work, and there was no more trouble. Next day we took two Arados from Grove to Schleswig and from Schleswig all the way to Farnborough. We had not come direct, but had dog-legged our course to avoid a long sea crossing. Moreover we had flown the last 100 miles below 10,000 feet because Marty had oxygen trouble. It was a very long trip for a small jet aircraft with no external fuel tanks and a very hot performance range when one considers that I still had a fair amount of fuel left after landing.

I had plenty more shocks ahead. The CO sent for me and said, 'You're the only man in this establishment with any flying-boat experience.'

I nearly laughed. My 'experience' was an hour or two in a Walrus and a Sea Otter, both nothing more than little amphibians.

I told him.

He said, 'Oh, that's all right. That'll be enough'.

'What's the job then, sir?'

'I want you to go up to Trondheim and check out a flying boat they've got up there – give me all the dope on it you can so that I can go and fly it back to Calshot.'

I was a little uneasy. 'Why this particular boat, sir?'

He said, 'Well, this is a very big boat, and I'd rather like to bring it in myself, you know'.

'What's the name of it, sir?' I feared the worst.

'It's a Blohm and Voss 222.'

It rocked me on my heels. This was nothing less than the biggest operational flying boat in the world, a six-engined Diesel machine with a very special and unusual control system.

I had to get some more experience of big boats urgently before I climbed into a thing like the 222, so on my way up to Norway I stopped off at Schleswig and took up a smaller machine, the Blohm and Voss 138, from the flying-boat base at Schleswig Schlei. I had never yet called on the German pilots for help, but this time I felt the need. I managed to winkle out a captured pilot from British Army Headquarters. A heavy guard of soldiers brought him down to the boat but could not be persuaded to fly with him. Even with his help I found the three-engined boat tricky to fly. I did not look forward to the 222. However, I persevered and flew a selection of Dornier boats as well until I felt I was groomed as far as I would ever be.

When I got to Trondheim I found that she was the only 222 left intact. I made another request for the loan of a German pilot to help me learn the taps, and was given a Luftwaffe major, who sat in the first-pilot's seat, with me at his side. He seemed to have been expecting me.

He started the engines and, with everything going flat-out, we were soon tearing up Trondheim Fiord. We roared on and on over the gleaming water. When we had gone what seemed for miles and were still flat on the surface, going very fast and taking a tremendous buffeting from the water, I realized that something was very wrong.

I grabbed the stick from the German and tried to ease it back. It was locked solid. He had not taken any of the control locks out. He was deliberately trying to wreck the boat. I cut the throttles.

I heaved him out of the seat, yelled to the crew to hold on to him, and got the control locks freed. I couldn't waste time taking him all the way back, so I taxied her a little way back down the fiord and started again. This time she rode very smoothly and I found her a pleasant boat to fly.

125

From her huge cockpit to that of a Seafire was a big jump, but nothing unusual. Back aboard the *Pretoria Castle* I did the first tail-down catapult launch in a Seafire, then changed to the new Seafire 46 for deck-landing trials.

It was July now. This month another peculiar experiment came my way. The Army had decided to operate the little Auster aircraft from tank landing craft. We erected a mock-up at Farnborough to try it out. The Auster was supposed to take off with its wheels in three-grooved rails laid on the LCT's deck. The trials were successful, but the Auster and I suffered a few shocks when she fell with a bump off the end of the rails. This sort of circus act needed a few rehearsals before we got it right.

We did tests with rocket-assisted take-off in which various rockets in the cluster were deliberately made to fail so that recovery could be tested. We would fail first one, then another on the other side of the aircraft, to find out the effect on the swing of the machine. In the final stage the boffins tampered with one or another of the rockets without telling me which were the faulty ones. This was as close as we could get to real emergency conditions, and it gave me some bad moments.

In between these adventures I hopped over to Grove for some more Arados, and on 10th and 11th August went to sea again to take the Sea Hornet through its first deck landings.

She was a real flying fish, bred to the sea. Take-off was remarkable. There was no swing, and the view ahead was so excellent that the tail could be held firmly down throughout the entire run and give the perfect unstick. Landings were as good, with a forward and downward view better than in the Mosquito – although the batsman still disappeared from sight too soon under the port engine – and the Hornet's oleo undercarriage had much less bounce than the Mosquito's rubber-block type, which had threatened some trouble.

The hydraulic pump failed during my second set of landings and I had to work hard pumping undercarriage and flaps by hand for each landing. There were some things to criticize, of course, but I had no doubt that the Hornet had set a standard for twin-engined naval aircraft which would be very hard to beat. Comparatively minor modifications would make her just about perfect. Robertson's trials with the Sea Fury proved that we had a winner in this machine as well.

It was back to Germany again, this time with a team of scientists from

The first deck landing of the Sea Hornet, developed from the Mosquito, on HMS *Ocean*, 10th August 1945.

the Naval Aircraft Department at Farnborough to look for German catapults. We had already captured some V1 catapults. Now we were looking
for the type they had used to get their big flying boats airborne from
narrow and restricted waters such as the Norwegian fiords.

Taking off from the tiny strip at Bad Oeynhausen, Army Headquarters, in the little German Siebel 204 D which I was using now as my
personal taxi, my port engine failed just as the wheels left the ground.

We were in a valley. If I went on I would hit the rising ground ahead.
If I tried to touch down again I would overshoot. Hayricks along the sides
of the runway gave me the answer. I headed straight into one of these.

The prop went in like a threshing machine. We stopped, undamaged,
but beautifully camouflaged with hay. It took the combined efforts of
some of Britain's most brilliant scientists to uncover the aeroplane again.
We pushed it back on to the runway. Everybody set to work with nailfiles,
pipe cleaners, penknives, to clean the plugs, and an hour later we got off.

We were congratulating ourselves, when we heard a loud and ominous whining noise. Inside the cockpit was a wood hornet, a vicious little brute two inches long with a sting which can prove fatal and is certainly incapacitating. With awful thoughts of what would happen to them if he stung me, the boffins set themselves as scientifically as they knew how to kill the hornet. They chased the little striped thing round and round the aircraft, trying to trap him. This failed, and they took to smoking furiously to try to choke him to death. This made the hornet angrier and the non-smokers sick and forced me to do some instrument flying. Eventually he was despatched by a blow of the flight-engineer's glove. The crude approach had triumphed over the scientific one.

We should have heeded these warnings of fate, but we pushed on. At Schleswig we were advised to look for our catapults in three places, at Oslo in Norway, and on the islands of Heligoland and Sylt. We flew over Heligoland, but it was in such a state of devastation it looked like the cratered face of the moon. There would be no catapults there. We landed at Sylt. There they told us that there had once been a catapult at the northern tip of the island, but that it had been blown up. At Oslo there were traces of one on the Bygdo peninsula, but it had been utterly wrecked.

In landing at Fornebu airfield we almost finished off a bad job in style. This field was a little runway jammed in between the sea at one end and a sheer rock face 200 feet high at the other. All landings, all take-offs, could only be over the sea end, whatever the direction of the wind.

But when we came to take off the wind was blowing very strongly from the land, over the sheer cliff. And we were very heavily laden. The boffins got out their slide rules. They calculated that our turning circle would be just enough to let us turn away in front of the cliff. We took off, their sums were right, except that they had not allowed for the strong turbulence over the cliff. We scraped clear, but we had a very exciting ride.

In Stavanger in Norway we already knew there were many Arado 234 Bs on the airfield. I went up to investigate. I found twelve of them fit to be flown back to England. 'Splendid,' I was told. 'You get them here'.

If I was to do this job on my own I had to get well organized. I borrowed a communications pilot from Farnborough and used my little Siebel as a mobile workshop. I took two German technicians out of custody in

Norway and co-opted Hauptmann Miersch, who had been maintenance test pilot for the airfield, to help me get the machines back to England. Miersch could not be taken on trust. He was generally a cheerful enough character, but he was somewhat recalcitrant, and showed definite flashes of Prussianism in his relations with the two technical *feldwebels*. But his help would cut the job in half.

My main worry as far as he was concerned was that the first part of the trip back to Farnborough was within easy flying reach of Sweden, and I was frightened that he would make a run for it. I told him that I intended to fly the jets out two at a time, with him leading me to the next airfield. I would give him the course and height, but no maps. If he drifted off course I would without hesitation ram him from behind. I don't know whether he really believed this unlikely threat – the pilot of an Arado sat exposed in a Perspex nose – but he seemed to be impressed by it.

We took two jets at a time to Schleswig until all twelve were assembled there, and he gave me no trouble at all. From here we were going to stage them on to Brussels or Britain direct, depending on the weather. It was October now.

On 3rd October I led Miersch off from Schleswig with a met forecast of clear weather all the way to Brussels. Gilze-Rijen in Holland was the intermediate safety stop.

It was five o'clock when we left. Dusk fell at Brussels at quarter to seven, so we had an hour and three-quarters to make a journey which, at fast cruise speed at low level, should only take an hour to Brussels, or less to Gilze-Rijen. The maximum endurance of the Arado was an hour and twenty minutes at low altitude, where jet engines are at their thirstiest.

All the way to the south bank of the Zuider Zee the weather was as Schleswig had forecast. But there we ran into thick sea fog, which must have built up in the previous half hour. I switched on my wingtip lights.

There was nothing to do but to turn back, twenty miles short of Gilze-Rijen. I knew I had insufficient fuel to reach any serviceable aerodrome on the return run. Miersch was out of close-formation practice and lost me as I turned. On breaking out of the fog there was no sign of him.

I estimated that I could just reach Nordholz near Cuxhaven, if I flew on one engine only to conserve fuel. Airfield conditions there were bad, and they would be unprepared for me, but it was my only hope. My speed would be cut drastically, and dusk at Cuxhaven was at half past six.

I reached Nordholz by ten to seven in darkness. Landing was a grim prospect.

But a British naval unit on the coast saw the flame from my exhaust up in the night. They deduced at once that I was lost, and with great presence of mind switched on two searchlights and used their beams to guide me towards the airfield. I restarted the shut-off engine and landed by the light of four jeep headlights which some Americans at Nordholz quickly directed on to the runway. I made a safe landing with 120 litres of fuel left in my tanks.

As the time wore on and I heard nothing of Miersch, I began to fear that he had gone into the sea. Then we had a phone call from a small airfield called Eelde in Holland to say that they were holding our German pilot prisoner there. Eelde was a little grass field completely pitted with craters. Nevertheless, Miersch, in twilight, had managed to make a good landing, picking his way between the holes. He would never be able to get the Arado out again, and in fact the Dutch made sure of it by cementing their trophy in. I don't know how long it remained there. They held firmly on to Miersch until we came personally to collect him.

We went on to deliver the remainder of the Arados safely. Miersch and the two technicians, Walter Rautenberg and Walter Renner, both brilliant men, were given a small hut in the centre of the RAE and allowed to work with us in reasonable freedom, on their honour not to escape.

When all these Arados were safely at Farnborough I was made officer in charge of the enemy aircraft pool, responsible for receiving, checking all enemy machines which came in, selecting certain models for research, and ferrying the rest to the storage depot at Brize Norton. We soon built up a very interesting collection. In all I flew fifty-two different types of German aircraft.

Chapter 10

M y vampire was ready. I began her test runs into the wires on the airfield, first into the centre of the wire at faster and faster speeds, building up the 'g', then moving out to fifteen feet off centre on both sides. This proved too much of a strain on the hook attachment. At 3.35'g' and fifteen feet off centre the fitting parted at the wing root. The machine went back to the makers for further strengthening.

I took the chance of hopping over to Germany to collect my Arado from Nordholz. With me in the Siebel went my German team as usual. At Nordholz the runway was theoretically too short for us to get out in this fast jet at full load. We worked it out that at the absolute minimum fuel needed to make Schleswig there should be about five yards of runway to spare provided wind and temperature remained just right. My two *feld-webels* were very worried about my chances. They had never seen an attempt to get a machine like this off the ground in such a short distance, and they did not think a British pilot like me, with so little knowledge of this German aircraft, could make it.

If anything did go wrong I should certainly be sitting very close to the accident. There was nothing but a sheet of curved perspex between me and the ground.

We waited three days for the right conditions. To help me get off I stationed one of my *feldwebels* at a point along the airstrip at which I estimated I must have the nose wheel off the ground to stand any chance of getting off at all. If the wheel was clear when I passed him he was to raise his arm in the air. If not, he would fling himself on the ground. It had to be some sort of violent signal which I could easily see as I flashed past him.

I started off and roared down the runway. I kept my eyes on him, but he did not move a muscle. Then I was up to him and I thought he never would. But he suddenly threw his arm up. It was a relief but it told me I had nothing to spare. The wire fence at the end of the runway rushed at me. Out in my perspex bubble I was over the end and looking down at the grass before I felt the wheels just stagger off the runway.

I got the machine safely back to Farnborough, but for me the most satisfying result of that episode was its effect on our little team. Now, as never before, we were able to work together in real mutual trust. The concern of my *feldwebels* for me I found quite touching.

The repaired Vampire came back and there was more arresting work to do. I was also drawn in to some testing on 'Britannia', the special Meteor with which Group Captain H. J. Wilson, the old CO of Aero Flight, and Eric Greenwood, Gloster's chief test pilot, were going to make an attempt on the world speed record.

It was a breathtaking machine to fly. It did not use reheat, which was still too dangerous, but the thrust in its engines had been very much increased, and the whole machine had been polished and lacquered down to the last rivet until it shone mirror-bright. Our job was to fly it at various speeds and heights so that the resulting figures could be compared with those for the ordinary type Meteor and an assessment of the reduction in drag made. In this splendid machine Greenwood became the first ever to exceed 600mph officially, and Wilson broke the record at a speed of 606mph at Herne Bay on 7th November 1945.

The Vampire trials this time were successful, and on 26th November I went to Ford in Sussex to work up for the landings at sea. There was by now far too much traffic at Farnborough to do it there. At Ford I met up with the batsman from the *Ocean*, on which I was to do the trials, and we started our practice. But so much work was piling up at RAE that I was almost immediately recalled there. Among many other chores came the

The special Meteor 'Britannia' on which Eric Brown did some testing before it went on to break the world speed record with a speed of 606mph (969.6kph).

Line-up of test aircraft at RAE Farnborough immediately after World War II.
Captured German aircraft are in the third and fourth ranks.

job of helping to organize a big static display of all our most interesting
captured German aircraft. The stars were the piloted V1 which Hanna
Reitsch had flown, the experimental Bv 155, high altitude fighter, and the
composite pick-a-back aircraft comprising a Focke-Wulf 190 perched on
the back of a Junkers 88.

The public exhibition of German aircraft and equipment took place
at RAE Farnborough in October/November 1945. It consisted of static
exhibits except for a final week of demonstration flights of the advanced
jets. I was one of the demonstration pilots, and also had to give my
impressions of these aircraft to members of the press.

I had an in-depth knowledge of the Arado 234B from my ferrying
trips. This fast photo-reconnaissance plane had never been used as far
as we knew operationally in any long-range role, except once in the
Ardennes in the last phase of the war. But in Stavanger they told me that
one of them had been over Britain. To prove it they produced pictures
taken from high altitudes of the Forth Bridge and the ICI works at
Middlesbrough. It had a very long range for a jet, and was very fast. It
came in so fast for its landing and needed such a long run that a tail parachute was developed to slow it down, a very advanced feature.

The twin-engined Me 262 was Germany's first operational jet, and it had a remarkable performance for its time. Although under-powered in its engines, its triangular-sectioned fuselage and swept-back wings showed us that we had a lot to learn about refinements in profile design, because this machine had a tactical Mach number of 0.83, very much higher than anything else in the world at the time. Its critical Mach number was 0.86.

It had a very bad accident history because of its poor single-engine performance. If one engine failed after take-off before the speed had built up to 190mph the pilot was in bad trouble.

A two-seat version had been found at Schleswig, where the 262 had been used very successfully against our Mosquito intruders attacking Hamburg. They also appeared on the western front during the invasion and were virtually untouchable. If the Germans could have produced them in large numbers we should have been in very serious trouble. Flying the 262 I found it an exciting and challenging aircraft.

In my opinion the Me 262 was the most formidable aircraft of World War II. The three features that made it so outstanding were its sweptback wings, its axial-flow jet engines and its armament of 4×30mm cannon which could be supplemented by the devastating R4M air-to-air missiles in racks of twenty-four under each wing. Yet it had its weaknesses too, the main one being the sensitivity of the Jumo 004 engines to any rapid throttle movement, which could cause flame-out.

The second weakness was that the designers of the first jet aircraft both in Britain and in Germany had not provided dive brakes, necessary to slow-up these streamlined machines in operations such as attacking slower targets, or giving positioning flexibility in formation flying, and critically for providing drag to steepen the landing path angle and control the approach speed as necessary.

Finally, the 30mm cannon were only accurate below 650 yards range, so a 262 attacking a bomber opened fire at about 600 yards but had to break off the attack at 200 yards to avoid colliding with the target, thus giving a firing time of only two seconds. However, leaving these shortcomings aside, the Me 262 was at least 100mph faster than any contemporary aircraft so could literally dictate its own combat terms.

Then I came to the Heinkel 162, the Volksjaeger or People's Fighter. This was a bizarre and infamous little machine, another of those fathered

Take-off of the Me 262 – the highest performance aircraft of the Second World War.

in desperation towards the close of the war, when it was becoming obvious that only a miracle could save Nazi Germany.

In the summer of 1944 the Me 109 and the Fw 190, the Luftwaffe's veteran fighters, were no longer able to combat the increasing low-level attacks over western Germany. Our air bases were so close to Germany that it was practically impossible to vector such fighters to a successful interception.

Shortage of equipment prevented the use of standing patrols, and it thus became absolutely essential for the Germans to develop a high-speed single-seater fighter fast enough to take off and attack when enemy aircraft were actually in sight. Owing to our heavy bombing of the larger German airfields with long runways this new fighter had to be able to operate from small emergency fields. Finally the mass production of such a machine had to be on such a scale that our aircraft could be engaged at any point in the whole of their flight.

The Me 262 had to be ruled out because it could not be produced in large enough numbers. Supplying two engines per plane was quite beyond the powers of the shrinking German aeroplane industry. It was difficult enough to provide even a bare minimum of the numbers of 262 needed to combat the Allied heavy bomber formations.

The demand for a single-engined jet fighter especially designed for attacking the Allied low-flying aircraft went through despite bitter opposition from various leading personalities in the German aircraft industry, particularly Professor Messerschmitt. In September 1944, after various

135

projects had been considered, an order was placed with Heinkel of Vienna for the delivery of no less than a thousand of a new fighter for this purpose per month, beginning in the spring of 1945.

The danger of a false step in such a rush programme was obvious, but it was hoped that the risk would be minimized by a special concentration of key technicians and development personnel, and by the imposition of realistic limitations on the design. It was possible to pool the best brains and skills of the German aircraft industry in the autumn of 1944 because the production of bomber aircraft had then been stopped. Nevertheless it was important that the project should not interfere with the existing air-defence programme, so it had to be carried out on an entirely separate basis.

The new fighter imposed some exacting technical requirements on the industry, including a very high speed at low and medium altitudes – a minimum of 750kph at sea level – unassisted take-off in less than 600 metres, a minimum production build-up to obtain the necessary large-scale production, the extensive use of wood in the construction.

The attempt to satisfy all these demands was a nightmare. The short take-off run restricted the all-up weight, which in turn affected the endurance and armament. Initially an endurance of twenty minutes was demanded, but by the time the contracts were placed this had been increased to thirty minutes. Eventually, by the use of wing tanks, Heinkel was able to guarantee an endurance of forty minutes, but this required more than 600 metres take-off run.

The armament was restricted to two cannon. The wireless was to be a small utility set for vectoring. Protective armour was only provided against direct frontal attack and only such instruments were installed as were absolutely necessary for engine and flying control.

The need for urgent delivery imposed further restrictions. All constructional, aerodynamic, or mechanical risks were avoided, a wing with a straight leading edge, for example being adopted instead of a swept-back one, which might have given a much improved performance. The single jet engine was mounted above the wing. This meant a loss of longitudinal stability but reduced the fire risk to the wooden machine. Existing components from other aircraft types, such as the undercarriage from the Me 109, were used wherever possible. Production was completely standardized round the BMW 003 engine, with no thought of advancing to more powerful types.

Eric Brown described the tiny Heinkel He 162 as having the finest controls of any aircraft he had ever flown, but required very careful handling. This plane crashed on 9th November 1945 at Farnborough, killing the pilot, Flt Lt Marks.

This He 162A assembly line was discovered by the Allies in the former salt mine at Tarthun, near Magdeburg.

Every possible corner was cut and the machine was delivered for tests. On the whole the result was surprisingly good, but the little humped monster with its engine on its back was tricky to fly, showing marginal stability, a strong tendency to side-slip, and an eagerness to spin.

And that was not all. I afterwards saw a film shot of its fourth flight in the presence of Goering. The plane is seen to dive towards the Reichsmarschal. Suddenly he ducks. Quite plainly the whole wing can be seen splitting along the leading edge, and the skin rolling back. The machine crashed. By the time most of its faults had been corrected the war was lost.

It was still tricky to fly. In fact it was the only German aircraft on which Aero Flight had a fatal accident. It was flown during a flying display by Flight Lieutenant Bob Marks, a test pilot who had only just returned from a POW camp in Germany and was new to the game. I had already tested it and found it, from the stability and control point of view, one of the finest aircraft I had ever flown. But I warned him that she had a very sensitive rudder and a very high rate of roll, and that he should be careful using rudder to assist rolling action.

I had flown the aircraft on the first three days of the display, but Bob had wanted to have a go on the last day. In his enthusiasm he must have forgotten the advice, used too much rudder, and made the whole fin and rudder collapse. The machine literally tumbled, head over heels, out of the sky, the only time I have seen such a thing happen. It crashed straight into Aldershot Barracks, where it killed a soldier as well as its pilot.

The Volksjaeger Salamander, with its pygmy size and very limited range, was an impracticable proposition. A more powerful jet and a swept-back wing might have made it a phenomenal machine, provided there had been more time to develop it properly. It was intended that the Me 262 and the Volksjaeger should be superseded by another single-engined jet fighter, but that one never materialized.

The Me 163B was another such 'shot in the dark' air weapon brought in during the desperate days of the retreat through Germany. It was specifically designed to combat the mass formation daylight raids of the American Fortresses. Initially the defending Me 109s and Fw 190s took heavy toll of the Forts. Then the Americans introduced the Thunderbolt and Mustang to give escort cover. The Mustang with its very long range and high performance was particularly successful in attacking the

The Me 163B flown in towed and gliding flight by the author, the Walter rocket motor having been removed and an auto-observer installed in its place to record test data.

German fighters, so that the bombers began to get through to their targets in large numbers, thus causing the Germans to resort to drastic countermeasures such as the Me 163.

It was an ultra short-range, single-seat, tailless interceptor fighter of mid-wing design driven by a Walter bi-fuel liquid rocket-propulsion unit in the fuselage behind the pilot. The fuels used were the T-Stoff and C-Stoff, the volatility of which had been demonstrated so effectively to me by Dr Walter at Kiel.

The 23 degrees swept-back wings were of wooden construction and the fuselage of all-metal with a single vertical fin and rudder. The under-carriage consisted of a retractable skid mounted on the jettisonable two-wheel chassis which was automatically dropped when the skid was retracted on take-off.

This machine was aptly known in the Luftwaffe as the Komet. Although it had an endurance of only four minutes at full thrust it could climb to 30,000 feet in two and a half minutes.

Operational squadrons of Komets first went into action early in 1945. If ample warning of raiding bombers was received each 163 would be towed up to about 20,000 feet by two Me 110Gs and released when the bombers were sighted. They would then start up their rocket units and climb above the bomber stream, then dive down through the formations without rocket power, firing as they broke through their ranks with either machine guns or a battery of rockets. Provided two minutes had elapsed the rocket motor would be started up again and a rapid climb was then made and the process repeated two or three times until all their fuel or ammunition was gone. The plane then glided back to base and made a motorless landing.

If no warning had been given the 163 could take off under its rocket power, although this was dangerous and reduced the number of attacks possible on the enemy bomber formation. They took moderate toll of the Forts, but suffered fantastically high casualties themselves. Eighty per cent of these resulted on take-off or landing due to explosions arising from the unstable fuels used. Losses in action were only about five per cent, and the other fifteen per cent resulted from fire in the air or loss of control in high Mach number dives.

Two pilots I interrogated said they had never stalled their aircraft, but seemed to have been quite confident in aerobatics with it and had never known of a 163 spinning. They were always instructed to jettison all fuel before landing, although one had crashed on a railway track with fuel still aboard without exploding.

The German propaganda service had put it out that Ernst Udet had been killed in a compressibility dive in a 163. In fact he shot himself, a truth depressing to the Luftwaffe which soon leaked out.

Other interesting points I learned about the plane was that ditching characteristics were good, but baling out was impossible above 250mph, as the hood could not be safely jettisoned above this speed. Another piece of depressing information by these operational pilots was the high rate of broken backs among 163 pilots due to heavy stall-in landings. Pilots would land with the undercarriage selector lever down instead of being returned to neutral, when the skid oleos are under hydraulic pressure and present a too rigid structure, or, worst of all, touch down with the skid retracted.

In retrospect I often wonder whether it was worth the very considerable bother to set up the powered flight I made in Germany, but I believe the boffins who encouraged me were right, because now I have a better appreciation of that unique aeroplane. Certainly it was sensational to fly, and risky too, because there was so much possible to go wrong and virtually no escape route. From an operational standpoint it was severely limited by its dependence on fair weather and its minimal endurance, but these facts are reflected in its combat record of sixteen kills and ten losses (six to fighters, four to bombers). It was the product of two great scientists, Dr Alexander Lippisch and Professor Hellmuth Walter, and two great test pilots, Heini Dittmar and Rudolf Opitz. It did not win the air war for Germany but it certainly influenced post-war aeronautical design.

We decided to start the tests in England with the aircraft used purely as a glider, towed by a Spitfire 9, and using the grass field at Wisley. The take-off was a tricky business, because the tug was invariably airborne before the 163, and so the tug pilot had to be instructed to hold the Spitfire down until I told him over the radio to unstick. In spite of the smooth grass I was bumped badly on take-off and my head often came into sharp contact with the cockpit canopy even when I was firmly strapped in. Directional control was very good with the steerable tail wheel mounted, and I made take-offs in a 35mph wind blowing at twenty degrees to the direction of take-off without any trouble or unpleasant effects. The view during the take-off was very good. The 163 would normally unstick at 105mph but it was dangerous to haul her off prematurely for fear of being forced back into the ground by the tug's slipstream, or forced to bank over and dig a wing into the ground as the ailerons were sloppy at low speeds. Many pupils had been killed on a towed take-off due to this wing-dropping characteristic causing them to cartwheel.

At a height between fifteen and thirty feet the skid had to be retracted and the trolley thereby jettisoned. This release had to be carefully judged. If it were done too low the trolley bounced and could hook up on the landing skid. If released too high it could bounce up and hit the fuse-lage fuel tanks, causing an explosion.

The 163 was normally towed at 168mph and had to be flown in a lowish position on a high tow otherwise an uncontrollable pitching could set in if too high, or alternatively the tug could be lost from view, as the downward view from the 163 was very bad indeed. In the correct tow position the aircraft handled splendidly. In rough air there were no control difficulties if the speed was kept above 135mph. Below this speed lateral control was sloppy.

At the 163's optimum gliding speed of 155mph the rudder was very light and effective, the elevators very sensitive and the ailerons light but not very effective. The plane was generally very unstable and had to be firmly controlled all the time.

Medium and steep turns revealed no abnormalities, and harmony of control was delightful. I made a fast glide at 281mph, and was thrilled with the way she handled and manoeuvred. I dived to 438mph. The plane was beautifully clean and accelerated fast and smoothly, but she was known to drop her nose violently in a 'graveyard dive' at Mach 0.84. On a stall she would dive in a deep spiral, but recovery was straightforward. She was in her element, and so was I.

Landing, without power and at a high approach and landing speed, required accurate judgement. View was very bad. For touchdown the plane could not be stalled on to the ground as the shock would have been very great. If it was held off very low and gently, then lowered on to the ground at 112mph, it did not bounce, but ran along on the tail wheel first before pitching forward quite abruptly on the skid. I once forgot to put the skid selector to neutral and had a very rough ride on a rigid skid framework instead of an absorbent oleo. I had heard of authentic cases of the 163 being landed on its sprung trolley when the latter failed to jettison, though it took a very long run to pull up.

I enjoyed my life with the birds in the 163, but it was obvious that operating the machine must have been as trying for ground crews almost as much as pilots. We had plenty of maintenance troubles, especially with the skid and tail-wheel oleos – and all without the rocket motor, the really big hazard.

The war was over now, but there seemed to be no end to the breakneck scuttling from airfield to airfield, from cockpit to cockpit. I was an RNVR officer, theoretically in for the duration only, and most of the others were rushing to get back to their civilian jobs.

But I knew now that this was my job. I had had several tentative offers from civilian aircraft firms which tempted me. There was a rosy and a highly paid future to be had there. But no aircraft firm could ever give me anything like the wonderful variety of flying experience which I was getting in the Service and which I was enjoying so much. Added to this purely selfish motive was the feeling that I owed the Navy a great deal for the exciting and rewarding life I had led for such a long time now. And I was in the middle of several important projects. I wanted to stay on, I wanted to go, I could not make up my mind. Then the Navy did it for me by offering me a four-year Short Service commission. I accepted right away.

My immediate future settled, I plunged back into work. On 2nd December I went back to Ford, did just one brief ten-minute session of ADDLS[1], and put my Vampire on ice in the hangar. I was desperately keen to beat the Americans at being the first to operate jets from carriers. I did not want to risk delay by damaging the machine on the airfield. I just could not wait.

I took off early on the 3rd, partly because I had a certain amount of fuel to burn off before I could get down to the right weight for landing on, partly because the plane was still a prototype and did not even have a compass. I took my own private wrist compass with me, but it was not the most reliable instrument in the world, and I had to find the ship in the Channel.

Because of my early take-off I missed a signal from the ship telling me to remain at Ford because the weather was too bad for a landing. The Captain – again Captain Caspar John – was actually just announcing over the ship's loudspeakers that I had been told to remain at Ford when I burst like a banshee on to the scene and screamed round the *Ocean*.

Caspar John was a very experienced carrier trials captain. He knew me, he knew the aircraft, he knew the ship. He very quickly weighed up the situation and ordered 'Land on'. This was a big moment for the Navy. If things went well today we should have moved into the jet age, the first navy to do it.

I was very conscious of all this as I prepared to make my landing. Coming round the ship I could see that she had a fair amount of movement on her. I realized that when I made my approach I should have to decide very quickly and very early on whether I was going to carry on or go round again, because at this stage in jet-engine development my Goblin engine was very slow in accelerating. This was the thing I had to watch most.

I settled down on to my final approach to the deck, and immediately realized that the ship was moving much more violently than I had thought before, pitching and rolling. But my Vampire was so steady in her approach descent and the batsman was giving me such a steady signal that it never even crossed my mind that I might have to go round again. I came straight in and made a very gentle landing, although

[1.] Airfield Dummy Deck Landings

camera shots showed that the pitching stern had hit my tail booms just before I touched down.

I refuelled and went straight on with the trials. The shortness of our take-off run astonished all the goofers on the island. We soared past them at captain's eye-level, twenty feet up.

On the fourth landing we had some trouble when the very large landing flaps struck the arrester wires and were damaged. The Vampire had to be flown ashore again and modified.

We were back aboard three days later with four square feet chopped off the flaps. We had no further troubles.

We had succeeded, we had arrived – but the Vampire never went into squadron service with the Navy. There were two reasons for this. First was the dangerously slow acceleration pick-up of her jet engine. The Vampire was in all other respects a perfect deck-landing plane, but we felt that at this stage no jet could be trusted entirely in an emergency requiring a sudden increase of speed. When a piston-engined machine was opened up suddenly on a wave-off the wings got an immediate increase in lift from the slipstream of the propeller. With a pure jet there was, of course, none of this. A pilot relied on getting his extra lift entirely by increasing the aircraft speed. The early jet engine's acceleration response was very sluggish as the Germans had already found out.

And there was another important snag. We decided that the Vampire's fuel capacity was too low for carrier work. Its radius of action would be far too limited for the long and uncertain hauls over the sea which naval flying often entailed, especially with the possibility of having to circle the ship and make several approaches to the deck before finally getting down.

The decision not to put it into squadron service meant that the Americans had jets operating from carriers before we did. But our caution turned out to be justified when the Korean War developed. The role of naval aviation in this 'brush fire' war was to give close support for the Army. The US Navy quickly found that their Banshee and Panther jets, with three times the fuel capacity of the Vampire, burned fuel at low altitudes so fast that their time over the support area was impracticably short. The Australians, too, with their Meteors, found themselves severely restricted, even operating as they did from land airstrips.

The Americans had to fall back on their piston-engined Skyraiders and

The world's first deck landing of a pure jet aircraft. Eric Brown landing a Vampire on HMS *Ocean* on 4th December 1945.

The Vampire leaps into the air on its first deck take-off.

Circling HMS *Ocean* at the conclusion of the successful sea trials of the Vampire.

145

take scores of their World War II Corsairs out of mothballs. The Royal Navy was already properly equipped for the job with the excellent Sea Fury. These conventional machines, free from the jets' big thirst, did all that was asked of them, and more. The Vampire would have been quite useless.

I flew back from the *Ocean* and next day was off to the Continent again with my German team, Hauptmann Miersch, *Feldwebels* Walter Renner and Walter Rautenberg. We went to Rheims in northern France where a most unusual German experimental aircraft had been reported. This machine, a Dornier 335, had landed at Rheims for some reason unknown to us – probably trying to escape to Spain, straight from its Bavarian factory.

We flew there as usual in my Siebel and found Rheims covered in snow. The airfield was completely disused and there were no Air Force units anywhere near, only a combined American and French supply organization whose main job was to guard hundreds of prisoners of war fenced off in a huge compound.

In a corner of an old derelict hangar we found the Dornier 335. It was a weird machine, Germany's fastest piston-engined fighter, with engines at the front and at the tail. It had several other very modern features, a tricycle undercarriage, a cruciform tail unit with a double fin and rudder, and hydraulically operated ailerons. It was the fastest piston-engined machine in the world.

Here it was lying cold and silent in the dust. We had no idea how long it had been there or what condition it was in. So we had to give it a complete overhaul ourselves on the spot, then fly it out.

It was a very tall order, especially for Renner and Rautenberg. We had no proper tools, other than what we had brought with us, and we would be working in the draughty old hangar with the temperature well below freezing point and no heating whatsoever.

And we had nowhere to live while we were there. I went to the Americans and asked them if they could put us up. When I told them who my assistants were they got very agitated and demanded that they should be put into their POW camp. I went back to the airfield. The only thing to do was to live in the Siebel for the next few days.

But when I got back I found that the two *feldwebels* had been active. Not only had they had the initiative to drain the oil from the Siebel before it froze overnight – both of them had been on the Russian front – but they had gone hunting and had discovered in a field next to the airstrip a very old disused workshop on wheels, a sort of caravan with a bench down one side and four bunks along the other. This was preferable to the aircraft. At least we could lie down in it. I went back to the Americans cap in hand and persuaded them to let me have some blankets and a big supply of canned food.

When I returned this time I found that Renner and Rautenberg had made some remarkable alterations in the caravan. They had made a rough sort of stove out of an old oil drum, and had divided the caravan into two sections. One was supposed to be the officers' sleeping quarters, the other their own. This was the Prussian-minded Miersch's doing. It was the only time we had words. He had completely ignored the need for cooking space. I had the segregation arrangement altered at once.

There we lived for a week. Outside the snow piled higher and higher. I begged some coke for our stove from the French, but I did not dare ask for food from them, which would have meant revealing the nationality of my staff. That would have meant goodbye to them. I had to scrounge food from local villagers.

We worked on the aircraft in appalling conditions. As we knew absolutely nothing about this particular machine, every single part from nose to tail had to be checked and put in working order. It called for great patience, will-power, and skill from my two young technicians. While they slaved away at the entombed fighter Miersch and I rehearsed what we could pool of our knowledge of the machine. I had flown a two-seater version of the thing briefly at Farnborough, but Miersch obviously had the better knowledge of the complex electrical and hydraulic systems of the aircraft so I decided that he should fly it out to Merville on the first lap of our return trip – although at the moment this seemed very far away, with the machine a cold and silent corpse in the hangar.

I myself became general scrounger. My main job was to persuade the French to send soldiers to sweep the one runway available to us clear of snow. Their gratitude to the British for liberating their country was so unbounded that they did this eagerly. But I had to be very careful to keep the three Germans out of their sight whenever the soldiers were on the field. None of my team could speak English, though Miersch was making strenuous efforts to learn, and they would have found it hard to explain themselves to the Americans or the French.

During the day we went about our various jobs to do with the aircraft, and time passed without much strain. But during the long nights of midwinter, with darkness from four o'clock in the afternoon until eight in the morning, boredom and cold between them threatened to make our lives a misery.

It was a grotesque situation. Here we were, a British ex-civilian and three German regular officers, victor and vanquished, trying to live together in a derelict hut on a deserted airfield in the snow. There was absolutely nowhere to go – the Germans dared not move from the aerodrome – and nothing whatsoever in the way of entertainment, not even a book or a pack of cards. There was only one thing we could do to pass the time. Awkwardly at first, we talked.

We were careful to tread warily in our topics of conversation. Miersch steered clear of politics and I did not bring up Belsen. We had a job to do and we had to live together until it was done. We could not risk falling out. These were the facts of life for us.

When we talked about the war it was from a strictly military standpoint. Miersch was very bitter about Germany's fate. To him it was totally unjust. He could not begin to see why the entire civilized world had joined together to crush Germany. Hitler, he said, had never wanted war with England. He grumbled bitterly about the 'English luck of Dunkirk'. Miersch was a very intelligent man, but with the deep, fanatical patriotism which only the older Germans had, loyal to his military leaders even in disastrous defeat.

His strict Prussian upbringing prevented him from ever bringing himself to a level where he could discuss anything spontaneously with the two warrant officers. The only time he ever addressed them was to say 'Rubbish!' to some opinion which one of them had advanced.

These two were of that sterling quality which makes the regular warrant-officer type the real pivot on which any military organization hinges – simple men, but fine soldiers and splendid technicians. Their defeat meant to them not so much a loss of national pride as the destruction of dearly loved material things, the deaths of so many of their friends, the savage blows to the remnants of the old German culture. One of them came from Augsburg and was worried by reports of the destruction there of many of the town's old medieval statues and buildings. They did not mind that the boundaries of Germany had been crossed by an invader so much. They feared that the character of their country had been finally destroyed.

Their explanation of the rise of Nazism was typical of the generation of Germans who had lived through the desperate state of Germany after the Great War. It takes real hardship to impress the minds of children, and both could remember vividly the awful poverty and despair rampant in a Germany brought to utter ruin. When a leader emerged who at last offered a clear-cut goal there seemed nothing else to do but to follow him. They still felt that Hitler had achieved a lot in putting the country back on its feet.

All three agreed that it was Hitler, however, who had made the fatal error leading to disaster when he had ignored Britain's threat to intervene if Poland were attacked, believing it to be a mere bluff. I was interested in finding out when they thought the first warnings of defeat had begun to appear. Their opinions differed. The technicians, who had been on the Russian front, thought that Stalingrad had marked the beginning of the end. Miersch, who had been mostly on the western front, surprised me by saying that he himself had first had doubts when the Americans had come into the war as far back as December 1941. He had also been profoundly depressed by Ernst Udet's suicide. This, he said, had had a very bad effect on the whole morale of the Luftwaffe. It suggested the beginning of a rot. Udet to his pilots was a folk hero, and quite irreplaceable.

We talked, we argued – but we did not fall out, and at the end of a week of it we were still working together in harmony. I used to wonder exactly what made Miersch, the ardent, arrogant Prussian, co-operate with me so thoroughly and efficiently. He was an enthusiastic aviator, and I guessed that eagerness to prolong as much as possible what would almost certainly be his last hours as a pilot had a lot to do with it, added perhaps to some feeling of personal gratitude to me for taking him out of the misery of a POW camp in Norway, and also some cynical determination to grab something out of the ruins, while the going was good. But I think that the mainspring was the inborn and sternly inculcated sense of duty which was so strong in him. Not only was it his bounden duty, under the rules of war, to obey the orders of his conquerors, I was also a rank above him. Neither he nor the warrant officers failed to salute me first thing in the morning, and there was always the stiffness of rank between us.

Nevertheless, a kind of friendship with sincerity in it grew up among

The Dornier 335 which Hauptmann Miersch crash-landed at Merville in northern France when he was unable to get the nose wheel to lock down.

us. If they had wanted to they could easily have disposed of me and made a run for it. But they carried our their duties to the letter, and often exceeded them.

Renner and Rautenberg were artisans of the very highest order, as good as our best at Farnborough. Starting completely from scratch they got the fossilized machinery of the Dornier humming. Meanwhile Miersch in the evenings told me some of the background of this advanced machine. There had been trouble from the early stages of testing. One of the first prototypes had crashed and the pilot had been picked up dead with both his arms missing. In a subsequent crash the body had been found with one arm missing. Eventually it was discovered that the method of baling out had been to blame for these gruesome and extraordinary injuries. In order to jettison the cockpit hood the pilot had had to grip two red levers at the front of the hood itself and exert all his strength to pull them. The hood tore off at once and so great was the pressure on it that he had no time to unclench his fists so that his arms were in danger of being torn from their sockets.

Quite apart from this dangerous feature, the Dornier 335 had the

The Dornier 335 which was flown by Eric Brown at Farnborough. It was in this aircraft that Alan Hards, the CO Experimental Flying, lost his life when a fire in the rear engine burnt through the elevator control cable.

most complicated system of safety devices ever employed to get a pilot clear in an emergency. On the starboard side of the cockpit was a row of buttons. Pressing the first one exploded a charge which threw the rear pusher propeller off. The second button operated another charge which blew off the top fin and rudder. The third armed the ejection seat. The pilot then tried to jettison the hood manually. If he was still alive after that he either pulled the face blind or squeezed a trigger on the seat arm-rest which ejected him.

We feared hydraulic trouble more than anything else, so Miersch, with his greater general experience of such German systems, carried out the first test flight. I thought that he was more likely to be able to preserve the machine than I, if anything did go wrong.

The flight was reasonably smooth. Hydraulic trouble did develop, and we had difficulty in raising and lowering the undercarriage properly. There were no jacks to prop the machine up and give the undercarriage a proper ground test. We just had to go on flying it until it was right.

I did the next flight. The Dornier was very fast and quite manoeuvrable. But the hydraulics were still not functioning properly. The undercarriage had to be raised and lowered two or three times before it would lock down.

But the Americans warned me that another heavy snow shower was due the next day. I did not want to become weatherbound there and decided that we must get the machine clear right away. I sent Miersch off on the first leg to Merville airfield in north-west France. We were to follow in the Siebel.

When we got to Merville we saw the Dornier sitting in the middle of the airfield with its front propeller buried in the ground. Miersch had been unable to get the nose wheel to lock down when he came in, so had cleverly decided to feather the front propeller and land on the grass instead of the runway to minimize damage. He made a very good landing and in fact did very little damage to the machine, which was completely salvageable.

The Do 335 was an unusual aircraft by any standards, being full of innovatory ideas – tandem engine layout, cruciform tail, 18° sweptback wings, powered ailerons, reverse thrust on the front propeller, and an unusual ejection seat system. However, the end result was the fastest production piston-engined fighter in the world at the end of World War II. It was a large aeroplane and essentially an all-weather/night fighter, and viewed in that light it would have performed well, but it was too stable and heavy on the elevators and rudder for a day fighter.

Chapter 11

IT WAS A NEW YEAR, the first year of peace. To us at Farnborough it brought many changes. Chief test pilot Roly Falk had already gone into industry. Tony Martindale had been invalided out with spinal injuries after a bad Spitfire crash. On 1st January a new Director, W. G. A. Perring, took over from W. S. Farren, and there were numerous other changes in personnel. It also brought us more work than ever, greater danger, and a string of tragedies.

Alan Hards, the CO Experimental Flying, was very interested in our experiences with the Dornier 335, and he asked me to give him a check-out in the two-seat trainer version we had so that he could fly it himself. I took a long time showing him the complicated emergency drills. Next day he went off solo.

He was coming back into the circuit ready for landing when we all saw to our horror that his rear engine was on fire. Every runway was instantly cleared, but he continued right round the circuit in the normal way heading for the duty runway, apparently unaware of his danger. When he was about two-thirds of the way round the Dornier suddenly plunged vertically into the ground and he was killed instantly. The fire had burned through the control cables to the elevators. Poor Alan. He had been a good friend of mine.

I began the first serious probings of the carpet-deck-landing technique by flying the Vampire along the runway at Farnborough with its wheels up at very low heights and speeds.

I was also carrying on with RATOG[1] and arrester work. We fitted rockets to the Sea Otter amphibian to see if we could get her off the water quickly. This was only the second time rockets had been used with a fabric-covered aircraft wing, and we set the Sea Otter's wings on fire. It was a very ugly rush to get round and down again before too much fabric got burned off the wings. Contrary to my hopes the airstream did not put the flames out but fanned them.

[1] Rocket-assisted take-off gear

At the same time we received a new naval fighter, the Seafang. This was a development of the Spitfire, with a laminar-flow wing. It was a machine which never made the grade at all. With the fast jets that were now flying, it was a little late on the scene anyway, and it had very bad stalling characteristics, making it very unsuitable for deck landing from a control point of view. I also ran into severe trouble when I tested her on the arrester wires. Going into the wires off-centre resulted in a long series of fin and rudder failures. The side loads straining the machine then were being transmitted through the sting-type hook on to the fin spar and causing very bad distortion. We persevered with the Seafang for a long time, but she just would not do.

We did the first full-scale experiments on the carpet deck project. A Hotspur glider fuselage was filled with concrete and dropped vertically on to a piece of rubber carpet deck. After a few drops I thought it would add a little more meaning to the experiment if I sat in the Hotspur and was dropped as well. I was foolish enough to do it sitting inside the bare fuselage on nothing but a ballast block of concrete. At ten feet per second the glider crashed on to the deck and for a moment I thought I had broken my back.

In March we had a visit from one of the test pilots of the Bell Aircraft Corporation of the USA. Just for a laugh I asked him to test my old Bell Airacobra, which I had been using for so many hops around the country. He took off, did one very quick circuit, and came back ashen-faced. 'I have never,' he said, 'flown in an aeroplane in such an advanced stage of decay. This machine should be scrapped forthwith.' So, on 28th March, I went up for a last aerobatic session in her, then bade her a sentimental farewell. The last laugh was on me.

The American was here to look into the results of tests we had been making with the unusual type of wing camber on a Bell Kingcobra to observe boundary-layer air behaviour over the wing, experiments which we had also done with a special high-speed wing fitted to a Hurricane.

For the tests we had to fly through a trail of chlorine gas laid by another aircraft in front. We inevitably flew in the very early hours of the morning, because it had to be cold enough to keep insects out of the air – one fly squashed on the edge of the wing was enough to ruin the whole experiment. The air also had to be still enough for the gas to lie undispersed. Although the chlorine was a deadly poison we did not wear gas masks because it was thought unlikely that the stuff could get at us in flight through our cockpits.

Nevertheless some of it invariably did, and the result was a blinding headache. The experiments were controlled by a very enthusiastic scientist named Bill Gray, who thought nothing of ringing up at a dismal four o'clock in the morning and getting us up in the air. We usually took turns, the man with the headache from the previous day flying the gas aeroplane.

The Kingcobra was bigger than the Airacobra to house the longer two-stage Allison engine, but there was only a 25mph increase in performance, and the handling had suffered slightly. It was never used operationally by the USAAF, but some 2,500 went to the Soviet Union under lend-lease, and 300 to the Free French Air Force.

About this time the Empire Test Pilots School, which had been formed at Farnborough, began to turn out its first graduates, and we received our first two in Aero Flight. One was a Canadian Air Force man, the other a naval pilot, Dickie Mancus, who joined me to help with my work in the Naval Aircraft Section. He relieved me of much of the tedium of slogging into the wires and other basic drudgery, so that I was able to devote more of my time to pure experimental work, in which he, too, shared.

Unfortunately, the Canadian was killed within a few weeks of joining us. He was carrying out compressibility investigation on the threshold of the sound barrier in a Mustang when he dived from a very high altitude straight into the ground. This fatality accentuated the unknowns involved in this work. Martindale had written off both his Spitfires in dives near the speed of sound and seriously damaged his spine in doing so.

On 18th July I took up a Vampire to test its behaviour at speeds near Mach 1 and I was diving at a speed of Mach 0.72 when suddenly without warning the aircraft started to porpoise violently, flinging me up and down in the cockpit, cracking my head against the canopy. I caught the plane on an upward swing, kept a steady backward pressure on the stick, and the motion ceased. But it would have been very easy to accentuate the swing by moving the stick out of phase with the fast oscillation. Then I should have been in real trouble. German pilots had described something very like this in their recollections of the Me 163 at near-sonic speeds.

I recalled this experience of mine instantly when on 27th September we

Geoffrey de Havilland died at the age of 36 in the tailless DH 108 in which he had been about to attempt the world speed record.

heard the shocking news that Geoffrey de Havilland had been killed in the tailless DH 108, in which he had been about to make an attempt on the world speed record.

His body was picked up on the mud flats at Whitstable, with his neck broken. He had not pulled his parachute ring. Could some of the Vampire characteristics at very high speeds have been transferred to the 108? Could de Havilland have experienced the same sudden shock as I had in my Vampire, only very much more violent in his advanced machine? Could he have died from a violent contact between his head and the canopy? It was impossible to be sure, because the plane had broken up suddenly and violently as well.

Thus the warnings which beset this last stretch of the path to the sound barrier multiplied. They were problems which test pilots were going to have to overcome, and soon. It was easy to see how, in the face of them, the Ministry could cancel a project so completely untried as the Miles Supersonic Aircraft.

Meanwhile there were still plenty of other ways for us to kill ourselves. The GAL/56, a new tailless, swept-wing glider inspired by German models, provided me with plenty of opportunity.

It was one plane in which I found I could not relax for a second, beginning right away with take-off. You could not lift it off the ground through the slipstream of the towing aircraft before the latter was airborne, which was the normal method, because as soon as it was clear of the ground effect – the cushion of air between wingtip and ground – the centre of pressure suddenly shifted and the machine dived straight back into the ground, to bounce on its very springy undercarriage wildly

The De Havilland DH 108 Swallow was a post-war research aircraft – converted from a Vampire fuselage – to investigate the behaviour of swept wings and the tail-less layout. After Geoffrey de Havilland's death on 27th September 1946 the RAE were brought into the picture and Eric Brown, with his experience on the Me 163B, was chosen to fly the Swallow. His impression of the aircraft was 'A Killer. Nasty Stall. Vicious undamped longitudinal oscillation at speed in bumps'.

157

The GAL/56 tail-less glider, considered by the author to be the most difficult aircraft he ever flew. When the RAE tests were completed Eric Brown flew the GAL/56 to Lasham airfield and handed it over to Robert Kronfeld, the General Aircraft chief test pilot and one of the world's most experienced glider pilots. Shortly afterwards he was killed in the GAL/56 when it spun into the ground.

across the airstrip. The only thing to do, I found, was to hold the monster down until the towing Spitfire had got off the ground, then jerk it sharply up into a position above the Spitfire tug. If you ever got caught in the latter's slipstream in the air the glider became completely uncontrollable. All you could do then was sit and wait for it to be thrown out of the slipstream again.

And it had the most incredible stalling characteristics. When you eased the nose up to slow the speed down, the plane suddenly took charge and continued to rear nose up until it was in a tail slide. Even pushing the stick right on to the dash made no difference. Then suddenly the stick movement would take effect and you would be pitched forward to fall almost vertically. General Aircraft decided to investigate this awful phenomenon after we had finished our tests. Their chief test pilot, glider expert Robert Kronfeld, went into a spin and was killed. The stalling characteristics also made landing very tricky.

I cast off one day with a female flight test observer, Miss Curtiss, in the second seat. The weather was very dubious and the cloud soon closed in completely below us. But I did not want to waste the flight, and I estimated that we were not very far from the field, so I decided to carry out our tests on the way down.

But the cloud was thicker than I had thought. When we broke clear of it the field was too far away for comfort. I would be sore pressed to make the nearest runway. I had to stretch that glide so far that I literally stalled it in over the boundary fence and it reared up at an alarming angle, then dived straight at the runway. Luckily there was not enough height for it to plunge vertically in. We struck at an angle of forty degrees and damaged the nose enough to put her out of action for about a month. Poor Miss Curtiss. For her first flight in a GAL/56 it had been quite an experience. She never uttered a single cheep during the entire flight. But she had kept the recording apparatus turning. Full marks for her but not for me.

To replace my old Airacobra I was given a German Fieseler Storch, that remarkable slow-flying plane. To baptize it thoroughly I took it to sea and landed it aboard the carrier *Triumph*. They put the barrier up for us, as the Storch had no arrester hook, but it was not needed. To the astonishment of the goofers the little plane landed and came to a stop right on the after lift, and was promptly struck down into the hangar. We paid our way while we were on board by using the Storch's incredible gift for hovering to photograph the approach path to a carrier, something which had not been properly done before, and were also useful in investigating roundown turbulence, the violent swirl of air which is set up round the after end of the flight deck of a carrier.

Eric Brown landing the captured Fieseler Storch on HMS *Triumph* – the first time such a machine had been flown aboard a carrier.

Chapter 12

With the old anxieties of total war receding, we began to receive a different type of work in Aero Flight, problems resulting from the new demands of peace.

During the war no testing or development of civil aircraft had been done whatsoever, and Britain was left to face the peacetime commercial markets with no new airliners, only drawing-board designs.

At first we made do with wartime conversions. The Lancastrian was adapted from the Lancaster, a civil version of the Halifax was built, and other stop-gap aeroplanes of this kind thrown into the race for aircraft and airline business.

We found the accent shifting slightly now to the testing of embryo new civil airliners and equipment. With a view to giving future civil airline pilots reasonably light controls on the projected huge airliners like the Brabazon – everyone was thinking big now – which were on the drawing board, we did some intensive development work with hydraulically powered controls fitted to a Lancaster.

Perhaps the rush to be first on the world's air routes was overdone. When the first big machine built exclusively for airline passenger use since the war came to us for testing it was in bad trouble.

It is a sad fact of life in the aircraft industry that a brilliant designer who one day produces a winner can next day father a problem child. Roy Chadwick, Avro's genius of the drawing board, had given us in the Lancaster one of the finest aircraft of all time. From the same brain came the Tudor.

Because I was by now the oldest inhabitant in Aero Flight it fell to me to deal with this luckless aircraft and try to help put things right.

There wasn't just one thing wrong with the Tudor. As it was when it came to us it had no hope of passing its Certificate of Airworthiness test nor indeed of crossing the Atlantic, which it had been designed to do.

Basically it suffered from excessive cruising drag, high engine-failure safety speed, bad stalling characteristics, and control difficulties on take-off. It was, to say the least, hardly the ideal passenger-carrying machine.

The RAE Farnborough was called in to help solve the problems which the Avro Tudor, the first British pressurised transport, was experiencing. Eric Brown first flew a Tudor I on 20th July 1946.

The bugs in it had worried even the makers and its designer to such an extent that they turned it over to RAE with a plea for help. We put a crash programme on it at once, partly because of its obvious importance to the economic future of the country, and partly out of our real desire to help the industry. There was then, if not now, a tremendous feeling of inter-dependence in the British aircraft world.

The whole problem was handed over to a scientist named Joe Lyons, who was left largely to his own initiative to work it out. He and I worked together very closely on it, dissecting every flight to get at the roots of the trouble. We did not stop to think then of the tremendous responsibility entrusted to us – two young men under thirty with much of the immediate future and good name of the British aircraft industry in our hands, but I did regard it as one of the greatest tests of my ability.

We went a long way towards solving the mystery, and were able to hand it back with a reasonably clean bill of health. But it was quite obvious that it would never be a specially good aeroplane. All we could do was to patch up most of its faults. What it really needed was some redesigning, and we said so.

It was to have a shocking career.

First, in a crash shortly after it had taken off from Ringway Airport at Manchester, it killed both its designer Roy Chadwick and Avro's chief test pilot Bill Thorn.

The terrible story continued. Two Tudors on the Bermuda run, *Star Tiger* and *Star Ariel*, disappeared without trace in reasonably good weather and without any radio distress calls when just short of their landfall. The causes of these two disasters have never been found, but something very drastic and violent must have occurred.

It continued its black history when it crashed at Llandow in South Wales, killing over eighty Welsh rugby supporters returning from an international in Dublin. This was at that time the biggest single air disaster in British aviation history.

The Tudor was restricted for passenger carrying, although Air Vice-Marshal Bennett of Pathfinder fame fought hard to clear its name. It was also used for freight carrying and did good work in the Berlin airlift.

On the civil side of our work we also started a long programme of high-altitude gust investigation. It was becoming obvious that we were moving into the jet airliner era, entailing flights at high altitudes. The limits of an airliner's strength depended very much on the stresses imposed on it in turbulent air. Normally turbulence was associated with cloud and high winds, but strangely enough some powerful gusts occurred in absolutely clear air at high altitudes, where the mysterious 'jet streams' were found. These were comparatively narrow bands of very high-velocity winds, which could stretch for a very considerable distance. They could be a hundred miles long and only ten miles wide, but the wind velocity be over 200mph.

We did this work in a Spitfire 19, a photographic reconnaissance machine with a pressurized cabin, capable of flying at over 40,000 feet. Every day for about two years we made two routine flights until the work was carried on by the development flight of BEA. Even today we are still not sure of the origins of jet streams, but we know enough about them for safety.

Alongside all this work for civil aviation I still had a military programme to carry out. The Fleet Air Arm, too, had moved into the ways of peacetime and the needs of the Navy in preserving it.

A new hydraulic-pneumatic catapult was installed which had to be proofed so that its performance could be checked before it was introduced into service. For the first launch with it we used an Avenger as being an old and well-tried faithful. It was a startling maiden effort. The aircraft was shot off so violently that the engine cut and the folding wings unlocked and folded back. It was a nasty sight from the cockpit. In this launch the catapult had produced 2.5 'g', but was designed to give much higher velocities. Obviously a much smoother acceleration was badly needed.

We worked hard on this task of smoothing out the acceleration curve, with frequent engine cuttings, and eventually got such good results that we were able to go up to 4.6 'g', the highest velocity ever obtained up to that time on a piloted aircraft.

During these tests the RAF Institute of Aviation Medicine, under Wing Commander 'Doc' Stewart, became interested in the physiological effects of such high 'g' launchings, and in their investigations decided to enlist the active help of my Norwegian elkhound, Chuck, to see the effect of 'g' on a creature whose heart lay, unlike a human being's, in the fore and aft plane. He collapsed instantly on the floor, but got so fond of aiding science that for a long time after these tests he continued to turn up at the site hoping that he would be needed.

Another willing sacrifice was my golden retriever Winston, a veteran air passenger and air-lift scrounger. Winston's main contribution was to suffer the effects of tight turns in a Wellington. We put him well at the back so that he would get the maximum 'g' effect, and he was supervised by the same gallant Miss Worthington who had flown before with me as an air sickness guinea-pig. He came quite unscathed out of the experiments, and was only once exposed to any danger, when he slipped off the catwalk and fell on to the framework of the fuselage, putting his four paws right through the fabric-covered geodetic lattice work. Miss Worthington had a hard time of it getting him out, but finally made a sling out of an enormously long college scarf she wore, slipped this under him, and hauled him clear.

Since the Mosquito and Hornet landings we had been investigating the problem of single-engined deck landings in twin-engined machines, which had always been regarded as a very hazardous business. The twin-engined American Grumman Tigercat was an attempt to solve the problem by giving the pilot a hydraulically-boosted rudder so that he could

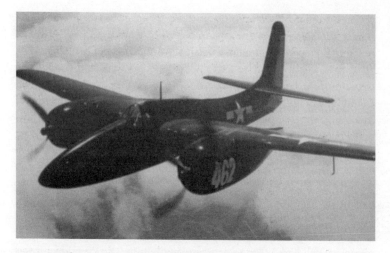

The main British interest in the Grumman Tigercat was to see how it could cope with a single-engine deck landing with its power boosted rudder. Six years after its tests at Farnborough the author was given the chance to fly a specially adapted Tigercat with a periscope sight, from a supine piloting position. He described it as 'a hair-raising experience'.

cope easily with the heavy foot-loads imposed upon him when one engine failed. It was not the answer however. It helped to keep him straight, but the single-engine safety speed was not appreciably lowered.

The British Short Sturgeon tried to solve it by fitting contra-rotating propellers, which had shorter blades than the normal type, thus allowing the engines to be brought much closer to the fuselage than usual. There was no swing on take-off with this machine, and it would probably have done quite well on the deck, in single-engined landing, but the jet age had already made the problem easier, and to my knowledge no twin piston-engined propeller type has ever made a single-engined deck landing to this day.

When 1946 came to an end I had been three years at Farnborough without any leave at all. Twice I had set off, only to be recalled within twenty-four hours each time. But when that bad winter of 1946 came and the RAE, like most of the rest of the country, was snowbound for a month and a half, I really thought that at last I would make it. I could not think of anything you could do in my job in the snow.

I had forgotten helicopters, and the research programme which was now urgent. We began investigations into helicopter rotor flow, which really tested the ingenuity of the boffins and the nerves of the pilot.

To start with a fifteen foot long hollow metal pole with holes along its upper surface was fixed to stick out from the side of the helicopter. Coloured smoke was then forced along the tube from inside the aircraft. The smoke drifted up over the rotor blades and the pattern of the airflow could be seen and photographed, but the weight of this pole and its drag was so great that the aircraft used to go into an uncontrollable turn towards the side on which the pole was fixed. We still managed to do some successful flights with it, but finally decided to imitate the technique we had used with the Kingcobra for our boundary-layer tests. Two Fieseler Storchs were taken over. One of them dangled three canisters emitting coloured smoke for the helicopter to fly through, and the second Storch photographed it as it flew through the smoke trail. Another method was to hang a smoke canister from the jib of a fifty-foot crane while the

Investigating the flight characteristics of early helicopters by flying in coloured smoke. The fifteen-foot-long hollow metal pole had been fixed laterally to the helicopter, but the weight and its drag forced the aircraft to go into an uncontrollable turn towards the side to which the pole was attached. It was also used vertically as depicted.

165

helicopter hovered underneath it. This was dangerous as the rotor tips were very close to the jib, leaving little room for pilot error.

The reason for these airflow tests was partly to investigate a region of the flight envelope we had encountered which gave rise to loss of control. This occurred in zero forward air speed descents under certain conditions of collective pitch movement, causing a nose-down pitching; full backward movement of the stick could not prevent the speed increasing rapidly and the helicopter rotating. In effect it was the equivalent of a stall and spin in a fixed-wing aircraft.

The vortex ring state, as this phenomenon was called, had not previously been explored, and our fundamental investigative work on it made an international impact, to such an extent that the great Igor Sikorsky visited Farnborough to have a demonstration. He was a delightful man with an old-world charm, and before our flight we swapped stories of our first solo rotary-wing flights. He wore his trademark trilby hat throughout our forty-minute flight and he talked for about two hours afterwards with myself and the relevant boffins about our research work.

Later, in September 1947, we pushed our work into the realms of blind flying, which is difficult in a helicopter by virtue of its pendulous longitudinal stability. We therefore adopted a more sensitive artificial horizon, and after some practice 'under the hood' I made the first actual cross-country flight totally in cloud from Farnborough to Beaulieu on 7th October 1947, involving forty-five minutes on instruments, and carrying a flight observer who recorded the whole flight on auto-observer. Then on 27th November I made the first night flight of forty-five minutes, and since there was no instrument panel lighting, this omission was compensated for by a torch held by my flight observer, the ever-trusting Bill Stewart.

So we passed that grim winter. But I received some compensation on the first winds of spring. At the end of March, when I was on board the *Illustrious* with a Sea Fury for side-wind catapult trials, I got a signal to say that I had been made CO of Aero Flight. It was a great honour for me, particularly as I was the first naval pilot to head this exclusively RAF unit.

And on the summer breezes I soared aloft on the upsurge of another adventure. We had finished our tests with German jets now, and from their snarling sound and fury we moved to the utter silence of the empty sky in the beautiful sailplanes we had captured. After the roar and violent motion of war planes, soaring and gliding in the singing altitudes with the pure flight of birds was very good for the soul.

Most fascinating of all was the Horten IV, a high aspect ratio all-wing prone-position glider. This striking little aircraft had been well tested in Germany, and it was known that on one flight it had been carried up to 26,000 feet by a strong up-current and the pilot had had to bale out as he had carried no oxygen equipment with him.

To me its most intriguing feature was not so much its performance as the pilot's prone, or semi-prone position. Flight in this position was a breathtaking revelation to me. Aerobatics came easily and effortlessly without any of the discomfort felt from high 'g' when in the usual sitting position, and landings could literally be judged to within inches once the pilot had got over the initial shock of seeing the ground rushing past right under his nose at high speed.

This aircraft so stimulated my feelings about the prone position for piloting that I persuaded the boffins and the Institute of Aviation Medicine to start a thorough investigation into its potentialities.

We had also brought back from Germany an aircraft called the Zaunkoenig or Wren, a parasol high-wing ultra light monoplane designed by Professor H. Winter, the designer of the Fieseler Storch, and built by his students at the Technical High School at Brunswick. This was built as a fool-proof trainer in which a pupil could be sent off to solo in safety after only one hour's ground instruction – the time was reduced to five minutes for those who had flown sailplanes.

The machine was tiny and weighed only 800lb. It had a little 50 hp engine. It had made a few flights in Germany with Professor Winter himself at the controls, but had got no further than the development stage.

We erected it at Farnborough and I made the first flight in it. It was without doubt as near foolproof an aeroplane as there will ever be. It was unstallable and unspinnable. Just to prove our confidence in it we sent off solo, Handel Davies, then Head of the Aerodynamics Section, who had previously flown only as a pupil in a dual control Miles Magister. After only half an hour's ground instruction he pretty well proved Dr Winter's thesis.

In gliders you work closely with the elements. But even in high-powered aeroplanes you are forever wrestling with the weather. Thunderstorms are a constant hazard, particularly in civil airliners, which are not stressed so highly as military planes against severe shocks.

The German Zaunkoenig (Wren), built as a fool-proof trainer by the students at the Technical High School at Brunswick. The intention was to design a trainer in which a pupil could be sent off to solo after only one hour's ground instruction – or only five minutes for those who had flown sailplanes.

There had been many cases, both military and civil, principally in the tropics, of aircraft entering thunderstorms and being hurled out again in small pieces. It was a well-known fact that the black heart of a cumulo-nimbus or thundercloud contained columns of air moving at very high velocities in opposite vertical directions, so that an aeroplane flying into such a centre was subjected to very severe stresses which could easily cause structural failure.

It now became our job to investigate this. For it we inevitably chose the Spitfire, one of the most highly stressed aeroplanes ever built. Our method was simply to wait for thunderclouds to appear, leap into the air in our Spitfires – we had two permanently standing by for this work – and charge in to the blackest centre we could find.

What happened then depended largely on your own wits – and the thunder. It was frightening work. It meant trying to control the plane in severe turbulence on instruments, many of which were giving completely false readings because they depended for their operation on reasonably stable atmospheric conditions.

These thunder cells were raging cauldrons of noise and light, the noise coming from the thunder and from the hailstones battering on the metal skin of the plane, the light from the lightning, which often struck the aircraft, but worst of all by its brilliance which often blinded the pilot so that he could not read the instruments in the cockpit for a few vital seconds.

We soon learned the hard way that the golden rule was to strap yourself tightly in the cockpit, turn on the cockpit lighting to ease the effect of the lightning flashes on the eyes, and fly steadily through on your gyro instruments concentrating merely on keeping the aircraft level without worrying about speed or height, which varied alarmingly throughout your passage through the thunder cell.

Both our Spitfires suffered severe damage from hailstones and lightning strikes, and two or three times engines cut due to icing. Whenever your machine was struck there was a horrible acrid smell, like fire and brimstone. St Elmo's fire would glitter round the cockpit rim and circle the spinning airscrew tip with unearthly sparkle, while inside the cockpit nacelle it would be as black as night.

In July we started serious work on the carpet deck, building our Stage III, the actual landing installation on the airfield, and starting measurements of our approach technique over the runways. I sat in a Vampire while it was dropped from a crane on to the 'carpet' from various heights to test the energy absorption of the carpet itself.

This was built up of the top carpet, composed of five layers of vulcanised rubber, above three layers of NFS hoses, inflated at varying low pressures. We subjected this to weather tests, and also tried the effect of the hot jet pipe – which in practice would be resting against the carpet on landing – on contact with the rubber.

Ever since the Vampire deck landings we had been struggling with the problem of lift control on jet aircraft with particular reference to quick pick-up from the deck in an emergency wave-off. Something had to be introduced to make up for the absence of slipstream effect which a piston engine provided in these tense circumstances. Quite a few ingenious devices were tried, but the best answer proved to be the improved acceleration response of the new Rolls-Royce Derwent and Nene series of jet engines.

In August we were able to try this improvement for ourselves when we received the new Nene-engined naval fighter from Supermarine, the

E1/45, or Attacker as it came to be called. This machine was unique in having the ordinary tail wheel undercarriage instead of the usual jet and tricycle combinations. Its wings were fitted with lift 'spoilers'.

I ran into trouble with the Attacker on its arrester-proofing trials when the arrester hook was sheered from the V-frame to which it was attached. But the fitting was strengthened and the sea trials took place in October aboard the *Illustrious*.

The landings were shared with Mike Lithgow, the firm's chief test pilot, himself an old Fleet Air Arm pilot, myself, and a pilot from Boscombe Down. Three opinions on the aircraft's deck-landing cap-abilities were better than one, and the firm was encouraged by having a direct interest in the trials.

Lithgow made the first direct landing, then handed over to me to make the first take-off, and the three of us alternated throughout the trials. We had some trouble again with the hook arrangement, and

The author making the first take-off of the Rolls Royce Nene-engined Supermarine Attacker. It became the Navy's first operational jet fighter, although it was not the complete answer to the problem of lift control on jet aircraft in an emergency.

The Eagle-engined prototype Westland Wyvern came to Farnborough for testing. It was then passed on to another service unit for its deck-landing trials before going into squadron service.

decided that a modification was necessary. This was done, and in two weeks we were back again in the ship to complete the trials successfully. The Attacker was never a brilliant aircraft, but it went into squadron service and performed reasonably well for the Navy's first operational jet fighter.

Three other new naval aircraft also appeared on the scene about this time, the Fairey Spearfish, the Westland Wyvern, and the Hawker N.7/46.

The Spearfish torpedo bomber had its troubles and never went beyond the prototype stage. We eventually used it as a hack for arrester gear and catapult development work.

The Wyvern strike fighter was designed to have a turbo-prop, but as this had not been perfected in time the prototype employed the Rolls-Royce Eagle, a huge, twenty-four cylinder piston engine. For Harald Penrose, Westland's chief test pilot, it presented the unusual and trying combination of a first flight in a new aircraft with a new engine.

The Wyvern gave no trouble on its passage through Farnborough, and as in this initial form it represented nothing unusual in aircraft design, it was passed on to another service unit for its deck-landing trials. It was a fair machine and went into squadron service.

The Hawker N.7/46, later called the Sea Hawk, started its flying life in the hands of Bill Humble, Hawker's chief test pilot. He and I had worked very closely together on the Sea Fury. When the N.7/46 showed rather peculiar vibration troubles on its first few flights Bill, whose jet-flying opportunities had been rather limited since this was his firm's first jet product, came along to ask me if I would do a hop on the aircraft and give my opinion on the vibration. It was a gesture typical of the personal liaison between us at RAE and the firms' test pilots.

So I carried out the seventh flight on the machine at Farnborough. Vibration there certainly was in plenty. It was finally traced to a near case of elevator 'flutter' – one of the dread words in a test pilot's vocabulary, because it usually implies a runaway vibration which ends in the break-up of the structure affected.

In this case, however, the vibration was not a runaway one and was reasonably soon cured by incorporating a streamlined torpedo fairing at the junction of fin and tail plane and also by replacing the rectangular heat shield fairings at the jet efflux by pen-nib fairings to cure flow breakaway. The Navy then received an altogether splendid machine, a beautiful piece of aesthetic and practical design which looked, and was, superbly airworthy. In full flight the Sea Hawk looked indeed like a graceful sea bird, when taking-off and alighting more like a spray-dodging flying fish.

In the autumn of 1947 I was called to the office of Morien Morgan for a discussion on my handling experiences with tailless aircraft, of which I had flown four such types. At the meeting were three other members of Aero Dept. Flight Section – Philip Hufton, Dr Karl Doetsch, a former aerodynamicist and test pilot at the German Aviation Research Establishment at Völkenrode, and Dr Dietrich Küchemann, a former wind-tunnel expert from the same establishment.

Morien explained to me that he was investigating the optimum aerodynamic shape for a possible supersonic transport aircraft of probable tailless configuration. A lively discussion followed, and the major contribution was Küchemann's argument in favour of the slender delta wing layout, although he did express some reservations on its likely slow speed handling characteristics.

There is no doubt in my mind that Küchemann's presentation was the inspiration for the wing configuration of Concorde, and Morien Morgan locked on to this immediately. He pursued it with his initiative to build the slender delta H.P. 115, a decision arising out of the first meeting of the Supersonic Transport Committee at RAE Farnborough, chaired by Morien, who was then Scientific Adviser to the Air Ministry.

Chapter 13

As far as I knew the carpet deck was the biggest job on the horizon for me. The installation being built at Farnborough was coming along well and would be ready soon.

I thought I had finished with my German aircraft tests. But now two German scientists who had accepted jobs at Farnborough came up with a design study of a transonic aircraft to break through the sound barrier. It was expected to reach a Mach number of 1.24, and a height of 60,000 feet. Basically the design was for a severely swept-wing aircraft built round a Rolls-Royce Avon jet engine, with the pilot lying in a prone position in a nacelle inside the air intake duct.

It was intended to land on skids rather like skis, which retracted into the underside of the fuselage. This form of landing gear was chosen because it was the simplest solution to the problem of housing the undercarriage. A wheeled undercarriage was much more complex and always more difficult to house. Wheels and tyres could not be made too thin if they were to absorb very high landing speeds, and they also needed very strong brakes to pull up fast aircraft. With the simple skids no brakes were needed.

But we did not know whether skids would stand up to the tremendous shocks which would be involved. So my old Me 163 was dusted off again so that I could make some fast landings on to the hydraulic skid which it had fitted. The landing touch-down speed of our transonic research plane would be about 160mph, and we decided to go on and land the 163 up to this speed, and if necessary push it to destruction in the process. It was the first time that I had seen under the heading 'Limitation Of The Test' the words 'Test to Destruction'.

So far all the tests we had done on the 163 had been carried out from the Vickers grass airfield at Wisley, but this was much too small for the tests ahead. So I was flown on tow by a Spitfire to the RAF station at Wittering, which was a grass landing strip used during the war as one of three special emergency landing strips for bombers returning from raids on Germany so badly damaged that a crash on landing was practically inevitable.

The airstrip there was originally five miles long and had two control towers. During its wartime life it had been staffed by special crash teams of doctors and technicians with special heavy lifting gear and everything necessary for dealing with a landing disaster involving heavy aircraft. Often after a raid so many badly damaged aircraft came in that the teams got the removal of wreckage down to such a fine art that the airstrip could be completely cleared of a mountain of wreckage in a matter of minutes.

By the time I arrived in November 1947 with the 163, two miles of this strip had been de-requisitioned and handed back to the local farmers, so that I was left with three miles of airstrip. It seemed ample.

I did the first landing at 135mph. There were no hitches. I made another touchdown, again quite smooth, this time at 137mph. But this one was much slower than I had intended, and I made the third landing at 158mph, which was about what we could expect the research plane to do.

It was too much for the hydraulic skid. It held briefly on the actual touchdown, but collapsed completely when we began our run across the rough grass surface. The skid was smashed up into the fuselage and rammed the hydraulic oleo legs up through the cockpit floor so that the rudder bar was completely jammed hard over to port and my legs were pushed up and jammed under the instrument panel. All the special fittings carrying our instrumentation for the tests came adrift and peppered me as we skidded across the field in a curve towards the boundary fence.

While we were still doing well over 100mph the ailerons ceased to operate and the port wingtip dropped to the ground. The quite gentle curving path became a vicious sweep towards the fence, which was looming up fast ahead.

I was not worried too much about the fence, which was only a wire-stranded one and unlikely to make very much impression on my thick bullet-proof windscreen. What bothered me was that I was already completely trapped in the cockpit and was taking a severe jolting in my spine. I thought of all the tales I had heard from German 163 pilots of 'Komet spine' and of the many unlucky ones who had broken their backs in landing and take-off crashes just like this one I was in, certain I was going to join them.

But the machine stopped just short of the fence, and it took only a few minutes to release me after all. At the time I felt no particular ill effects other than being slightly cut by debris in the cockpit, and I flew myself back to Farnborough in a Viking that evening together with all the boffins and their camera records.

Next morning I woke up to find myself completely black and blue from the base of my spine to the hairline of my neck. I was X-rayed at the RAF Institute of Aviation Medicine and relieved to find that there was no compression fracture.

I was in the air again by midday the same day, but for a few days I restricted myself to the milder job of teaching other RAE pilots to fly the helicopter. This was another chore which had been added to my already bulging schedule. In all I taught six pilots to fly and although I never fancied myself as an instructor, at least none of my pupils ever came to grief.

By the middle of December only the weather held us up from going ahead with the carpet – or flexible deck as it was now called – trials. The deck installation was ready, but we were forced to wait until wind conditions were right. The bad weather lasted, and it was not until after Christmas that we were able to start.

December 29th was rather a dark day in my life. Early in the morning my father, who had been staying with us over Christmas, was taken seriously ill. I was waiting anxiously by his bedside for the doctor's verdict about eight o'clock in the morning when Charles Crowfoot, who ran the flight tests in the Naval Aircraft Department, called to say that wind conditions were ideal for the first attempt at landing on the flexible deck.

I explained my domestic crisis but said I would see how my father was feeling. I told my father that I was required for a special job at RAE. He knew how long we had been waiting to start this important trial. He said he was feeling fine and that I was to go along straight away. With anything but untroubled feelings I went off.

By five past twelve I was in the air circling RAE for the first pass at the deck. I did one dummy run over it just to see that conditions were quite right, then settled down to the approach.

The approach path was by no means ideal. It had to be made over buildings and down a sloping gradient before coming to a flat run-up of about 200 yards before reaching the flexible deck itself.

I always liked to keep the margin of stress on an aircraft to a minimum in case of mechanical failure, and I had got the approach speed

THE FIRST ATTEMPTED FLEXIBLE DECK LANDING

ENDS IN DISASTER AT R.A.E. FARNBOROUGH — 24/12/M

From the author's scrapbook; a complete photographic record of the first attempted landing of an aircraft with no undercarriage on a flexible rubber carpet, allowed the RAE to make a detailed investigation into the causes of the crash.

176

down a little lower than usual, but still within the safety limits which had been calculated by the boffins. Just before reaching the flat stretch of ground I felt the plane sinking rather faster than usual and I opened up the engine to give me extra lift.

This had always done the trick before. But this time, although the engine power increased I did not accelerate at all and the sink became worse.

I knew I was very near the ground by now. In fact my hook was actually trailing in the grass. The rate of sink was stopped by the ground cushion effect of air being compressed between the wings and the ground so that I remained with my hook still trailing in the grass without being able to gain an inch of height as I rapidly approached the deck.

The deck itself was raised above the ground but at its approach end there was a ramp leading up to it in a gradual incline. Between the ramp and the deck was a ridge.

The hook clanged against the ramp but stayed firmly down until the plane crossed the boundary between the ramp and the deck. The hook caught in the ridge and was flung up against the fuselage, and the tail booms of the Vampire hit the ridge.

The impact damaged the after end of the plane and jammed the elevators. The aircraft was pitched nose-down towards the deck and it crossed the arrester wire in a dead level position instead of being in the correct nose-up attitude.

The nose swung on downwards towards the carpet. The arrester wire scraped along the underside of the fuselage and would easily have been picked up by the hook had it been free. But when the hook had been thrown up by contact with the ridge it had locked back up in its housing. This should have been impossible as the mechanism was designed to prevent this very thing, but it had failed.

This converted what could have been a successful landing with minor damage to a major crash. After crossing the arrester wire the plane continued to swing nose-down towards the deck and plunged into it with such violence that the nose completely vanished and penetrated right down to the bottom layer of the NFS hoses under the topmost strata of rubber.

Then it was thrown harshly up again in a nose-up attitude. I opened it up to full power and was climbing away safely when I realized that the stick was jammed solid, with the elevators keeping the plane in a nose-up

177

attitude. I throttled back gently and she settled on to the grass ahead of the deck. The crash split the cockpit all round me, though I was unhurt.

I was rushed to sick bay for a quick check up, then met with the boffins to hold a short post-mortem. By the time I was ready to go home it was quite late. I found when I got to my house that my father had died as I was on my way there.

Fortunately we had full camera coverage of the accident. We found that my approach speed had been a little lower than normal but should have been safe enough to allow the aircraft to pick up speed comfortably when the engine opened up. Some unknown effect had destroyed lift control at this stage, and this unknown had to be determined.

We started a series of tests with tufts of wool placed on the wing roots to find out what happened to the airflow. We soon found that in the approach speed range which we had been using any increase in engine power caused a change in airflow behaviour around the wing-root air intakes which aggravated rather than improved the lift.

We also decided that a pilot should not be left to make his approach unaided, but that a Deck Landing Control Officer should be provided armed not with the usual bats but with a microphone for talk-down control through the plane's radio.

We tried to discover what had made the hook jam up in the fuselage and see whether it might do the same if it hit the arrester wire or anything else less solid than the ramp. We got the hook to jam up into the housing again in conditions just like this, so a big modification was obviously needed.

We were not ready to land-on again until March of the new year, 1948. I was actually in the air on the approach path when the whole thing was called off over the radio as the windspeed had suddenly dropped and would give me too high an entry speed into the wire. But I was not perturbed. The omens were good. My son was born on 1st March.

On 17th March I made a landing, flying into a 12mph wind.

As I came in the batsman gave me last-minute corrections, unable to keep the excitement out of his voice. He lined me up nicely and my first sensation was that of the wire rushing up very quickly, its black and white stripes – painted on it for judging height – glaring.

Then it whipped underneath me and I knew that in a fraction of a second I should know whether I had snagged the wire or not. Almost at once I felt the machine check and she settled squarely but heavily on to the deck with only a very little pitching movement. The Vampire dropped like a body hitting a tightly stretched trampoline. I did not cut the engine until the plane had actually stopped, in case I had to go round again. But this time the landing was perfect.

I was relieved rather than elated this time, because I felt that, although all the scientists connected with the job knew that the previous crash had not been my fault, there were others not in the know who thought that my personal worries that morning had warped my judgement.

From this date on throughout the spring and summer of 1948 we continued to increase our knowledge by lowering the windspeed at which we landed to zero, then finally landing with tail winds behind us. On some of these later landings the arrester gear 'bottomed' or pulled right out against its stops, and on others the arrester hook attachment bolts were strained. Our limit was reached with over 5.6 'g'. The gear bottomed, the hook was torn clean out of the aircraft and sent hurtling backwards by the taut wire like a stone from a boy's catapult. Luckily there was no one in the way.

I made forty of these landings in all, many of them in front of VIPs of various sorts. Nothing was ever specially rigged for them, and these were only demonstrations in the sense that sometimes times of tests would be adjusted to suit the important visitors. Of course it was an extra strain, to start with at any rate, to have to concentrate on serious work like this with an audience looking on. With the new techniques we had developed since that first unsuccessful landing we could now be confident of getting down without any trouble. I reached the stage where I could judge almost as accurately as the instruments the amount of 'g' I was taking on each landing. It was always far in excess of that experienced in a normal deck landing but not in the least uncomfortable provided you were very tightly strapped in. Any slackness in the shoulder harness would allow it to cut into your shoulder when the full 'g' came on.

The ordinary work of deck-landing assessment was not neglected during these experiments. On 27th February a special hooked Meteor was delivered to us for experimental deck work, a machine with the larger wing of the standard Meteor 3 but the powerful engines and stronger undercarriage of the Mark 4. She gave us no troubles at all in

ABOVE: Meteor EE337 touches down on HMS *Implacable* – the first deck landing of a twin-engined jet aircraft on a British aircraft carrier.

RIGHT: A Meteor with two Rolls-Royce turbo-prop engines. This type of power plant had many advantages over the standard pure jet engines for use on naval fighters.

the work-up stage and on 8th June I successfully landed her aboard the *Implacable.* This was the first twin-engined jet ever to be put on board a British carrier. Although it was never intended as anything more than a research aircraft, it was simple to land on the deck and a great improvement on the Vampire in the excellent acceleration which its Derwent 5 engines gave for going round again.

I also flew a Meteor with two Rolls-Royce turbo-prop engines, the first machine with this type of power plant to fly in this country. This plane removed all the acceleration problems of a pure jet, which was important to us for deck landing.

There was the usual flow of interesting work other than naval business. I took on some more rogue aircraft, with a preponderance of heavy, four-engined ones. My naval uniform produced some eyebrow lifting at Handling Squadron's headquarters at West Raynham when I turned up to test their rogue Lancastrian, and even more at Central Bomber Establishment, where their much publicized world-travelling Lincoln aircraft, 'Crusader', had run into stability troubles. Few of these hardened veterans of Bomber Command could resist asking whether I hadn't come to the wrong place.

Another RAF machine in serious trouble was the new elementary trainer, the Percival Prentice. It had been exhibiting very dangerous spinning characteristics and had killed a number of students and instructors. After a few turns of a spin the aircraft suddenly flattened its attitude. This is the most dangerous type of spin, when the rudder, which is needed for recovery, is blanketed by the fuselage.

It would not recover with full application of rudder alone, but also required a two-handed, full-blooded push on the stick, hardly the thing you could expect an embryo pilot to do after a mere twenty hours or so in the air, and unlikely to inspire much confidence in the instructors either. We were eventually forced to change the face of the Prentice completely after a series of flights with different modifications running into double figures. I could have written a manual on spinning after that. I had great admiration for the boffins flying with me. Often we would do more than fifty spinning turns in one flight, a sick-making thing for a passenger.

One day in a Farnborough barber's shop a boffin named F. E. Lamplough came up and introduced himself to me. He was an elderly man, who had been living in retirement and come back to RAE during the war. His speciality, he said, was optics, and he had been wanting to speak to me for some time to enlist my support for an application of his work to aircraft.

He outlined his plan, which was nothing less than the incredible idea of photographing the actual shock waves occurring on an aircraft wing near the speed of sound. He was going to use the principles of an apparatus called a shadowgraph recorder. It would necessitate flying at high Mach numbers at dusk so that the light of the setting sun would throw shadows on to the wing and thus allow his apparatus to photograph the shock waves on the wing.

He pointed out that the real problem was that the sun would be so low on the horizon at this time of day that the aircraft would have to fly at very low altitudes, and that a period of about a quarter of an hour only

Aero Flight Section, led by Morien Morgan and the author, taken at RAE
Farnborough in October 1948. In the background is a Lancaster II .

would be available before the sun disappeared completely over the horizon. The pilot's worry would be that compressibility effects are at their most dangerous when they occur near the ground at very high airspeeds. Stresses on the aircraft structure are then at a maximum and time to recover from trouble at a minimum.

We started tests on a Vampire and I made the first proper flights in April. That first evening I reached a speed of 540mph at 2,000 feet, and went home with no knowledge of whether it would produce any results at all. When I arrived at RAE next morning I found the place agog with excitement at the startling results. Lamplough had produced pictures of the shock wave which were quite unique and created a sensation in aeronautical circles throughout the world. To this day they remain a classic example of this vital kind of research.

In February the two German scientists, Winter and Multhopp, published their note on the Transonic Research Aircraft which had caught my imagination when it had first been discussed. We had by now done some background work on the skid undercarriage. The design also

The Reid and Sigrist Desford trainer was chosen for the first British prone piloting trials. Eric Brown left Farnborough before the tests were completed. They were successful but the RAE Transonic Research Aircraft (below), with prone piloting position and an Avon jet engine, was abandoned.

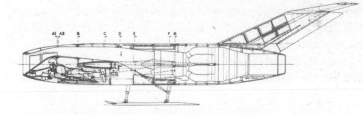

called for the prone position for the pilot, an idea which had fired my enthusiasm after my flights in the Horten IV glider. The very first drag estimates had shown that the profile of the fuselage had to be kept free from all disturbing elements, and an external cabin hood could not be fitted. The only possible place to put the pilot seemed to be in a prone position in the air intake duct in which he could have a reasonable downward view for control.

I had already been stirring up interest in the prone position among the scientists of Aero Flight, and on 10th May I was asked to a meeting called by the Ministry of Supply to discuss the prone position idea. I was asked whether I thought any flying should be done on the subject at RAE. I suggested that we should convert a suitable tandem-seat trainer so that the front cockpit was occupied by a pilot in the prone position and the rear one by a safety pilot in the usual sitting position, and recommended the Reid and Sigrist Desford Trainer for the job. This was agreed and I was sent to make a check flight. The Desford, of which only a prototype existed, flew as I had hoped and was turned over for conversion. As a secondary step we selected the two-seat Meteor trainer to take over from the Desford if the first tests proved successful.

I was disappointed to have to leave Farnborough and part company with the project before these tests were made. They were very successful, but the Transonic Research Aircraft itself was abandoned because it was thought to embody too many unknown factors, of which pilot fatigue in the prone position was found to be an important one.

While all this frantic search after the Holy Grail of supersonic speed was going on, a Mosquito aircraft from RAE took a radio-controlled, rocket-powered model of the Miles M.52 in its bomb bay up to 36,400 feet over the Isles of Scilly, where it was dropped on 10th October 1948 and achieved a Mach number of 1.38 in level flight. This underlined what a fantastic opportunity had been missed by the earlier cancellation of the full-scale M.52. Britain could have – and should have – been the first nation to break the sound barrier in manned flight.

In the summer of this year we had another fatal crash in Aero Flight when Squadron Leader Dick Whittome plunged into the ground from a compressibility dive in a Spitfire. This plane had been specially modified so that when it was diving really fast the airscrew could be stopped and feathered. This was done to stop the recurrence of a runaway propeller bursting the engine as it had done in both Martindale's bad crashes. The cause of Whittome's accident was never known, and another death was chalked up to the unknown devil of the sound barrier.

At the same time I was surprised to be given the job of doing compressibility dives in, of all things, the Tudor. There was a reason for this, as a special research four-jet version of the Tudor was going to be built, provided the airframe stood up to the sort of strains it would then have to undergo. My past experience with the Tudor had marked me out for this experiment.

It was planned most carefully by the boffins. The crew of the aircraft was kept to the absolute minimum of two pilots, one flight engineer and one supervising scientist. The machine was stripped to an empty shell so that we could take it to maximum height for these potentially dangerous tests. We practised our test procedure rigidly on the ground so that every man knew exactly what to do in any one of the many emergencies which we knew could develop. I, for example, was to take control of the throttles and controls entirely during a dive, but if stick forces became so heavy that I needed both hands the flight engineer was to take over the throttles, and if I still could not pull out the second pilot had to be ready to add his strength.

We got the Tudor to 32,000 feet and worked up in steps from 0.6 Mach to 0.7, which may not sound very much on paper but was only fractionally below the Mach number at which the early Vampire had been in trouble, and above that at which some current fighters had gone out of control. We only stopped at this speed because the pull-out had become a two-man affair, and we decided our safety margin was running out.

The four-jet Tudor was built and renamed the Ashton, and it gave much valuable information used in jet airliners, in which Britain took such a startling lead with the Comet.

Preparations were building up all the time for the first landings on the flexible deck at sea. I trained a cross-section of naval squadron pilots for the job, including an American on exchange duty. By the end of September everything was ready.

But on 1st October I ran into some serious trouble on another job which looked as if it might knock me out of the trials altogether.

I took over a Meteor which had been fitted with the new Griffith Suction Wing, a forerunner of the present boundary layer suction control system. Roughly speaking, this consisted of a series of holes on the wing surfaces and ducted to the jet-engine compressor so that the layer of air which sticks to a wing's surface and sets up drag can be sucked away through the holes by suction from the jet engine and blown out over the ailerons through the slots near the hinges. This improves lift and control simultaneously and would thus be a most effective way of reducing landing speed for carrier-deck operation.

I took up the Meteor with the underside aileron slots sealed over with rubber so that measurements could be made and compared with the figures arrived at with the rubber removed.

Although great care had been taken to make a perfect seal, all the rubber blew out on the starboard side. This set up a violent aileron oscillation and over-balance of the control so that the ailerons themselves could only be seen as a blurred mass and the wings were flexing alarmingly. At the same time the plane was rolling violently from side to side and sometimes going over the vertical. I put up with this for a while, then decided that I had better get out before the situation got out of hand – if it hadn't already.

I called Farnborough and announced my intention of baling out. They said, 'Okay. Another aircraft in your vicinity is being homed on to you by radar to keep a watch on your bale-out.'

Within seconds another Meteor appeared, flown by one of the pilots in my own flight who quickly sized up the situation and noticed as the wings rolled into a near inverted position that the rubber was also beginning to peel off the other wing. Very intelligently he told me that if I could stay with it a few moments longer the remaining seals might all come off, and at least the rolling would disappear.

This is what did happen. Although the aircraft was still not pleasant to handle it was controllable, and I was escorted back to base by the other Meteor.

Now my way was clear for the sea trials of the flexible deck, on which I and many others had already spent so much time and effort.

The trials began on the light fleet carrier *Warrior* on 3rd November. For the first flights I had to use, not the proper Sea Vampire 21, but the ordinary prototype Vampire. This version was not fitted for catapulting, and would have to be flown off from the mere 300 feet of steel flight deck left free for'ard of the flexible-deck installation.

The whole flexible deck stood two feet three inches above the steel flight deck, with its for'ard end in line with the after end of the island, where a swivelling crane was conveniently situated for handling the aircraft at rest after landing. The after end of the flexible deck stopped in front of the after lift and aft of that a special raised roundown was built.

The sea trials of the flexible deck; the prototype Vampire, flown by Eric Brown, landing on the deck installed on HMS *Warrior*, after two practice dummy runs over the deck.

During a previous visit to the ship in July I had had this roundown painted all white, and twelve-inch white lines painted athwartships under the arrester wire and at a point ten feet aft of this, all to act as markers on the approach and run-up. There was a twelve-inch white line painted the whole length of the ship indicating the centre of the rubber mat, and the central span of the arrester wire was painted black and white alternately in two-foot lengths.

I made two dummy practice runs over the deck, then came in for my first landing. On the approach at about 118mph I aimed at the white-painted roundown as the spot at which I would start levelling out to give myself enough run-up.

The motion of the ship and the turbulence over the roundown forced me to cross the stern at sixteen feet, higher than I had anticipated. I started to hold off and from the hundred-foot mark assessed my height by sighting on the arrester wire until I was about two-thirds of the way along the run-up, when I had to transfer my gaze to a spot ahead as the wire was swiftly disappearing under the nose of the plane and I might have unconsciously eased the stick forward and nosed towards the deck.

The plane's belly scraped the wire, the hook caught. The arrester wire and the deck had been deliberately set hard and the shock was uncomfortable, though only for a split second.

Drawing confidence from this first good landing I went on with the series. I had some trouble on my fourth landing. The deck was pitching and heaving slightly and I just failed to pick up the arrester wire. I struck the for'ard end of the flexible deck with sufficient force to record 0.4'g' on the accelerometer, which was still switched on, but the machine bounced off into the air at a fairly steep angle of attack and remained airborne with a little forward pressure on the stick. I went round again and this time landed smoothly. It was a reassuring outcome.

On the fifth landing the port wingtip hit the arrester wire which was rising on the ship's roll, but minor damage to the wing did not prevent a normal landing. To give greater wingtip clearance the wire supports were moved in towards the centre by seventeen feet. It meant that there would be less leeway for an off-centre landing, but we thought that this would be adequate.

On the next two attempted landings I ran into more serious trouble. Each time I picked up the wire but it whipped out of the hook after about twenty feet of wire had pulled out. Moving the supports had put greater tension on the wire and it had been forced out of the hook by its whipping up and hitting the tail booms of the plane.

We had been doing the tests with restricted amounts of fuel for safety, and I was down to seventy gallons. The ship now reported that some very peculiar reaction had obviously developed in the wire and that I must return to Lee-on-Solent. On seventy gallons I would be lucky to make it.

There was worse to come. When I was half way there Lee came up on my radio … 'We are clamped solid with bad weather. You'll have to divert to Tangmere'. I made Tangmere with nothing showing on the fuel gauge.

The hook was altered, checked by two landings on the flexible deck at Farnborough, and the trials resumed. We stepped up the weight of the aircraft, reduced wind speed, and made off-centre and side-wind landings up to all possible limits. It was so easy to line the aircraft up perfectly on this deck that landing deliberately off-centre I found difficult, but we had little or no trouble altogether. On the twentieth landing the Vampire took a thirty-knot, eighteen-degree side-wind and the machine fell out of my hands just after it had crossed the roundown. It sank straight on to the arrester wire, which whipped up and dented the underside of the port wing and the starboard dive brake before going into the hook. The plane slid placidly on to the rubber mat. After the fourth landing I had used the Sea Vampire 21, which was fitted for catapulting, and with her made what was actually the first launch of a jet and tricycle aircraft from a British ship. All our further take-offs were catapulted.

As the trials gathered momentum we brought the other pilots I had trained into the act. At Lee-on-Solent one of these pilots took over an aircraft which had originally been meant for me but which I had rejected till an engine fault was cleared. He was making his landing on the flexible deck when the claw of his hook sheered clean off. He bounced on the deck and was able, luckily, to go back to Lee. Shaken by this, and with the flexible deck very much on his mind, he landed on the runway with his wheels up. When the damage was checked it was found that the bolt connecting the claw to the V-frame was sheared. The break was such a clean one that we were rather puzzled. Nothing further was discovered, but our security measures for guarding the aircraft were tightened up.

I finished the trials with a feeling of satisfaction. 'I feel,' I said in my report, 'that the principle of flexible deck landing for undercarriageless aircraft is fundamentally sound … The experiment is probably ahead of its time in that it apparently does not offer much gain to the conventional type of jet aircraft in service at the moment, but it should offer a lot to an aircraft specifically designed for flexible-deck operation, provided that arrester gear development can keep pace with increasing approach speeds … It may even be that future swept-back and delta plan form aircraft will be forced to adopt this method of landing on carriers, since all calculations point to serious wheeled landing problems on such aircraft …'

To date my eager prophecy has not materialized. No one in military circles has denied that the flexible deck works but it seems that the idea came at the wrong time, when the urgent programmes of the war years were finished and economy had become the watchword.

The scheme had real advantages. Dispensing with a heavy, bulky undercarriage not only saved space and weight for more fuel and armament, it also meant that the aircraft could be stacked up instead of stored sprawling over the deck and many more of them housed in a ship's hangar. The method would also have reduced landing accidents considerably, and the flexible deck itself would have been more easily and quickly repaired after battle damage. For use on land, particularly in campaigns like the Korean War, fought over rugged country at a rapid pace, it could have been invaluable, especially in conjunction with carriers similarly equipped working off the coast, as the whole installation could be transported in three two-ton lorries. The scheme demanded take-off by catapult, but there was no great difficulty about providing a field catapult.

But a plane without an undercarriage using a flexible deck must have the same facilities wherever it goes. It cannot land in a farmer's meadow in an emergency or an airfield which is not equipped with the rubber mat. And re-equipping all our airfields, not to mention scrapping existing conventional aircraft, was not calculated to appeal to a government facing the tremendous task of putting a nation's whole economy back on its feet. There were more urgent things to do with the money.

The scheme is not dead, however. The Americans have experimented with it from time to time, particularly the Marine Corps, and it is not forgotten in many progressive minds.

One benefit that came out of the flexible deck project – almost inadvertently – was the concept of the angled deck, probably the most significant contribution to the advancement of naval aviation, particularly from a safety standpoint. It came about like this. After the successful flexible deck ship trials on HMS *Warrior*, a meeting was held at the Ministry of Aviation to discuss issues that had been highlighted, one of which was how to land and catapult aircraft as a simultaneous operation in view of the fact that no crash barrier was envisaged for the flexible deck.

During the meeting in August 1951 Captain Dennis Cambell was in the chair, and during discussion, made pencil sketches on a pad in front of him without really appreciating the practical significance of his doodling ideas. At the meeting was Lewis Boddington, the Head of Naval Aircraft Department at RAE, and his quick mind saw the potential in the sketch proposals for normal carrier operations. Back at Farnborough he produced a design for a ten degrees angled deck to be suitable for a carrier such as *Ark Royal*. This arrangement would allow landing and catapulting to be independent of each other's operation, and would eliminate the need for a crash barrier to deal with a missed arrester wire pick-up by the landing aircraft merely carrying on round again for another attempt.

Chapter 14

IN THE RUSH FOR SUPREMACY in the world of post-war aviation, there were many false starts, many failures. For six years all development in civil aviation had ceased, and designers in general were out of practice and out of touch in this field.

I had experience of some of these ambitious flops. I also had to fly military types which were anachronistic hangovers from the war. Some of these were good aeroplanes but of a specification no longer needed, others were poor deck performers anyway. A case in point was the Blackburn Firecrest. Its predecessor the Firebrand had not come up to expectations as a naval aircraft, and the Firecrest was too similar in performance to be of any use.

Early in 1949 I went to work on the new control system for the Bristol Brabazon, which was nearing completion at Filton. The system was designed at RAE and I tried it out for the first time on a Lancaster. I then took it to Filton so that Bill Pegg, Bristol's chief test pilot, could try it out for himself. There I got my first look at the 'Brab'.

The size of the giant plane was breathtaking, dwarfing even the huge Blohm and Voss 222 which I had flown in Norway. But instinctively I felt what many other aviators must have felt – that it was just too big. Where were the runways and taxi tracks big enough to handle it, the hangars to house it? There were only one or two airfields in the country large enough. And such a huge machine would have been very sensitive to heavy gusts at high altitudes. Ill-fated argosy, as archaic as the dinosaur.

Delightful, however, was the new Hawker P. 1052, a swept-wing version of the Sea Hawk. Here we had an aeroplane which could give a new lease of life to our compressibility work, which had got stuck at about Mach 0.9. We succeeded in pushing our top speed to Mach 0.94, but to our disappointment, not beyond. This was not because the P. 1052 had any nasty characteristics, but strangely enough because the reverse was the case – instead of trying to nose over in a compressibility dive it made every effort to nose up out of it. It was obvious to me as I flew this beautiful aircraft that it would be ideal for the first swept-wing deck-landing

The elegant Hawker P.1052 arrived at Farnborough on 1st June 1949 and Eric Brown was asked to assess it for use on aircraft carriers. He found it a delightful aircraft to fly, but after he left the RAE his successors experienced a number of forced landings and it never entered service.

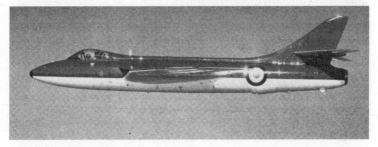

A Fleet Air Arm Hawker Hunter. Eric Brown's first flight through the sound barrier in a British aircraft was made in a Hunter.

The De Havilland Swallow was a brave attempt to solve some of the many problems involved in breaking the sound barrier.

trials, and my successor at Farnborough came in for the job. Good as it was the P. 1052 never went into squadron service, and was eclipsed by Hawker's new pride and joy, the splendid Hunter.

But all these things became minor matters when in July the De Havilland 108 with newly strengthened wings arrived at Farnborough. It was delivered to us for the twofold purpose of probing the sound barrier and investigating the cause of Geoffrey de Havilland's death in the previous high-speed 108.

It had already had an exciting life since then. When it was again released in its strengthened form John Derry was reputed to have taken it through the sound barrier. The story was much ballyhooed in the press and the facts distorted.

I had long talks with John Derry on his experience so that we could benefit from it before our own tests. He told me that he had been pushing the aircraft hard in a dive to get a high Mach number just below the speed of sound when he let go of the stick with one hand to switch off the recording cameras and the machine ran away from his control. For a split second he saw the Machmeter needle flicker over the magic number 1 before he regained control with the greatest difficulty.

Unfortunately his cameras were switched off and he could not switch them on again as he had his hands very full with the ugly situation which had developed. So there was no instrumented proof that he had been through the sound barrier. John Derry himself was the first to appreciate this and never personally pushed this claim in opposition to that of the Americans when they smashed the sound barrier in the Bell X-1. There is no doubt that he did exceed the speed of sound, but not in controlled flight.

I had already flown a slow-speed version of the 108 and was quite familiar with its characteristics at that end of the scale. I had realized at an early stage that this was a tricky aeroplane that had to be handled very carefully. Already during stalling tests in the slow-speed version I had got myself into an inverted spin, an undignified position I had not been in since my elementary training days. The spin was very flat, which normally means that recovery is going to be difficult, but in the case of the tailless 108 the high rudder was in the perfect position to be clear of any blanking effect from the rest of the fuselage when inverted, and so the rudder was effective and I recovered. Nevertheless this feature claimed another of the pilots in Aero Flight later in the year when he got into similar trouble and spun into the ground.

As I was already familiar with the low-speed characteristics of the 108 I started off immediately with the high-speed tests.

The first object was to get the plane going as fast as possible as high up as possible, and then gradually step down the height just as Geoffrey de Havilland had been doing when the aeroplane broke up at 7,000 feet at Mach 0.875.

Our first series of tests were made at 35,000 feet, and I reached Mach 0.985 after a dive from 45,000 feet. At this speed I had the stick right back against the stop, so it was obvious that this was the absolute limit that could be reached in controlled flight. It was exasperating to be so near the magic figure of Mach 1 and yet be so far – and all too easy to see how John Derry could have gone out of control in such a situation.

Then we repeated the tests at a medium altitude level of 25,000 feet. But this time I reached only 0.94. I was deliberately jerking the stick backwards and forwards to simulate the effect of the bumpy air which would have been met with at low altitudes such as that at which the world record run would have taken place and Geoffrey de Havilland had been flying when he was killed. Even with the slightest sharp movement fore and aft the aircraft began to oscillate to an extent that was becoming dangerous at this speed.

I had had no trouble of this kind at 30,000 feet, but here was a warning signal that the Swallow lacked longitudinal damping at the higher indicated airspeeds met at lower heights. A long plank will always balance better than a short one, and in a conventional aircraft with a normal tail unit the inherent stability usually damps the oscillating motion before it becomes really dangerous. But it had long been suspected that a tailless aircraft would lack this steadying feature. It is rather like cutting off the tail of an ordinary machine and trying to rebalance it at a point much further forward.

With this very much in mind I descended to 4,000 feet, knowing well that it was in this region that Geoffrey de Havilland had met disaster.

At Mach 0.88 it happened. The ride was smooth, then suddenly went all to pieces.

As the plane porpoised wildly my chin hit my chest, jerked hard back, slammed forward again, repeated it over and over, flogged by the awful whipping of the plane. My thoughts were grim.

This was how it happened. This was how he had died. In the same

195

second his head had cracked the canopy top and broken his neck, the wings had gone, the plane broken up.

He was a big man, I was short. And I had had my seat lowered as far as it would go, with this in mind. I wouldn't break my neck yet. This was the moment of truth.

But I was going under fast, I couldn't keep this up. The whole plane was oscillating as fast as a hand can wave goodbye. The 'g' was murderous and getting worse.

Like another hand guiding me the drill we had practised so hard took over. Both hands went out, both hauled hard back, one on the throttle, one on the stick.

The motion ceased as quickly as it had started.

I sat, head bowed, shaking. If this hadn't worked I would have been finished.

But it was QED. We knew our enemy. Next time we would be better prepared. That is test piloting.

By now my Farnborough days were numbered. On 5th April I was given a permanent commission. At the same time I was warned that I would have to leave RAE. I had been there nearly six years and this was a long way past the normal duration of a naval officer's appointment. From a career point of view I had to go and gain experience with a front-

A week before the author left Farnborough, a test flight in the unorthodox SR/A1 twin-jet flying-boat fighter almost ended in disaster. Landing in Cowes Roads the flying boat hit a large piece of wood and overturned with Eric trapped upside down in the cockpit. He was rescued by Geoffrey Tyson, Saunders-Roe's chief test pilot.

line squadron. On 11th August I was posted to the School of Naval Air Warfare at St Merryn in Cornwall to be brought up to date on front-line weapons work.

But my last days seemed to have been set in a violent pattern.

The day after my appointment I went to the Saunders-Roe works at Cowes to fly their unorthodox SR/A1 twin-jet flying-boat fighter at the invitation of the firm. I had acquired a reasonable amount of experience on flying boats during my German period, and I was quite confident about this job.

I was given a run over the controls by Geoffrey Tyson, Saunders-Roe's chief test pilot, then set off for my first take-off from Cowes Roads. Take-off in this boat was not easy, as the firm had readily admitted, but I had no special trouble, so I set about checking the aircraft's handling characteristics in the air, including its behaviour during a dive at Mach 0.82.

Everything went well and at the end of the flight I came in to land in the same direction as I had taken off, but was told by radio from the patrol launch to land along a direction at ninety degrees to that of the take-off, as there had been a wind change.

I saw the launch moving out to this new position and turned in to land parallel to it. For some unknown reason I decided, contrary to my usual jet practice, to land with the cockpit hood open.

I touched down normally at about 100 knots and the boat seemed to be running sweetly on the surface of the water when suddenly I caught a momentary glimpse of a dark patch ahead of me.

There was a tremendous crack as something hit the underside of the pressure hull, and as it was compressed between the hull and the water shot out like a shell from a cannon and knocked the starboard wing float clean off.

The starboard wing dipped at once and the aircraft swung violently to starboard, then cartwheeled to port and over on to its back.

She skidded along on the surface of the water for about fifty yards then came to rest. Upside down in the cockpit I saw the water first rush past, then pour in as we stopped. I undid the safety straps hoping to fall out of the cockpit, but was firmly held by the parachute harness, which I could not unbuckle.

With a great struggle I got free, gulping water to relieve the pressure on my bursting lungs. Somehow the water gave me extra energy and I kicked myself free of the cockpit, but every time I tried to get clear I hit something solid.

I realized it was the upper surface of the wing. Struggling to the trailing edge I surfaced. But by now I was in such poor shape that I could not even manage to inflate my Mae West. I started to lose consciousness rapidly, and all I could do was to stick my finger hard into a drain vent hole which I could see just within reach in the side of the fuselage, hoping that this would hold me fast when I passed out.

My next recollection is of Geoffrey Tyson supporting me in the water. It was only a flicker of consciousness before I passed out again and finally came to in Cowes Hospital, spouting water like a whale with someone giving me artificial respiration.

Tyson had in fact leapt fully clothed from the launch to grab me just as I was about to vanish under the water again. As the launch got near to the overturned machine they saw that two large holes had been knocked in the bottom of the hull. Apparently a large piece of wood, probably from a dismasted yacht taking part in Cowes Week the week before, had embedded itself in the hull. Normally the take-off and landing lanes were carefully swept by the patrol launch but this time the sudden wind change, plus the fact that the SR/A1 did not carry enough fuel to keep it circling in the air, had meant that there had been no time to sweep the newly chosen landing lane. I left hospital next morning and was fit enough to fly myself back to Farnborough. After another week, I left to start a new phase of my life.

The thought that I would no longer be a part of RAE was almost impossible for me to grasp. I had been there so long and become so very deeply absorbed in the work that I had come to feel a permanent feature of the place. Mixed up somehow with this was the instinct that I was indestructible. I had had so many brushes with disaster, seen so many others killed – but I had lived. Perhaps it was high time to go. But I just could not take it in. It had been my life, and I had lost it all.

Not only had the actual work been utterly fascinating to me and without any sense of strain – only to my wife, who never complained of the long and dangerous hours I spent away from my family – but I had made so many good friends among those dedicated people at RAE whom I admired so much.

The fact that my background had not been that of a young professional naval officer, but that of a student, probably made me so much more *en rapport* with the scientists. I also found it very easy to get on well with the RAF, among the serried ranks of whom I was on paper very much the odd man out. I was fortunate to have such fine COs as Alan Hards, Dick Ubee, Silyn Roberts, and Alan Wheeler.

All the civilian test pilots I met and worked with were completely devoted to the job, and seemed to be happy only when they were together talking shop. Among them there were some great names in the test-flying world. It was always a thrill to me to meet and talk flying business with men like Geoffrey Tyson, Harald Penrose, Jeff Quill, Mutt Summers, Bill Pegg, and George Errington. All these men had been heroes in my private hall of fame long before I knew them personally. As a goggle-eyed schoolboy I had watched Geoffrey Tyson pick a handkerchief off the ground with his wing tip as he played the star part in Sir Alan Cobham's flying circus. His picture along with those of Harald Penrose in the Westland-Hill Pterodactyl and Jeff Quill in the Spitfire, with which his name will always be associated, decorated my bedroom wall in my student days.

These three, giants in their profession, were all men of slight build, and of tremendous natural modesty, in many ways the antithesis of the glamorous movie test pilot.

Of a late 1930 vintage, matured through the war years, were Geoffrey de Havilland, Bill Humble of Hawker's, and Alex Henshaw of Supermarine's. They were men of great dash, splendid demonstrators of their firms' products. I can never think of them without visualizing a high-powered piston-engined fighter screaming vertically up into the blue, gyrating like a spinning top.

More contemporary with me as regards age were Mike Lithgow, an ex-Fleet Air Arm pilot, Peter Twiss, who had been on my original naval flying course, John Cunningham of Comet fame, John Derry, Neville Duke, and Roland Beamont of English Electric. These are the test pilots I associate with the onset of the jet age. They differed from their predecessors perhaps most noticeably in their more studied approach to the business. They all had, as I think even their illustrious forerunners will admit, a more technical approach to their profession. Progress demanded it. The jet age had brought simplicity in engine design and complexity in airframe design. Together these things had widened the field of test flying considerably.

'Jerry' Sayer, the Gloster test pilot who made the first British jet flight in the E.28/39. His only criticism of the plane was that the elevators were very sensitive.

There are many test pilots, both civilian and service, I have not mentioned, not because they were any less competent than the others, but only because they are not associated so strongly in the public mind with a particularly exciting machine or incident. Sometimes even such an historic occasion as the first jet flight in Britain does not carry its pilot's name along with it. 'Jerry' Sayer of Gloster's is the example here. Whatever it was that obscured his name, wartime secrecy or the fact that he lost his life in a non-jet crash so soon afterwards, I have always felt that here was one of the 'greats' in the game who was never accorded the high place he deserved.

Behind the pilots are the aircraft designers, the immortal R. J. Mitchell who gave us the Spitfire, Sir Sydney Camm of Hawker's, R. E. Bishop of De Havilland's, and Roy Chadwick of Avro's, to name only a few. Again I can quote a great man in this field whose name should have been a household word but never was. It was the lot of Joe Smith of Supermarine's to follow a man who was probably the greatest of them all. R. J. Mitchell had put British aviation on the map with his Schneider Trophy winning aircraft and then his final masterpiece, the Spitfire. Joe Smith took over the reins as World War II burst upon us, and he perpetuated this great aircraft through an astonishing number of variants before bringing out on his own account such jets as the Attacker, the Swift and Scimitar. I admired everything about Joe Smith. I only wish more people knew what a debt this country owed him.

It is a hallmark of all great designers that they are perfectionists and are not afraid of criticism. My personal experiences with them always revealed kindly men, who showed the greatest concern for their test pilots and expected only truthful information, no matter how distasteful, in return.

Another group that must be mentioned are the boffins – and boffinettes. If ever I met dedicated men they were the Farnborough boffins. In my time the Welsh and Scots seemed somehow to have cornered the market. Aero Flight had such brilliant aerodynamicists as Morien Morgan, Handel Davies, Dai Morris, and P. A. Hufton. When I see the illustrious positions they held in the aviation world, I wonder how often I must have held their lives in my hands and vice versa. They flew on every possible type of test flight involving the experimental work for which they were responsible. No less so did the boffinettes like Mrs Gwen Alston, Mrs Anne Burns – of gliding fame – and Mrs Dorothy Pearse, who was the first woman certificated aero-engineer in Britain and teamed up with the famous woman pilot Pauline Gower to run a private air charter company.

For sheer inventive ingenuity the Naval Aircraft Department team, led by the genius of Lewis Boddington, was supreme. The names of Dr Thomlinson, John Noble, Charles Crowfoot and others of this Department must go on record as those responsible for giving the Royal Navy a technical lead in aircraft carrier equipment which it still holds to this day.

These men and women were civil servants, but they worked hours, took responsibility, and produced results far beyond what their country paid them for. To me they represent the true measure of Britain's greatness.

Chapter 15

A^T ST MERRYN I went to school again in a class of potential squadron COs and senior pilots, for gunnery, rocket-firing, bombing, and tactical exercises. It was one of the most high-powered courses in the Navy, involving intensive flying and desk work, and the pass standard was very high.

You were treated as a raw student, and it was very good for any ego that might have become inflated. I really needed more re-adjustment than most of the others, after such a long time in the workshop of aeronautical science, where everyone is equal. There I had mixed all the time with civilians. Now I was harshly reminded that I was in the Navy, that the basic reason for my being in the uniform I wore was to fight in an aeroplane.

Air gunnery had not changed very much since my operational days, nor had bombing techniques particularly, but I was new to the business of rocket attacks. I found it very exhilarating to let loose against the collection of old army tanks set up for us on the Cornish coast.

Another thing which had changed was the type of basic formation, the finger-four having replaced the old vic of three, although the pair, which I had been used to in *Audacity*, remained the basic fighting unit. In that ship we had used the pair under force of circumstances, and it was not being preached at the time as a tactical doctrine. The RAF were then using the vic of three.

This was my first taste of Cornish weather – fair, but with the treacherous quick mists creeping in from the sea. We had to get used to diverting to other fields, with St Merryn covered in.

I was at the School of Naval Air Warfare for only three months, but during that time two COs of Aero Flight at Farnborough were killed, both in DH 108s. My successor dived into the ground in the high-speed version, while his successor spun in on the slow-speed model. Both had been RAF pilots under my command and good friends of mine. It was a sad blow.

When my new appointment came in December it was a very unexpected and pleasing surprise. I was to go back to my old *Audacity* squadron, 802, as a senior pilot. The wheel had almost come full circle. The squadron's twelve Sea Furies were based temporarily at Culdrose in Cornwall and formed the fighter part of the 15th Carrier Air Group, which also included a Firefly anti-submarine squadron. The Group was attached to the light fleet carrier *Vengeance*. To round off my feeling of having come home, Commander (Air) at Culdrose was my second *Audacity* CO, Donald Gibson.

The squadron was divided into three flights. One was led by the CO, one by the senior pilot, one by the next senior in rank. It is the senior pilot's job to be responsible to the CO for keeping the squadron up to peak operational efficiency by organizing all aspects of its training and arranging the flying programme accordingly. There was a very wide field of training to be covered, including navigation, gunnery, bombing, rocket firing, night flying, deck landing training, tactical formation, instrument flying, and photography for reconnaissance purposes.

There is usually a hard core of about four or five experienced pilots in a squadron, while the remainder cover varying lesser degrees of experience down to the odd one or two whose first operational squadron it is. It is interesting to be able to mould these new boys into fighter pilots very largely after one's own pattern. Although certain tactical procedures are standardized in air-combat work, the Fleet Air Arm has always encouraged squadrons to employ their own initiative, as this encourages the type of flexible thinking which is essential in operating from carriers at sea.

It was wonderfully refreshing to be back with a squadron. I had almost forgotten the particular feeling of camaraderie in such outfits. Apart from the flying there were, for example, the wild squadron runs ashore in the usual collection of ancient vehicles, not a single one less than ten years old. I suspected that some of the squadron's maintenance effort went into keeping these old crocks on the road instead of the planes in the air, but as senior pilot, largely responsible for the morale of the squadron, I had to turn a blind eye to these non-union practices. Fortunately for me I was not responsible for training the pilots to drive their cars as well as their aeroplanes, because if our aircraft accident rate had matched our driving wastage the Navy would have called a Board of Enquiry forthwith.

The carrier air group system was a comparatively new institution at this time. It meant that two squadrons were banded together under an air group commander to become the property of one particular carrier as its air force. Time spent ashore was merely filling in between embarked periods in the ship while she was in for leave, refitting, and maintenance.

The job of air group commander was an unenviable one on the whole. As an executive officer he was lost between the Commander (Air) of the ship on the one hand and the two squadron COs on the other. The latter, with the best will in the world, more often than not found it galling to share their leadership of the squadron with another who was not of it. In practice the air group commander was the administrative head of his group rather than its operational leader. Although the group was supposed to be a team, there was hardly ever an occasion when a team effort was called for. Even in a big concerted strike, when the Fireflies were used in their ground support role and the fighters gave them cover, an overall CO was really superfluous to the squadron COs, and there were never very many of these mass strikes, even in Korea.

The air group commander never even possessed a personal aircraft, but had to go begging, whenever he needed one, to either of the two squadron COs, usually to the one whose type of machine he was most used to.

The scheme was never popular in the Fleet Air Arm and was doomed to failure. It was scrapped later. But it did have one good effect, in that it brought the fighter and the anti-submarine people together and gave us a much better appreciation of each other's problems.

Life in the squadron now became a series of long periods embarked in our carrier, interspersed with short spells ashore. Our first trip in the *Vengeance* was to the Mediterranean, and on the way I made my 2,000th deck landing in the Bay of Biscay, my old stamping ground in *Audacity* days.

It was an old established practice for an aircraft carrier to work up in the Mediterranean because the weather there was always so good and not only allowed plenty of flying but was a morale booster as well.

We had some good runs ashore in the sunshine. On our first trip we called in at Leghorn. From here we made excursions to Florence and Pisa – though the pure educational value of these was doubtful. We made an interesting contact with the Italian Navy, whose academy was at Leghorn, and which was just beginning to build up again after the war.

Their surface ships had had a particularly disastrous history in World

War II, but their submarines, and in particular their midget submarines, had put up a good fight, and our Firefly boys were especially keen to get what information they could on Italian underwater experience.

Another visit to remember was to Sardinia. This rugged island had been, until recently, one of the worst malarial areas in the world. The work of a Rockefeller health team had removed this blight just after the war, but in spite of this we found Sardinia a rough and unattractive place.

Perhaps it was pure bias. While we were there Cagliari's rugby team, proud of its reputation as Italy's number one team, challenged the Fleet. We turned out a very strong team, but to our horror we were confronted with a ground which was nothing more than a piece of fine gravel, with not a blade of grass to be seen anywhere. When we looked at the Italians we saw that they were as thickly padded as an American football team. Our captain watched all this in horror, and then was given a bouquet of flowers and a kiss on both cheeks, which rattled him even more. In spite of this we ran up a score of thirty-two points, but I, at scrum-half, like everyone else in the team, was cut to ribbons.

On our return to England we were disembarked for a spell in Germany, where the squadron was to be based for two months at Wunstorf, near Hanover, to take part in large-scale army exercises on Luneberg Heath. We arrived just after the Berlin airlift had been completed, and lived in the sort of magnificent mess and living quarters which Goering had built for all his Luftwaffe stations. All these messes had a wonderful bowling alley in the cellar. Here, nightly, we pitted ourselves against the RAF or the Army units who had taken part in the exercises with us.

At sea the fighters had the job of protecting the parent carrier, the Fireflies that of hunting submarines, but both had the parallel function of ground attack in support of army operations. For this purpose an army officer was allocated to each carrier. This 'carrier-borne ground liaison officer', as he was called, had a small team of two soldiers, and their job was to brief air crews on army-support operations or often go ashore in their special radio-equipped jeep to go into the battle area and call down the strike aircraft on to 'targets of opportunity' as the local army commander required.

We had taken our pet soldiers with us to Germany, and the liaison officer spent his time thinking up exercises for us with the local army groups.

The Sea Fury was a good looking aircraft with the fine lines typical of all planes designed by the famous Hawker designer Sydney Camm. It was a first class naval aircraft.

On a typical day he would brief us about 8am for an assumed tactical situation. He would then disappear in his jeep to join up with our own Army force, and we set up an operations room and stood by at readiness just as if it were the real thing.

A flight of four would be sent up to keep a standing patrol over our own forces to try and beat off any RAF aircraft which, acting as the enemy, were trying to attack our ground forces.

Our major job was to await calls from the jeep to attack certain targets allocated to us. The Army usually left an old tank or a hut for us to attack with practice bombs. Occasionally, in certain areas, we were allowed to strafe lines of old disused army vehicles representing a convoy. These were very popular exercises and reasonably realistic, although of course we met no flak. It was all very timely, as it turned out, for Korea was not far away.

Throughout such a day the standing patrol would be relieved at intervals of one and a half hours, and this was kept up until about dusk, when the Army CO usually called for a full squadron strike on an important target, and off would go the twelve aircraft together.

We had with us a two-seat Sea Fury trainer for instrument-flying training and we used to give the Army COs rides in this over the battle area to let them see how it looked from our end, and many valuable lessons in camouflage were learned this way. In exchange the Army used to let us drive their tanks, which was good fun and added some variety to the routine.

After a short spell ashore in England again while the ship went in for maintenance, we were off to the Cape Verde islands. Our main purpose here was some oceanography work, badly needed as the charts of this part of the ocean were seriously out of date. Many of our ships spent their time taking soundings and exploring the nature of the sea bed. Only a few yards from the shore, where these huge chunks of volcanic rock rise in places sheer from the ocean floor, they recorded some tremendous depths of water. There was little for us to do ashore there. The only Europeans were a group looking after the cable and wireless station, and the islands were rife with all the worst forms of tropical disease.

We were glad to be off and heading for Casablanca, glad too to resume our daily flying routine. It was exhilarating work in the keen airs of the Atlantic or the sunny Mediterranean. The tenseness of the war years was gone, of course, the hours of anxiety when the air had been loud with engines and screaming bombs, but we practised hard and thoroughly our task of providing the carrier force with the best possible air defence and strike capability.

An exercise might begin with the Fireflies taking off at dawn to carry out an anti-submarine patrol of the area round the ship, then forming up some 100 or 150 miles away and coming in on simulated attacks against the ship.

One flight of our Sea Furies would be sitting on the deck ready for immediate take-off if and when the alert came from the Fighter Direction room.

The alarm goes. You grab up your helmet and maps and run the length of the flight deck to your aircraft, feeling the whole deck begin to pound under you as the ship starts to pick up speed for the fly-off.

You plunge into your cockpit, give the flight-deck officer the thumbs up when you are ready to start. When everybody has given the signal he passes it on to the bridge. Commander (Air) presses his button. The klaxon squawks raucously. All together the pilots fire their Coffman starter cartridges to kick the engines over, a shock of sound. The ship is turning into wind, and your aircraft tilts on its oleo legs.

The flight-deck officer begins his traditional action ballet. He waves the men lying prone on the deck in the tearing slipstream to pull their chocks away, then roll aside. He rotates his flag to tell the first plane, already ranged on the centre line with wings spread, to open up against the brakes. The engine roars, the aircraft trembles and quivers, and he chops his hand across in the signal to go.

You are off and tearing down the deck. You do a quick turn off the deck on to the heading for interception, flying at three-quarters throttle while the rest of the flight catches up with you.

Meanwhile the flight-deck officer has waved the next machine forward on to the centre line from its perch, wings folded, to one side of the deck. He pushes down with one hand, telling the pilot to brake on that side to swing himself properly round. He gives the sign to spread the wings, the run-up signal when the aircraft is ready, the curt drop of the flag, and the pilot is off to join his flight leader.

As you head for the interception everybody peers for the 'enemy', who is coming in low on the water, difficult to spot. You sight him, turn in to attack, careful not to get caught in his slipstream at this low height and spin in. You press your button and the camera records your shot.

Then you go back to the ship for the land on. You circle the ship until you are called into the landing pattern. Each flight comes down into the pattern in turn. You fly down the starboard side of the ship in echelon formation. Just past the bows the leader breaks away to port into the circuit, flying down the port side, lowering wheels and flaps ready for the landing. His number two heads on past the bows for another ten seconds, then he turns to port, followed by the others at ten-second intervals.

A good squadron will achieve a landing interval of thirty seconds between each aircraft. This calls, of course, for good judgement by the pilots, but also for fine team work by the flight-deck party, who have to unhook the plane, restow the hook, lower the barrier, get him for'ard into the deck park, reset the arrester wires, and raise the barrier again, all in swift seconds, with the batsman bringing the next plane in automatically, glancing briefly for'ard to see that all is ready. This might be a morning's work, succeeded in the afternoon by a practice shoot at a splash target streamed and towed behind the ship, with the men off watch making bets from the roundown.

On the way down to Casablanca I returned from one trip to find that on the approach to the deck my elevator was so stiff that I could not get the stick far enough back to bring the tail down into the proper deck-landing attitude.

I came in hoping that the length of the hook alone would be enough to pick up a wire.

But when I touched down the tail was still too high in the air. I cleared all the wires and sailed on towards the barrier.

A barrier crash is never pleasant. Although it happens quickly there is time for the pilot to realize he is in for it. All he can do is brace himself for the shock, waiting for the horrible noise when his big metal prop chews up the steel-wire strands of the barrier and the machine shoves the whole terrible tangle up the deck to the sound of rending metal, wondering whether he will be lucky and just tilt on to his nose and fall back, or whether he will stay over, or, worst of all, go right over on his back, when the pilot will be in a nasty position, especially if fire breaks out …

I was one of the lucky ones this time. My Fury slammed into the barrier, tipped up, fell back. It was a mess, but I was unhurt.

We had one very spectacular barrier crash in the *Vengeance*, however. A Firefly bounced clean over the first barrier and looked like clearing the second barrier as well until its hook caught in the top strand of the barrier mesh.

This stopped the machine abruptly. Then the hook broke off, and the Firefly, the last aircraft to land on from this exercise, careered straight into the deck park of about a dozen Fireflies and Sea Furies, most of which still had their pilots in the cockpits and their ground crews milling round them.

Such a catastrophe I have never seen before or since. The Firefly hit the rear parked machine, a Sea Fury with its pilot in the cockpit, set up a chain shock which pushed the front three aircraft right off the bows, and its flailing propeller crunched its way up the fuselage of the Fury, throwing off thousands of lethal slivers and splinters of jagged metal. It came to rest with the propeller boss skewered right up against the armour plate behind the pilot's seat. Amazingly, no one was killed, but there were some fantastically narrow escapes.

Fortunately this kind of accident is rare, thanks to the strict training the Fleet Air Arm receives. In the case of my barrier no one could be blamed on account of carelessness or inefficiency. When the plane had been disentangled from the barrier we found a steel bolt lying in the hinge shrouds of the elevator, restricting its proper movement. How it got there still remains a mystery to me.

About this time, after our return from Morocco, I decided to start a formation aerobatic team within the squadron. This was something I had long wanted to do, and I reckoned that I now had the right material to start with.

The three pilots I chose were all on their first operational tours in a front-line squadron and had all the required dash combined with flying skill that I was looking for.

The first one was my own wingman 'Boot' Nethersole, an ex-Dartmouth lieutenant who had shown a particularly good flair in his air-weapons work. The other two were both Commissioned Pilots and were quite different in temperament, but equally matched and above average in flying skill. Johnny Walker was a typical 'press-on' fighter pilot of the tireless, happy-go-lucky type one associates with The Few in Battle of Britain days. Bill Newton, on the other hand, was a more studious character who had a more business-like approach to his flying as his recognized profession, and was always trying out new tricks of his own to improve his ability.

Aerobatic teams were nothing new, and if we were going to impress our audiences more was wanted than just good tight formation flying. We had to think up some unusual manoeuvre. If we didn't have any new gimmicks we were not going to score.

In the normal run of things an aerobatic team consisted of four aircraft arranged in 'box' or 'diamond' formation. We decided to perform our manoeuvres stepped down in line astern, each with his propeller about one foot from the elevator of the man ahead of him. That was our gimmick. Besides satisfying the uninitiated by having a different look about it, the professional would appreciate that it made tremendous demands upon the rear man, particularly in such figures as a barrel roll.

In this stunt, although the leader would only be describing a cylinder of reasonably small circumference, the latter would grow with each man until number four was being asked to fly round a wide cylinder in which any faults in the flying of those ahead of him would be exaggerated when they reached him.

In formation aerobatics smooth flying by the leader is essential if the whole thing is not going to look ragged. He must also fly at very much reduced engine power so that those astern of him will have a margin available to adjust their position. In our line-astern formation the number four was at full throttle throughout the manoeuvre, while the leader was only at about half-power.

After experimenting quite a bit we sorted ourselves into the best flying order. I led, with Boot behind me, then Johnny, and Bill as rear man. We had to practise at least three times a week to keep up to exhibition standard. Sessions had to be reasonably short, as the concentration required was tremendous and the margin for error absolutely negligible. I could tell when the boys were really bunched up behind me because I could feel the pressure on my tail from the whirling propeller of the man immediately behind me.

Naturally we started off practice at a safe height until the whole manoeuvre could be accomplished every time without anybody falling out of formation. Then we came lower and lower until we reckoned we could start the whole thing from a few feet above the ground and perform, if necessary, under a low cloud base of 500 feet. Absolute faith in the leader is required when this stage is reached. It is fatal to take even a fleeting look at the ground, which is so perilously close, with the plane in some peculiar position. Once a pilot takes his eye off the man ahead of him he is courting disaster, not only for himself but for the whole formation.

We worked up our routine on passage with the *Vengeance* and treated her to displays frequently. The object of this was to get the other aviators on board to criticize until we had acquired the high degree of polish we were aiming at.

When faced with a proper display before the public I always visited the display site the day before and flew round assessing the obstructions in the area, the position of the spectators, and the position where the sun would be at the time of our display. All these factors had to be taken into consideration if the presentation was to be as good as we strove for. It was no good, for example, asking the spectators to stare into the eye of a burning summer sun to watch a manoeuvre.

Then on the morning before the show we would have a full rehearsal with the entire team. During this time freedom of talk on the R/T was allowed amongst the team. Johnny might complain that Boot was slightly out of line, or Bill would yell at me that I was not leaving him enough power margin to keep up at the back end.

'Ease it off, boss, I'm on the stops!' would tell me this, or someone might call, 'Can't we angle this another fifteen degrees out of sun – I'm getting blinded on the last quarter of the roll!'

We did not stick entirely to our own new formation, but flew the box type as well. With this the problems were not so difficult, as I could then see my two wingmen and feel the position of the man behind on my elevator controls.

During the actual performance nobody spoke except me. I would call what each manoeuvre was to be as we ran in towards the display area. This was normally only a reminder of the routine we had mapped out before-hand, but something, probably a weather change, might force us to alter the routine. The appearance of heavy rain clouds, for example, might make me cancel a looping manoeuvre which required 2,000 feet of height. We would do instead, say, a rolling manoeuvre under the clouds, then do the loop if and when they had passed over.

After our Moroccan trip we went, early in 1951, to the RAF station at Wattisham near Ipswich for another of the Fleet Air Arm's normal spells with the Air Force. It had always been our policy to liaise very closely with the RAF so that operating procedures could be standard-ized and we could support each other at any time without a lengthy period of adjustment. This practice had paid off, for example, in the Battle of Britain, when Navy pilots had taken to duty with Fighter Command very smoothly and distinguished themselves. Today the RAF still carry out the basic training of all Fleet Air Arm pilots – although we do have some flying instructors in the RAF schools – with standardiza-tion as the primary object. We had many combat exercises with the RAF B-29 Washingtons, which confirmed our opinion that the Sea Fury was out of its element at high altitudes, but could look after itself remark-ably well low down.

From Wattisham we were packed off to sea again. This occasion was rather a special one, as we were selected to go to Sweden in the *Indomitable* on the first visit of a British carrier to that country.

Before the ship entered the very complex Stockholm Archipelago our aerobatic team was flown off to give a flying display over the Royal Palace. The local papers gave us a magnificent write-up afterwards, except one Communist journal which complained that the display had endangered the whole population of Stockholm. Apparently their reporter had been standing on a bridge overlooking the Royal Palace and at one stage had had to look down to follow us.

We seemed to impress the Swedish Air Force, and were asked to tour their airfields in the Stockholm area. This liaison was very satisfactory, and finished up with many of the Swedish Air Force and the members of 802 Squadron doing an unsteady conga round the traffic policeman in the centre of Stockholm at four o'clock in the morning. After our week's stay in Swedish waters the King came to sea with us to watch a day's flying operations.

Chapter 16

I HANDED OVER to my successor at the end of July 1951. The squadron was leaving for Korea, I for America. I was going on exchange duty to the Flight Test Division of the Naval Air Test Center at Patuxent River, Maryland.

So it was back to test flying. I was delighted to find that the CO of my flight was Lieutenant-Colonel Marion Carl, US Marines, whom I had met when I had been in command of Aero Flight at Farnborough. He had been the first American pilot to land a jet on a carrier, and had also broken the world speed record in the Douglas Skystreak.

It was a very happy omen for me, and he welcomed me as an old standing member of his team instead of a new boy. The two of us were by far the most experienced test pilots there, many of the others having recently come straight from the Test Pilots School at Patuxent River.

Unlike the set-up at Farnborough we were assigned projects on particular aircraft and stuck very much with these projects right through their test programme. It was not usual to hop from one aircraft to another as I had done at RAE, although as a visiting airman I was given at least one or two flights on all the types we received. Our offices were shared with the project engineers, as the Americans called their boffins, so we were if anything in closer contact with them than under the British system.

I was back on jets again, and it was exhilarating to be able to break the sound barrier on my very first jet flight – in a Sabre – in the USA. This was an everyday occurrence in our division, and sonic bangs were always shattering the peace of Chesapeake Bay.

As soon as I saw the Sabre I instinctively knew I was looking at the Spitfire of the jet age. This particular aircraft was an F-86A-5 kept for chase-plane duties in Flight Test. It was a product of German technology learnt from the Messerschmitt 262, and had 35 degrees of sweepback on its wings which were fitted with full-span slats, power-boosted ailerons and elevators and an adjustable tail-plane.

My first flight was like an initiation ceremony, because the Flight Test pilots were all daring me to boom the base commander's house in a

Eric Brown flew the F-86A Sabre at the US Naval Air Test Center at Patuxent River. He described it as 'the Spitfire of the jet age', and it was in a Sabre that he first experienced supersonic flight.

supersonic dive. This is easier said than done because the sonic bang does not hit where the aircraft is pointed, so I reckoned the Admiral's house was safe. This in fact proved to be the case, but I got a bull's-eye on his garden hothouse. I had only been on the base a week and had not yet met the Admiral, so my interview was accelerated. He knew of the transonic work I had been doing at Farnborough and was very sympathetic, but discipline had to be upheld so he fined me twenty dollars for the damage to Navy property. However, the Flight Test boys decided to pay up their bets and so I was in surplus on the whole deal.

Later I got to fly the F-86E fitted with a 'flying tail' which was hydraulically powered, and I consider that aeroplane was the finest jet aircraft I ever flew from a handling standpoint.

Patuxent was a vast airfield on a spit of land sticking out into the Bay; it was a fourteen-mile drive right round the perimeter of the whole airfield complex. It was ideal for a test establishment, being right out in the sticks, and its air space was one of the few on the eastern Atlantic seaboard not criss-crossed by airways. Like Farnborough there were catapults and arrester gear sited in the middle of the field.

My first project was on the Grumman Panther, the counterpart of the Sea Hawk and of about the same performance. I found that the American testing methods both in the air and on the ground were very similar to our own except that they had the practice of using 'chase' aircraft to accompany a test flight in a machine which was considered to have more than the usual element of risk. We all had to take this duty of chase pilot, which meant taking up an aircraft of similar performance to the one under test and keeping very close to the latter, observing him throughout. The object was to have a first-hand eye-witness account of any incident causing the loss of the test aircraft or to render any help possible by giving information to the control tower or test pilot.

I took the Panther, Banshee 3, and Skyknight through their flight handing and performance tests. Another unusual facet of American test methods was that the new aircraft would be given a quick limited flight clearance to go into squadron use while the extended flight programme then continued at Patuxent – the Panther, for example, was in operational use in Korea while I was testing it. Increased flight clearance would be given as the tests proceeded.

This system meant that the squadrons got the feeling of being right up to date. Having a 'hot' plane straight from the factory is a great morale booster to a fighting pilot. It also gave very valuable operating and maintenance experience which test aircraft working in specialized conditions cannot give. Its disadvantage is that sometimes machines are released to front-line squadrons with many bad flight characteristics still not ironed out.

Just after I arrived our Flight had a big panic, which spread like a forest fire, when a small A-bomb fell off one of our aircraft during routine tests near the airfield. It was being carried under one wing to see how its drag affected performance. Within hours of its falling the National Guard had sealed off an area of seventy-five square miles.

It should give everyone confidence to know that not only did it not go off, but it was recovered from a farmer who had found 'this piece of junk', as he called it, in one of his fields, heaved it on to the back of a farm cart and was driving it over rutted roads to dump it when he was intercepted by the searchers.

One very frustrating thing about flying in the USA is the enormous amount of paperwork and clearance procedure to be gone through before a pilot can fly from A to B. In America military aviation definitely takes second place to civil as regards priority use of air space in peacetime, whereas the reverse has always been the tendency in Britain. This

r two of the American aircraft which the author flight tested at Patuxent River were the
ian Panther (top) and the McDonnell Banshee 3. It was the Panther which he used to
strate the new British steam catapult on HMS *Perseus*.

Testing the hydro-skis at Patuxent River. They were to be fitted to land planes so that they could operate from a beach or strip of sand.

different British attitude is no doubt brought about by our proximity to troubled Europe.

Flight Test Division was composed of four flying sections, Carrier, Patrol Plane, Carrier Suitability, and Rotary Wing. My section, Carrier, tested flying characteristics and performance. Patrol Plane tested all non-carrier types and seaplanes. Carrier Suitability carried out all arresting and catapulting trials. It was irregular, but I actually flew in all branches from time to time.

Working with Patrol I found fascinating at this time because the US Navy was just beginning to experiment with hydro-skis, which were designed to be fitted to land planes so that they could operate from a beach or strip of sand. The idea was to taxi down and take to the water like a duck – landing and beaching in the same way – although the aircraft could not be stopped on the water as it would sink if the speed sank below reasonable taxiing speed.

Rotary Wing was particularly active at this time, and I was welcomed there as an extra hand, useful to relieve the pressure. The helicopter pilots were working absolutely flat-out to supply the big demands for the 'pinwheels' then being made. Their helicopters were far more advanced than any I had met with and much easier to fly than the early models I had been weaned on.

In the February of 1952 HMS *Perseus* arrived at the US Navy Yard in Philadelphia to demonstrate the new British steam catapult. The carrier had brought her own Sea Furies with her, but the Americans wanted to see how the new device handled their jets.

I was chosen to fly the Panther for them, as it was my project, and an American pilot was to handle a Banshee fighter. The first trial looked like being an exacting business. The carrier was to stay alongside in the Navy Yard while the aircraft for the test were to be lifted on board by crane from the airfield inside the dockyard, shot off from this position, then immediately landed back on the airfield and the test repeated. After some launches from the field at Patuxent I flew up to Philadelphia.

On the day set for the trials the carrier was alive with VIP American brass and officials. To everyone's chagrin a five-knot tail wind was blowing over the flight deck – instead of the ten-knot *head* wind which had been hoped for.

A huddle of frustration gathered. The Americans shook their heads firmly at the idea that a jet could be shot off with the ship tied up and a tail wind blowing over the catapult.

But Commander Mitchell, the inventor of the catapult, was there – a man with whom I had worked closely many times on catapult trials in Britain. Without a flicker of emotion he said, 'Of course we'll launch. These are just the sort of conditions this catapult likes'.

The Americans protested. The risk was unjustifiable. Then the *Perseus*' Engineer Commander spoke out of the awkward silence. 'We'll risk the British pilot if you'll risk the aircraft.'

There was a hush. I had not been consulted, of course, but the gauntlet was down now. The Americans agreed.

So I, the innocent in this drama, climbed into my cockpit and was flung off at 4.3'g' at a speed of 126 knots through a maze of dockyard cranes and workshop chimneys.

We had proved our British invention. Trials continued into the next day, when the awkward tail winds increased. Eventually I was shot off at 4.5'g' and 132 knots – and thanks to the new machinery it was the smoothest catapult ride I had ever had. In fact a launch from this steam catapult was so smooth that for a second one imagined it had misfired. In contrast to the ordinary catapult, which starts with a fierce kick up to the 'g' level, the new one took one gently up to 'g', then held it until the plane was airborne. Afterwards we went to sea and continued trials in Chesapeake Bay, with the aircraft loaded up to maximum weight. There were no hitches.

British naval aviation was bursting with new ideas at this time. When I left Britain I had been briefed by the Admiralty to take with me details of a new idea to revolutionize carrier-deck landing. This was the principle of the canted or angled deck, based on an idea by Captain Dennis Cambell, a former naval test pilot, and converted into engineering practicality by Lewis Boddington, who had been Head of the Naval Aircraft Department at Farnborough during my time there.

The feature of the idea was a second landing path superimposed on the normal one and leading off to port of it. This scheme was seized on eagerly by the Americans, and it is typical of their speed that they actually had the carrier *Antietam* with this deck built on her almost ready for trials in nine months from the time I had first brought the idea to them. Before that the Carrier Suitability Branch flew a variety of jets on to the *Midway*, on whose huge standard flight deck a simulated angled deck had been painted.

They made touch and go landings along this painted deck, but of course could not be arrested because the wires had not been angled. The pilots were wildly enthusiastic about the idea and its great advantages. The angled deck leading off to port allowed a pilot to go round again if necessary when the carrier was operating its aircraft without any obstacle, and the dreaded barrier was done away with. Then, on the clear space for'ard and to starboard of the angled deck planes could be parked and, more important still, aircraft could be catapulted – all while aircraft were landing on. It greatly improved the safety and efficiency of flying operations.

These were proud and exciting days for me. At the same time I continued my more normal work. 1st April 1952, was a day full of incident. Marion Carl had been doing a final series of check spins in the new Grumman Guardian anti-submarine attack aircraft. We had already all spun this machine and successfully recovered, with the Guardian specially fitted with an ejection seat and a tail parachute. The tests were completed and the tail parachute removed, when Marion suddenly decided to spin it again to see if the loss of the tail parachute and its gear had altered the spinning characteristics. I was to fly the chase plane for him.

We climbed to 10,000 feet over Chesapeake Bay and I started to circle round him. He called, 'All set,' and went into a spin.

I circled him down. When he had reached 4,000 feet and was still spinning I got worried.

I called to him to jump as we passed 3,000 feet because he was obviously stabilized in his spin without enough recovery height. But he continued spinning straight into the Bay, with no sign of a bale-out.

As I circled the ring of the splash I saw a parachute canopy in the centre of it, floating on the water. Then Marion's head appeared and he gave a frantic wave. I radioed base to send a flying boat at once and stayed over him until it arrived some twenty minutes later.

He told me that he had tried to operate the ejector seat when I had called him, but when he pulled the face blind it ripped away in his hands and the seat failed to fire. He then tried the recommended method of getting out on the inside of the spin and found himself being forced back by the airflow. He finally got out on the other side and pulled his ripcord. He felt his parachute open literally as his feet touched the water. He had fallen straight into the splash of his own aircraft, which was why I had not seen him hit the water.

The success of this bale-out provided factual proof of something which wind-tunnel tests had suggested at the same time – that the old method of getting out on the inside of a spin to avoid being hit by the tail was just a long-accepted fallacy.

In America I followed with particular interest their high-speed work on the rocket-propelled Douglas Skyrocket at Muroc in California, and on the tailless Northrop X-4, which was similar to the DH 108. I learned from the National Advisory Committee for Aeronautics that their experiences with the X-4 were amazingly similar to our own. Because of undamped, small amplitude oscillations about all three axes at high Mach numbers, tests were not carried beyond 0.93.

There was no dearth of unorthodox projects going forward in the USA, and I had the opportunity of flying two in which I was particularly interested. One was called the 'circulating control system', which was really a refined application of the principle behind the Griffiths Suction Wing, which had given me some trouble at Farnborough. On the Cessna 170 I flew this high lift device, which decreased take-off distance by some forty per cent and landing speed by about the same value. Its benefits to naval aircraft are obvious, and the principle was used on the Royal Navy's brand new Buccaneer strike aircraft.

Carl Bails Out Of Plane At 500 Feet Over Bay

Nation's Top Test Pilot Narrowly Escapes Death

Lieutenant Colonel Marion E. Carl, U. S. M. C. of the Patuxent Naval Air Station, one of the first men to break the sonic barrier, that is, to travel in an aeroplane faster than the speed of sound, had a thrilling escape from death last week, when he was forced to parachute to safety after his plane failed to respond during tests above the Chesapeake Bay.

At an altitude of 11,000 feet, Colonel Carl, flying an AF -2-S Grumman "Guardian", began a series of spin tests. When he attempted to pull out of a spin, the plane refused to respond to his touch of the controls, and he rode the plane down to about 500 feet before leaping for safety. His chute opened seconds before he hit the water.

A check showed that the chute used by Col. Carl was the first one ever packed by John H. Gihlfstord, PRAN, of Redwing, Minn., a recent graduate of the Parachute Rigger's School at Lakehurst, N. J.

Picked Up By Martin P5M

After landing in the Chesapeake Colonel Carl spent the next 25 minutes in a life raft until a Martin P5M, piloted by Commander P. E. Stevens, picked him up and returned him to the Naval Air Station.

Hits Silk Before

Col. Carl is an ace of World War II, having accounted for 18 Jap Planes off Guadalcannel. He was forced to hit the silk once before, off Guadalcanal.

He is now Senior Project Pilot at the Naval Air Station, and to him falls the responsibility of testing everything that goes aboard a carrier type aircraft. He is now engaged in working with Grumman Aircraft Engineering Corporation, doing tests on performances and high speed characteristics of an aircraft model this company is perfecting, a new swept-wing Jet fighter.

In Ranks of Leading Test Pilots

Col. Carl is considered one of the leading test pilots of the country. He broke the world's speed record and held the record for a 12 month period when he attained a speed of 650.6 miles-per-hour in a Douglas Skystreak on August 25, 1947, at Edwards AF-

LT. COL. MARION E. CARL

From Eric Brown's scrapbook: the newspaper report of Lt Col Marion Carl's narrow escape from death when his Grumman Guardian spun into the sea at Chesapeake Bay.

The other fascinating project was in connexion with the prone position. The US Air Force had had a prone position experimental jet fighter built by the Stanley Aviation Corporation and it had flown successfully. The Navy, however, had turned its attention to the supine position and installed such a pilot's seat in the rear cockpit of a Grumman Tigercat. This is the best 'g' resistant attitude. The seat was adjustable from the fully upright to the supine, and had two upright hand grips, the right one of which was an auto-pilot control stick and the left a master throttle lever. There was a periscope sight for use when supine.

I found the take-off and landing in the supine position a hair-raising experience. In normal flight it was still uncomfortable, and positively alarming in acrobatics in the looping plane when I found myself going vertically uphill standing on my head. Of course the Navy's intention was only to use the supine position for long-range cruising, the three-quarter position for combat, and the upright position for take-off and landing.

In the Flight Test Section casualties were very high in the year and a half I was there. Five pilots were killed. I had more jet-engine failures there than I had had even in the early days of jet-engine testing at the RAE. This was particularly surprising as the engines were basically Rolls-Royce ones built under licence in the USA. I was so puzzled that I wrote to Rolls-Royce to find out why we were having this bother. Eventually it was discovered that the American company building the engines had made a local modification to them and this was the cause of the trouble.

My main impressions of the US Navy jets were that they were slightly superior to ours in performance and in particular had longer range, but from the pilot's point of view did not have such good handling characteristics. The new aircraft like the North American Fury, the Grumman Cougar, and the Douglas Skyray, coming into service as I left the States were certainly jumping ahead of our contemporary ones and taking bigger steps in performance. The US Navy, with more funds and more types at its disposal, does not stick so long with any one type of aircraft. They will keep one type in operation for, say, two years, when we will continue with a good machine for a period four times as long.

The huge American carrier fleet is a big customer for their aircraft industry, as also is the Marine Corps, whose flying branch is itself bigger than the whole British Fleet Air Arm. The Marines placed particularly big orders for helicopters, which they were using for commando assault in Korea at this time. Much of our work was the result of problems which had arisen on the battlefield there. Helicopters, for example, operating at high altitudes in the Korean mountains had been unable to get off the ground with full loads in the rarified atmosphere at these heights. We fitted RATOG – called JATO in America – to helicopters and solved the problem. I found it exhilarating to be accelerated vertically instead of horizontally by rockets.

Another interest the US Marines were showing as a result of Korea was in operating aircraft from restricted spaces. With this in mind the Chief of Naval Operations, Admiral Fechteler, sent for me to discuss the potentialities of the flexible-deck system. This was my first trip to the Pentagon, and I had to work my way through an incredibly complex security network before I met the Admiral. Besides the subjects on the agenda, he and I ranged over a great many topics involving naval aviation, and he expressed his gratitude for the way in which the British had co-operated in handing over the steam-catapult, the angled-deck and the flexible-deck ideas.

My relations with the US Navy were most amicable, and when my wife and I left the States we were showered with presents from the many friends we had made. I found that the average American aviator knew less about us than we did about them, and while they were always highly co-operative, at times I was exasperated by their slightly condescending attitude towards our smaller British naval air arm, which was evident in the lower echelons but disappeared in the higher ones. The standard of flying was as high, but certainly no higher than that of the Fleet Air arm, even though the US Navy was operating their carriers in a permanent semi-wartime environment and in a high state of readiness.

American carrier life is very different from ours. Their ships are of course 'dry', and their wardroom life has much less of the pleasant club atmosphere found in a British carrier. The captains of all American carriers are always ex-aviators, while this is not necessarily so in British ones. In fact some of our best combinations have been that of a salthorse captain and an aviator commander (air).

There is little basic difference in our operating methods, but there was a big difference in equipment, in which our carriers in many ways came off best. However, a great effort is being made now by both navies to standardize so that cross-operating is possible. Exchange postings such as the one I was on were designed to foster a better understanding of each other's problems, and they have gone a long way to help in this objective.

Chapter 17

Although in the immediate post-war period I had extensive experience of flying captured German aircraft, I had not flown any Japanese aircraft and was very interested in remedying this in order to assess their flying qualities and performance.

My first opportunity came somewhat by contrived good fortune. From Farnborough I was sent to Renfrew airfield near Glasgow in April 1946 to deliver a US Navy Grumman Tigercat, which had been on loan to RAE and was to be prepared at Renfrew for return to America on a ship already in the River Clyde. It was also my brief to examine a captured A6M5 model of the infamous Japanese Navy's Zero fighter, which had established a formidable reputation in the Pacific War. This aircraft had arrived some days earlier aboard the same ship that was to carry the Tigercat, and the Americans had given permission for it to be disembarked for examination and any necessary anti-corrosive treatment before it was reshipped to cross the Atlantic.

The shipment preparation was being undertaken by a small detachment of US Navy mechanics assisted by a party from the nearby Royal Naval Aircraft Repair Yard at Abbotsinch. I soon found out there were no specific instructions that the Zero was not to be flown, although it appeared to be the US Navy's intention to test fly it in America. Indeed it might already have been flown by the Americans as it had some of their instruments replacing Japanese ones in the cockpit.

The situation was therefore ripe for the Nelsonic eye treatment and this was not difficult in the circumstances. I arranged for a good look around the aircraft including an engine run-up in the early afternoon. I then arranged a further detailed inspection in the late afternoon, when the aircraft was left outside the hangar. I was given enough time with only the Royal Navy mechanics to sort out a quick flight without a US Navy presence.

The most astonishing features of the Zero were its absence of a bullet-proof windscreen, lack of armour for the pilot's seat, and no self-sealing for its three fuel tanks; furthermore the cockpit hood could be opened but not jettisoned. Obviously, Japanese combat philosophy for the fighter pilot was to fight to the death.

The design philosophy employed by the American-trained designer, Jiro Horikoshi, was to keep the Zero's weight to a minimum to obtain the manoeuvrability demanded as a prime requirement by the Japanese Naval Air Staff. Part of the technique of keeping down the Zero's weight involved the liberal use of the newly created extra super duralumin to lighten the airframe.

In the air the lightweight Zero was remarkably nimble, with a high rate of climb of the order of 4,500ft/min and superb manoeuvrability. I was most surprised by the noise emanating from the fuselage, rather like the sound produced when one pushes on the side of a large biscuit tin, caused probably by the 'panting' of the light-gauge alloy skin.

The handling characteristics were somewhat marred by the imperfect harmony of control, which gave only a moderate rate of roll and with a rather sensitive rudder to deal with considerable directional control changes with power and speed. Also the acceleration in the dive was rather slow and was to prove a bit of an Achilles' heel against the heavy American fighters such as the Hellcat, Corsair and Thunderbolt.

In assessing the Zero as a fighter, it must be remembered that it ruled the air in the Far East from 1939 until mid-1943. It had the impressive combat kill ratio of 12:1, and it was not until the Grumman Hellcat appeared on the scene that it found itself bettered in the Pacific War theatre. Whereas the Zero always sought to fight in the horizontal plane where its remarkable turning circle gave it the advantage, the Hellcat countered this by initiating combat in the vertical plane by diving on the Zero and picking up so much speed in the dive that it could follow the Jap fighter round a third of its tightest turn; this gave enough time to aim a devastating burst of fire from its 6×0.5 machine-guns into the frail shell of the Zero. Using such tactics the Hellcat shot down 5,156 Japanese aircraft, giving it the superb kill/loss rate of 19:1.

I had to wait till the early 1950s, when I was in the United States, to get any further opportunities to fly other types of Japanese aircraft, which by that time were virtually museum pieces.

I flew three single-seat fighters – the Nakajima Oscar, the Nakajima Frank and the Kawasaki Tony, all of which were operated by the Japanese Army. The Oscar was remarkably similar in appearance and performance

The nimble Japanese Zero was one of the most enjoyable aircraft flown by the author despite the continuous noise emanating from the light alloy skin fuselage.

to the Zero, but its armament was only 2 × 12.7mm machine-guns in the fuselage and synchronised to fire through the airscrew. The Frank was really a development of the Oscar, with more powerful engine and greater firepower, and was comparable in performance to the later marks of Spitfire.

The Tony was unusual for a Japanese fighter in having an in-line engine based on the German Daimler-Benz 601A. It handled like a Hurricane and was really comparable to a 1939 fighter in Europe.

I also had a go at the Mitsubishi Dinah twin-engined multipurpose Army aircraft, which was quite impressive and comparable to the Mosquito in most respects. However, I was not impressed by its Navy stable mate the Mitsubishi Betty medium torpedo bomber, which had the same weakness as the Zero – an inability to absorb punishment. Although carrying a lot of fuel to give it a good operating range, its fuel tanks were not self-sealing, nor was any protective armour supplied for its seven crew members. On top of these serious shortcomings was the fact that it was inadequately armed, making it a fighter pilot's dream target.

Finally I came to what looked an obsolescent aircraft, the Aichi Val dive-bomber of the Japanese Navy, but I reserved judgement on it till I had flown it, as I was aware that such aircraft had formed the major part of the force that attacked Pearl Harbor. This low-wing monoplane had a fixed undercarriage and single slat-type dive brakes similar to those of the German Stuka. Indeed comparison with the Stuka was inevitable;

227

both had to operate in an environment of air superiority, otherwise they were going to suffer severe losses, but both were very effective dive-bombers. Whereas the Stuka was a genuine vertical 90 degrees diver, the Val was around 75 degrees. Both were slow to accelerate in the dive, and the Val's bomb load was only half that of the Stuka. The Val was more manoeuvrable than the Stuka, but had poor defensive armament; however on the plus side it had good range and was easy to deck land.

Overall I got the definite impression that the Japanese did not lag much behind the Germans in aircraft design at the beginning of World War II, but got rather left behind as the war progressed, and indeed never got into the jet age.

This brings us to the thorny question of what were the 'greats' in my golden age of aviation from the mid-1930s to the 1970s. Here is my top twenty list, based on wide handling experience of aircraft of that era and judged by the sheer joy of knowing one was flying a real crackerjack:

AVRO LANCASTER – just to sit in the cockpit was sheer joy. It exuded self-confidence.

BOEING B-29 SUPERFORTRESS – gave a feeling of impregnability.

BÜCKER JUNGMEISTER – an aerobatic gem.

DE HAVILLAND HORNET – overpowered perfection.

DOUGLAS BOSTON – its take-off acceleration was a taste of things to come.

FIESELER STORCH – a virtuoso of slow flight.

FOCKE-WULF 190D-9 – German fighter technology at its best.

GLOSTER GLADIATOR – last of the great biplane fighters.

GRUMMAN BEARCAT – a pilot's dream machine.

HAWKER HUNTER – flies as good as it looks.

JUNKERS 88 – efficient in all its multi-roles, and a delight to fly.

LOCKHEED CONSTELLATION – a standard bearer for long-haul passenger airliners.

MACCHI C.205 – a wonderful combination of Italian styling and German power.

MCDONNELL F-4 PHANTOM II – exciting performance and a thrill to fly.

MARTIN-BAKER MB.5 – a real beauty that arrived too late for World War II.

MESSERSCHMITT 262 – a quantum jump in fighter performance in World War II.

NORTH AMERICAN F-86E SABRE – handling perfection with help of a 'flying tail'.

NAKAJIMA FRANK – a lively performer that was a revelation to fly.

SUPERMARINE SPITFIRE XII – Jeff Quill and I enjoyed this most of all the Spitfires.

VICKERS VISCOUNT – set a new standard for short-haul passenger airliners.

This list stirs up some wonderful memories for me, and in aviation as in most things, perfection is seldom achieved, but if I was asked to pick out the nearest I've come to it in flying, I would not hesitate to select the DH Hornet as my favourite piston-engined aircraft and the North American F-86E Sabre as my favourite jet.

Chapter 18

MY FLYING LIFE seemed set in a pattern of peaks and pleasant valleys. There was a kind of agreeable deceleration in going rapidly from sonic bangs in a fast new jet over Chesapeake Bay to the heaving, water-bound deck of the anti-submarine frigate *Rocket*, which I did at the beginning of 1953.

I was on board to qualify for my watchkeeping certificate, an essential for my career as a naval officer. I went from being a fairly senior air hand to the status of the greenest recruit on board. But I thoroughly enjoyed it all, and it did me a great deal of good in reminding me that an aviator was still an integral part of the Navy.

We were based at Londonderry, and I had some interesting duties, as *Rocket* was the senior ship leading the 3rd Anti-Submarine Training Squadron. This meant that we were at sea on average five days a week and there were plenty of manoeuvres to exercise a would-be officer of the watch. We co-operated with aircraft in many of these exercises, and I got a good look at the problems from the other end of the string.

We attended the Spithead Review of 1953, and later took the Queen down the River Foyle to Londonderry on her state visit to Ulster. I was given charge of the Royal Guard and for some time lived in terror of my bull-voiced G.I.[1]

It is a commonplace among naval aviators to say that driving a ship is like flying a plane – in slow time. I found out the hard way just how far this is from the truth.

From *Rocket* I was moved to the *Illustrious* for a month and a half as an additional member of the ship's staff for the big NATO exercise 'Mariner', held in northern waters off the Norwegian coast. I found myself almost entirely on helicopter duties, which was interesting to me because, although I had done plenty of helicopter flying, none of it had been from a carrier before. We acted as safety helicopter for the fixed-wing aircraft while they landed on, carried mail from the sorting centre in *Illustrious* to all our escort frigates, and on one interesting mercy

1. Gunnery Instructor

Acting as safety helicopter for the fixed-wing aircraft landing on HMS *Illustrious*.

mission I picked up an officer from the submarine *Tally-Ho*. This was the first helicopter pick-up from a submarine's deck at sea.

From *Illustrious* I was sent to 806 Squadron at Brawdy in Wales to familiarize myself again with the Sea Hawk, which 806 had been the first squadron in the Navy to receive, and from Brawdy I went up to Lossiemouth in Scotland on 30th November to command 804 Squadron.

The squadron was in an unusual situation. It had lately returned from Korea and was equipped with Sea Furies. I arrived as the only jet pilot in the squadron to convert the remainder of them to Sea Hawks. For this job two instructors and two Vampire trainers were attached to the squadron, and two pilots were trained at a time until each one had about twenty hours jet time in his log book and a jet instrument-flying grading. This pair was then passed to me to convert to Sea Hawks and to train operationally.

While the first two were being converted I was busy enough carrying out acceptance check flying on the twelve new Sea Hawks which were

804 Sea Hawk Squadron at Lossiemouth. Starting the Sea Hawks up in unison was quite a spectacular affair as the turbo-starter cartridges fired and jets of smoke spurted skyward from the fuselage behind the cockpit.

delivered to us. At the same time I had to keep the other pilots awaiting conversion in flying practice in their Sea Furies. We remained a hybrid outfit for about three months while this conversion task was under way.

It was an interesting experience because it showed how very quickly a trained front-line pilot could move from piston-engined aircraft to jets. During the nine months in which I had command of 804 we were accident-free, except for one minor incident which was repairable within the squadron.

Next door to the squadron was my old 802, who were still on Sea Furies and waiting to follow us on the same jet-conversion plan. We shared the same hangar, and a great friendly rivalry grew up between us, particularly on the sports field. It was very valuable to have another operational jet squadron on the same airfield when it came to exercises in the air.

While I was on Christmas leave at the end of 1953 I was promoted to Commander. I heard the news with very mixed feelings, certain that it would mean the loss of my squadron almost before I had got it. But a precedent was set and for the first time a Commander was allowed to stay in charge of a front-line squadron.

The basic difference between jet and piston-engine training is that jets work at higher altitudes. We had to learn the tricks of formatting and fighting at great heights. It is one of the greatest difficulties in starting this work to realize that visual sighting of another aircraft at high altitude is very hard in comparison with low altitudes. In the cloudless and horizonless stratosphere the human eye tends to focus at a natural distance of only a few feet, and there is nothing outside the cockpit to draw this focus out to a greater range. So it is not unusual for two aeroplanes to pass each other at high altitude a mere few hundred yards apart without seeing one another.

All flying on the Sea Hawks at high altitude was in the transonic range, so that compressibility effects were always at hand. These can affect the

804 Squadron Sea Hawks taking off in formation. Eric Brown was appointed to command the squadron on 30th November 1953. As the only jet pilot in the squadron he had to convert the other pilots to flying jets.

fighting qualities of a pilot very badly unless he is taught to fly his aeroplane with a high degree of skill so as to keep just outside the trouble boundaries without constant reference to his cockpit instruments.

Another new feature of the jets' entry into front-line work was the fact that large formations of aircraft were no longer used operationally, since at high altitude such 'balbos' are too big to give the flexibility of movement needed for air combat in these regions. With jet fighters the largest formation to be used tactically at high altitudes is the 'finger four', and more usually the basic section or pair.

Training in formation flying follows the normal pattern used for piston-engined fighters, even when practising for mass air displays, of which we had quite a few including the royal fly-past over HMS *Britannia* in the Solent on 14th May 1954, to welcome the Queen home after her world tour. On this occasion there were four jet squadrons involved, and plenty of rehearsal was necessary beforehand. The wisdom of this was seen on the day when bad visibility and drizzling rain set in over the Solent. These were no conditions for any pilot in a mass of forty-eight tightly packed jets to have any doubts as to what to do next.

My pilots made their first jet deck-landings on the *Illustrious* in the

Moray Firth within a few weeks of having been converted to Sea Hawks, and all without any trouble.

Later we had another period of deck landings to try out the new landing technique evolved for the angled deck. This involved altering old methods.

About 1950 the Fleet Air Arm had decided that it must have a common operating procedure with the US Navy for carrier work. The two navies had operated together in the Pacific during the war and the differences in deck-landing technique had caused difficulties when they had tried to use each other's ships.

The Americans did not use the British constant rate of descent approach to the deck from about 400 feet, but came round in a descending turn to a position about 400 yards aft of the deck at some forty feet above deck level. The final run-in was made holding this height all the way until the batsman gave the cut just before reaching the roundown. The pilot then cut his engine, pushed the nose down and dived gently towards the deck, pulling out just above the deck level to a three-point attitude so that his arrester hook would catch a wire.

This was a system I for one heartily disliked because I felt it was inherently wrong in that it left far too much to the combined judgement of the pilot and the batsman to make a decent landing. It also meant that a lot of heavy landings were made on the main undercarriage wheels because the pilot had misjudged the difficult flare-out just before contact with the deck. British undercarriages were not designed to such robust standards as American, so that they were either damaged by heavy contact with the deck or they bounced the aircraft back into the air so that it cleared the wires and went into the barrier.

As far as I know no one in the Fleet Air Arm preferred this system to our own, but we had to give in to the Americans and take over their cherished method if we wanted to be able to cross-operate with them. It was a case of converting a few hundred British pilots to new ways instead of several thousand American. Now at last this was dropped. We all breathed a sigh of relief.

By the early spring of 1954 I had picked out some pilots from my squadron who were good material for a formation aerobatic team. We had been warned that we would be expected to take part in many flying displays that summer. Again I was fortunate to find skilled performers.

804 Squadron aerobatic team. It was in the realm of aerobatics that the Sea Hawk excelled and it says a lot for its good handling qualities that the young pilots with no previous jet experience were able to be moulded into a first class aerobatics team.

My wingmen were Paddy McKeown, a Northern Irishman who was a natural pilot and a most happy-go-lucky character, and Nick Cook, who had come back as a RNVR for the Korean War and was now on a short-service commission, as also was my box man, Graham Foster. Nick and Graham were two sophisticates who tended to put on an act as drawling men-about-town.

Shortly after we had started our work-up, an Australian called Pete Seed was attached to us and he was such a good aviator that I decided I had a basis for building up my team in excess of the standard four. Soon I was working with seven aircraft. It became our gimmick to open the display with all seven, then break down to five, and finishing with the original four making a low, screaming run-in towards the crowd and pulling up vertically in front of them from ground level, disintegrating north, south, east, and west in a bomb-burst figure.

For this manoeuvre we thought that smoke trails would create a spectacular effect. We tied ordinary smoke generators to the arrester hooks and fired them electrically from the cockpit. In the light of the huge aerobatic formations operated in modern air displays, with their coloured smoke issuing from the exhausts, ours seems a very basic beginning – like all new ideas in retrospect.

One of the hazards we came across with our jets which had not bothered us in piston-engined days was collisions with birds. This remains a troublesome thing for a jet pilot. Jet noise gives a bird less warning than propeller noise, jet speed less chance to get out of the way. They never hear what hits them. It is such a serious matter today that bullet-proof windscreens, which in these days of air-to-air guided missiles could otherwise be discarded, are being retained as a protection against the other winged enemy and at Farnborough a man is employed specially to fire a Very light to scare off the birds when they gather too thickly. I myself have had my side screen shattered by collision with a bird.

Absence of propellers in a jet has enabled tighter flying in formation to be done, and has also improved the safety factor slightly – I have been nudged in my elevator by my line-astern man without any drastic effects. That such a thing has more serious results with piston-engined planes was demonstrated in a naval air display at RNAS Eglinton in Northern Ireland when, during a vertical climb, the box man in his Sea Fury chewed his leader's tail off with his propeller. The formation disappeared into cloud still going vertically upwards, with debris showering off the stricken plane. The leader then reappeared on the end of a parachute and the box man made a spectacular wheels-up crash landing on the runway. The Irish cheered this magnificent stunt to the echo, and there were several requests to repeat it on next year's show.

In the late summer of 1954 I had my swansong with the squadron in the Air Day at Lossiemouth when I led a formation of forty-eight jets in a fly-past. Then I was off to RNAS Brawdy in Pembrokeshire to take up my new appointment as Commander (Air).

This was a fighter station, so I was determined to arrive with a flourish and led my aerobatic team down, arriving in a formation landing of four.

My first week was a dramatic one. While I was having a look round the area in a helicopter we got a call to go immediately to one of the local beaches where a young girl was drowning. We flew there absolutely flat-out and got there just as she was being pulled out of the water by a rescuer. As we touched down the district nurse, who happened to be on the beach, was giving her artificial respiration.

We got the child and nurse aboard and while the nurse continued with the artificial respiration, assisted by my crewman, I called for the naval ambulance to be at Brawdy Control Tower to meet us with oxygen apparatus and a surgical team.

The flight back took ten minutes and when we landed the team of doctors was already there. The child was lifted on to the grass and immediately given oxygen. This still did not have any effect, so the surgeon opened up her chest with his knife and massaged the heart. Unfortunately the poor girl was past recovery.

This was to be only the first of many such rescues the Brawdy helicopter was called on to make during the summer months when the splendid beaches were covered with holiday-makers eternally in trouble, bathing or rock climbing. There seemed to be some sort of panic daily.

Brawdy is situated in such a position that the nearest active operational airfields are almost a hundred miles away. This was a big headache to me in the winter months when we suffered rapid deterioration in the weather. In a matter of minutes the airfield could be covered in sea fog without any warning, and jets with very little fuel reserve left would have to be diverted over these long distances.

So we decided to devote much of our training to Ground Controlled

Approach in bad weather. The aircraft was brought to within a few feet of the runway entirely by radar. Perfect teamwork is essential between pilot and ground controller to make this work. In extreme conditions when nerves are string-taut success may depend on such a thing as the note of confidence in the controller's voice. The latter must talk, and talk confidently, all the time. I have seen pilots open up and go round again when a controller's flow has faltered for a second.

We went further than usual. Landing an aircraft by GCA is a slow business, and our concern was to be able to get a lot of jets down as quickly as possible, so we practised getting our machines down in formation pairs with an interval of thirty seconds between pairs.

Our nearest flying neighbours at Brawdy were the Sunderland boys at Pembroke Dock, and we had very close liaison with them. We used their flying boats as targets for our fighters while their gunners got in some practice on us. It is surprisingly difficult to shoot down a large slow target like this flying at fifty feet above the water. A light jet fighter coming up from astern to attack invariably gets caught in the powerful slipstream from the big boat's four propellers, which can be very dangerous at this height.

In this lonely part of Wales our helicopters were also very busy during the winter months carrying supplies to the little rocky islands and lighthouses lying off the Atlantic coast. We also had frequent ship distress calls. Once a Greek tanker broke in two just off our coast in a 75mph gale with her crew roughly divided between the two halves.

The local lifeboat, with which we had very close liaison for rescue work, set out but as usual asked us to go along as well. The wind was so high that we dared not start the helicopter rotor turning in the open for fear that the blades would be shattered, so it was started up in the hangar with the doors closed and then flown out.

When it got to the ship the Greeks refused to have anything to do with the rescue strop which was lowered to them, but waved the helicopter away. We thought that this might be due to their not understanding how to put on the rescue harness, so we told the pilot to lower a bag with the pamphlet in it showing pictorially how to put it on.

The Greeks untied the bag from the wire rescue line, then, to the pilot's horror, clipped the rescue hook to the ship's rail. The helicopter was now firmly moored to a sinking ship. Eventually the shaken pilot had to cut the wire with the emergency cutter fitted to the aircraft and return to base. Luckily the lifeboat was able to rescue most of the crew, but others refused to leave the two halves and we had to keep a sort of running watch over them as they swept northwards for the next twenty-four hours, each getting farther and farther away from the other. Finally we landed salvage crews aboard.

It was clear that in this part of the world our helicopters were going to be a great asset to the community at large, but their operations were restricted to daylight hours. So I started to experiment with small spot-lights attached to the undercarriage and angled so that their beams met at some ten feet beneath and to one side of the cockpit. In this way I learned to hover over the sea in pitch darkness and to pick up an object in the water with the rescue scoop net. My aircrewman, Chief Petty Officer Shiel, was an Irishman of great inventive ability and pioneering turn of mind, so he revelled in this sort of thing.

One of his contraptions was a witch's broomstick which could be slung under the helicopter. It had a bicycle saddle and on this rode an intrepid sailor fully rigged out as a witch. We were in great demand for air displays with this, and we even got the broomstick so stable in flight that batting along at fifty knots at 500 feet was a regular feature of our show. Naval Regulations do not mention witches, so ours never got any flying pay for this daring act.

As Commander (Air) I was rather ruefully resigned to a full pro-gramme running the day-to-day air business of the station, with no excitement in the air. I had just two exceptions to liven up my time while I was at Brawdy.

The first was in February 1956, when one evening just as the last aircraft were returning to the airfield we had a phone call from a lady schoolteacher near Fishguard to say that she could see a flying saucer. My scepticism almost made me laugh outright as I listened to her, but I promised that I would ask one of the returning aircraft to have a look.

Jokingly we told one of our pilots over the radio what had been reported. To our surprise, he said, 'Yes, and I can damn' well see it, too.'

Again I was anything but convinced, especially as he said it was rapidly moving out of his sight. Minutes later one of our air traffic controllers called down to my office to say that he could see it with the naked eye from the control-tower roof. I shot upstairs and saw what did look like a saucer in the air.

I decided it was interesting enough to go and have a look at it, and leapt off in a Vampire to see what I could make of it. I climbed to about 40,000 feet but the shape was still above me and moving fairly fast, and in the now half-light of dusk I could not identify it. But I am certain it was not a cosmic research balloon, which was the only tangible thing I thought it might be.

The shape continued to be identified along the entire Bristol Channel coast that evening without any explanation of it ever coming out. Where I once scoffed – I now have an open mind.

Three months later I did chase a real balloon, a captive one from the missile range at Aberporth on the Welsh coast which had broken away in a high wind, trailing about 600 feet of heavy steel cable. It was being blown eastwards and was crossing the area where the Duke of Edinburgh was scheduled to fly across about that time.

We were asked to go and shoot it down and as this involved firing over land I thought I had better take it on myself.

I was homed on to the gasbag by radar and intercepted it in my Sea Hawk at 13,000 feet about fifteen miles west of Hereford. It was an ideal place to shoot it down, being over completely wild country, and as long as I fired towards the west there would be no risk of my bullets falling near any populated area.

I gave it one very short burst at absolutely point-blank range to keep my firing to a minimum. Although I could see my bullets going in I was surprised that it did not collapse immediately. Only its big tail sagged, but this was enough to make it start losing height fast, so I left it alone and it hit the ground thirty miles from Hereford. As a piece of action it was rather a comic turn, but it was more excitement than I was entitled to expect and it refreshed me.

Brawdy was remote and its winter weather was decidedly unattractive, so we could get on with the full-time job of flying without too many unoperational interruptions. I could, I discovered, clock up almost as much flying as the squadron boys. This paid dividends in giving me a closer look at their problems. It gave me a big kick too, when they invited me to join in their spells of deck-landing training or their weapons-training programmes. Normally a Commander (Air) at a 'main line' air station such as Ford was lucky if he had time even to write the training programme, far less participate in it.

After about two and a half happy years at Brawdy I moved on to a year's 'coursing'. My first six months was at the Joint Services Staff Course. There was an airfield nearby – Bovingdon – and I found out that flying was available to airmen on the course. Whether anyone had classified naval airmen as eligible I am not sure, and I gather there was a certain amount of tooth-sucking in the Admiralty when they were presented with my flying bill. However, it was well spent, as I went straight from this course to the Royal Air Force Flying College at Manby in Lincolnshire.

This was a high-powered course and not the thing for anyone out of flying practice. We flew Meteors, Hunters, and Canberras as pilots as well as acting as navigators in Canberras, Lincolns, and Valettas. In addition there was a full ground instructional programme on all aspects of air warfare. If you weren't burning the midnight oil writing a staff requirement for a future fighter you were at 50,000 feet over the French Alps in pitch blackness on a December night. It was just the sort of course either to make you think that flying was the most wonderful experience in the world or to bring on premature old age.

There was a complete disregard for rank, age, or experience, which can be extraordinarily good for the soul. You could be shot into the air in a Hunter at crack of dawn and be kept in the cockpit till late afternoon if the programme necessitated it. Not once in my entire time there did I make lunch in the mess on flying days. I was far more likely to be found eating my sandwiches in the cockpit surrounded by the aroma of kerosene as my Hunter was being refuelled.

In July of that year, 1957, I made my first flight through the sound barrier in a British aircraft, although I had been supersonic many times in the States. It had taken me almost exactly seven years to graduate from Mach 0.985 in the DH 108 at Farnborough to Mach 1.05 in the Hunter 4 at Manby – seven years for an increase of a mere 0.065 Mach. This illustrates just how tough it was to get over the transonic hump on the way to supersonic flight.

Chapter 19

THIS STORY CONTINUES in Germany, a country that has had a strange influence on my life.

My father had told me many tales of life in the trenches as an infantry-man and later in the air as a balloon observer in World War I. Always he presented the German enemy as an enigma – fine fighting men with a strange mixture of chivalry and callousness in their make-up, readily subservient to iron discipline, and looking always to a leader to provide the authority that gave their lives a purpose.

I was intrigued to find out more about this people. My first contact with Germany was brief but significant. On a Scottish schoolboys' cruise in the SS *Neuralia* to Scandinavia in 1934 the ship passed through the Kiel Canal early in August on its return trip to London. There was no opportunity to get ashore in Germany, but as we passed under a bridge a newspaper boy dropped a sheaf of small handbills which fluttered down on to our decks. They read simply 'Hindenburg dead. Hitler President'. I still have two of those bills.

During my last year at school in Edinburgh I decided to study German as an extra-curricular subject. Its intricacies fascinated me. Perhaps here was a key to the complexity of the German national character.

In 1936 I persuaded my father to take me on a holiday to Germany. Through an old RFC friend of his we had an introduction to Ernst Udet, then a newly promoted Major-General in the Luftwaffe. This volatile man made a tremendous impression on me. He was the complete extrovert, warm and friendly, exuberant with an enthusiasm more befitting my eighteen years than his elevated rank. He had always liked to mix with foreigners and he saw at once that I had more than a passing interest in his own all-consuming passion – flying.

He invited me to go on a flight with him. It was in a Bücker Jungmann, a neat little biplane trainer, and Udet made it behave like a performing flea. I suppose by all the rules I should have been airsick. I was too breath-lessly enthralled for that. When we landed – off an inverted glide – my mind was already made up. I would learn to fly at all costs.

I would have been staggered then to know the kind of future which this flight was to open up for me, to forecast my close identification with the cream of German aviation after our second terrible war against them – and my own individual war effort against Udet's young fliers.

Even when all this was over I was not finished with Germany. It was Christmas 1957, and I had just finished the magnificent course at the RAF Flying College when I got a call from Admiralty.

'How would you like to go to Germany to help set up and train the German Naval Air Arm at Kiel and Schleswig?' It was the full turn of the wheel.

Early in 1958 I left for Germany as the Head of the British Naval Air Mission. I went first to Bonn to meet the German Naval Staff, headed by Vice-Admiral Ruge, former naval adviser on the staff of Field Marshal Rommel.

Within his own service Admiral Ruge was known as 'The Professor'. He was a scholarly man, who spoke many languages fluently and had written a number of historical books about World War II. He received me in most friendly fashion and introduced me to his Chief of Staff, Rear-Admiral Wagner, a fine-looking man with a mane of white hair and jet-black eyebrows. The latter's open, cheerful manner belied the permanent bitterness that must have lain in his heart, for he was the only surviving signatory to Germany's unconditional surrender on Luneberg Heath on that May day in 1945.

My mission was to comprise technical officers and NCOs as well as two flying-instructor officers. We were to be fully integrated into the German Navy and serve virtually as Germans under the officer commanding their naval air arm. I felt this was a sensible approach, and Ruge and Wagner thought so too. It was a delicate period, requiring great diplomacy and tact. There were of course many who regarded even controlled militarism in Germany with grave suspicion.

I moved on to the German Naval Air Arm Headquarters at Kiel. There I met the Kommandeur of the Marineflieger, Captain Walter Gaul, a man of tremendous charm and personality. He had worked in the Historical Section of the British Admiralty for a number of years immediately after the war, so he knew something about the British.

We had a tough job ahead of us. Holtenau, the airfield we were to use at Kiel, had not been touched since it had been left derelict at the end of the war. The other one at Schleswig had been in use by the RAF, but had been gradually allowed to deteriorate.

The German squadrons of Sea Hawks and Gannets were training in Britain during the first half of 1958. My team was at this time split between helping the German squadrons training at Lossiemouth in Scotland and Eglinton in Northern Ireland. There were only three of us in Germany, and we had to get an airfield ready to receive these squadrons by 1st August. Much of the subsequent scramble to hit this target involved winkling our own British people out of buildings and areas which had been held since the days of the Occupation. This was never too difficult a task once the magic words 'in the interests of NATO' were flashed around.

During this hectic period I felt we desperately needed some communications aircraft to get us about, as we were covering hundreds of miles in our search for the right people and the right equipment to help us in our task. Our journeys were mostly by staff car, and on this account alone I felt I must find an aeroplane – in the interests of survival. Our German driver seemed to count it a point of honour never to be overtaken.

I found that in fact the German Navy had had a Pembroke delivered, but had handed it over to a Luftwaffe technical school, as the Navy had no airfield of its own. I appropriated this aircraft, with Captain Gaul's blessing, from Fassberg airfield and parked it temporarily at Cologne-Bonn civil airport. I then looked round for a likely airfield near Kiel, but the only one in operation was a small Luftwaffe grass field near Hamburg. This field was used by light Piper Cub elementary trainers, and its CO was not at all happy at my request to use it. There were no radio communications, and the longest run available seemed to him tight for a fully laden Pembroke. However, we finally convinced everyone that our proposition was feasible and operated there for some three weeks.

Encouraged by our operations the Luftwaffe sent a Pembroke load of VIPs to this field. It overshot into a lake near the airfield and gave its passengers a ducking. From that moment we were looking for a new home.

Fortunately Holtenau was handed over to the German Navy at this time. Here in lonely state we set up flying house. The airfield was just an oval-shaped grass field perched on a hundred foot high rise on the North bank of the Kiel Canal. The longest run available was 800 yards, with a deep ditch at one end and at the other an almost sheer hundred-foot drop to the concrete area of the old Kiel flying-boat base.

There were no control tower, radio facilities, or aircraft spares. We kept the Pembroke in an old leaky hangar on the flying-boat base and taxied it up and down an inclined concrete ramp joining the seadrome to the aerodrome. Every time I took off I felt like one of the Wright Brothers launching himself off the slopes of Kitty Hawk.

What I did not appreciate at this time was the pride taken in this solitary aircraft by the German Navy. It was the first to operate exclusively under their own command since the disbanding of the old air component or Seeflieger of the German Navy by Goering in 1935.

Goering had reckoned that everything that flew in Germany, with the possible exception of the birds, must be under his control. Hence the navy pilots were all requisitioned by him and became Luftwaffe officers. This schism had a far-reaching effect and was still felt in the upper echelons of German naval aviation. Many of the older naval pilots lived through the hey-day of the Luftwaffe when nothing was too good for Goering's men. Perhaps it is not surprising therefore if they tended to approach naval aviation operations with a slightly landlubber outlook.

During the June of 1958 I was asked to arrange a transit of our first four Sycamore helicopters from the Bristol works to Kiel, using only German facilities to save costs. These aircraft had no radio, as they were to be fitted with German sets after their delivery to Germany. And we did not have any Sycamore pilots. There were, however, three such pilots finishing their training in Bavaria at this time. I obtained their services and we set out for England, together with a young pilot from the Luftwaffe who was also coming to collect a Sycamore.

It was obvious that five radioless helicopters would not be allowed by the Air Traffic Control authorities in Britain to set off on a journey to Germany. The Bristol Aircraft Company provided the solution by lending me a small portable radio set. Thus equipped as mother hen I set out with my four mute chicks in formation.

We were determined to make Antwerp that night and reckoned to get there just before dusk. We had been warned that Antwerp-Deurne was a difficult airfield to find, and that we should be relying on radio guidance to land. I contacted Antwerp as we neared the town, which was shrouded in thick industrial haze. Back came the reply, 'Hear you okay, but my direction finder is unserviceable so I cannot help you'.

This was just the sort of news to cheer me up. Antwerp Control kept calling, 'We can hear you but can't see you'. I knew I would never find that field.

There was only one thing for it. I chose a church steeple as a landmark and indicated to the others to circle it while I landed to check our position. Four heads nodded acknowledgement, so down I went. It was a small field, with cows in it, but beggars can't be choosers.

As I settled on the ground I heard a tremendous rush of sound, and there were my four chicks packed tightly round me, our five sets of rotor blades practically enmeshing. Those Belgian cows looked as if they felt crowded.

We had to get out of there fast. We had barely got off when I was almost hit by a Very light arcing up out of the gloom. It was the airfield. We had landed virtually just on the wrong side of the boundary fence. For new boys these four German pilots were putting up an impressive display of allied unity. They were not going to lose their guide, even if the guide was lost.

Next day we made Kiel. The first operational unit of the German Naval Air Arm was on German soil. There were some thick heads on the staff after the evening's celebrations.

At the end of July the German Sea Hawks and Gannets arrived at their home station at Schleswig. The Marineflieger were really in business.

There was a hard haul ahead of the German naval aviators. One night that winter I walked into our one and only usable hangar to investigate the cause of a light I had seen. There amongst the tightly packed rows of aircraft were camp beds with young officer pilots asleep in them. It was bitterly cold and the hangar was unheated. But German hardiness, ingenuity, and industry soon overcame such early hardships.

My duties brought me into contact with many interesting German military figures such as Otto Kretschmer, top U-boat ace, a man who exuded quiet efficiency. He devoted himself to the study of naval history in his unending quest for perfection in his profession. Then there was the flamboyant, cigar-smoking Adolf Galland, top Luftwaffe fighter pilot, looking in the flesh just as every schoolboy imagines a fighter pilot to be.

But my strangest meeting took place one day in Captain Gaul's office. He called me in and said, 'I should like you to meet someone you have long wanted to meet. This is Colonel Horten.' The tall, handsome Luftwaffe officer was the second of the two brothers, the one I had looked for unsuccessfully in 1945. We had a long chat and a laugh over those days.

We had nine different types of aircraft of five different nationalities of origin in the German Naval Air Arm, so there was plenty of variety in our flying, including jet, turbo-prop, and piston-engined aircraft as well as amphibians and helicopters.

I doubt if ever in my life I have been called upon to cover such a wide field of flying jobs. I instructed pilots in type conversion, tactics, instrument flying, maintenance test flying, and helicopter flying; and observers in radar and navigation. In addition I spent a fair amount of time as VIP communications pilot, maintenance test pilot, and trier-outer of new types of aircraft of interest to the German Navy. In the latter capacity I got the chance to fly jet helicopters and boat-hull amphibious helicopters for the first time.

But what captured my interest most were my periods of attachment to the Focke-Wulf Company for spells of test-flying duty. My first visits to this famous aircraft firm at Bremen revealed a solitary office building surrounded by the ruins of bombed hangars housing beautiful new jet aircraft hiding pathetically under tarpaulins. There was nothing particularly unusual about such a situation in Germany at the time, but I was really amazed two years later to see on the same site new hangars, workshops and offices, with a magnificently organized production line churning out new and overhauled aircraft. Even my test-flying routine there now became a slick, streamlined affair, with all my results being tape-recorded over a radio link, instead of the laborious old system of writing on my knee pad in the air. This power to revitalize its broken body is perhaps Germany's most amazing characteristic.

Up to now my visits to Focke-Wulf had only been to carry out air tests on Sea Hawks and Gannets after major overhauls, but suddenly I was approached by management to see if I would be willing to help out for a spell as their company test pilot since theirs had been suspended for security reasons as he had near relatives in East Germany.

I explained that I was virtually under contract to the Marineflieger and they must consult with them on this issue. Captain Gaul saw that if he did not agree, his supply of aircraft would dry up at a critical time in the training programme, so he worked out an arrangement with Focke-

Instructing German Navy pilots in the Fouga Magister.

Wulf that I could spend two or three days every week till this situation was resolved by finding a new test pilot.

In the event it lasted almost three months, but I enjoyed it as I found that I could have access to the company's wartime files, which had been recovered from various sources after defeat in 1945, and were now mainly of historical interest concerning proposed future projects to defend the Third Reich.

My flying with Focke-Wulf did not involve testing their own products, as they had not reached that stage in their rehabilitation, but only checking out foreign aircraft which arrived crated at Bremen, where they were then assembled by the company for acceptance flights before onward transmission to the Luftwaffe or Marineflieger.

The proximity of the East Zone of Germany posed special problems for German fliers. It did not take a big error in navigation in a 500mph jet to overshoot one's home airfield, when it lay some thirty miles from the forbidden frontier. A hot reception awaited a pilot who made such a mistake.

Our training of the German pilots was done on the Baltic shore of Schleswig-Holstein, where on clear days one could look straight into the

East Zone and where on misty days one wished one could. Mist and fog are as characteristic of Schleswig-Holstein as its flat marshlands.

We had two age groups of pilots to train. There were the old hands who had flown in World War II and were brought back to form the nucleus of the new German squadrons. On the other hand were the young boys of the post-war generation who were new to aviation. There was a world of difference between them.

The old pilots had had a gap of fifteen years in their flying lives, during which aviation had made astonishing progress. Most of these men had never flown jets until now, and they usually found themselves thinking and reacting too slowly to keep pace with their fast aircraft. They also tired more easily under intensive instruction, and lacked the dash of the younger men. Worst of all, their tactical thinking was still very much of 1939–45 vintage. However, these older ones had to supply the leadership at the outset, as some sort of steadying influence had to be brought to bear on the young fledgling pilots. I made many friends among these veterans as I helped them with their problems.

The young pilots were no different from young pilots in Britain. They had the same bubbling enthusiasm, the same restless impatience with class-room work, and the same impetuousness which, if carefully nurtured, produces the fighter pilot of calibre. They were good material, and given luck and time would mature enough in two or three years to replace the old hands as flight and squadron leaders. I would have preferred a longer period, but in a new and expanding force it has to be thus.

I enjoyed teaching these young pilots the tricks of the trade, and they taught me a lot, especially to keep my wits sharp.

On one flight I was in the front seat of a light jet trainer monitoring the performance of my pupil, who was 'under the hood' in the back seat struggling with the final stages of a blind instrument approach. This test had to be conducted at a strange airfield, and we had chosen a Luftwaffe fighter base near Hamburg. The pupil was doing well and we were about 800 feet up from the runway with the undercarriage lowered but fortunately not slowed down to landing speed.

Suddenly without warning he rammed the stick hard over and rolled us upside down. By the time I had grabbed the controls and wrested them out of his resisting grasp the nose of the aircraft had fallen and we had lost so much height that I dared not roll back right way up in case we slithered into the ground. I pushed stick and throttles hard forward and we staggered across the airfield with our wheels pointing skywards and struggling to gain just enough height to get ourselves sorted out.

As if this were not enough, over the radio came the guttural voice of the German Air Traffic Controller, 'Navy One Nine Nine (my call sign) … you are violating airfield regulations. This will be filed against you.' Fortunately I was too occupied to reply. But it brought my pupil out from under his hood. The shock of seeing concrete runway where there should have been sky petrified him. His explanation was that he had had an attack of 'vertigo'. This happens when a pilot suddenly gets an over-powering feeling that his blind-flying instruments are reading wrong. His sense of balance tells him urgently to disobey them. If he gives way to this feeling the results can be disastrous, as they nearly were for us that day.

These were the trials which paved our way towards teaching the German Navy to fly. But we overcame them, and it was a proud day for my Mission and myself when the squadrons were finally assigned to NATO in 1960.

It was the end of a long phase in my own life. I was to move on now to a new job where for the first time in twenty-one years I would not have an aeroplane strapped to my rear end.

As a postscript to my time in Kiel it is worth recounting two of the diplomatically difficult situations that confronted me. Firstly, in late 1958 a prominent German submariner died locally and was to be buried in Kiel cemetery. The Marineflieger were asked to provide about twenty officers as a naval presence at the interment, and I was invited to be present. I took advice on this from the British consul in Kiel and was given clearance. However, what nobody seemed to be aware of until the last moment was that the Grand Admiral Doenitz, former Head of Submarine Command, C-in-C of the wartime German Navy, and finally successor to Adolf Hitler, had decided to make a personal appearance on this occasion.

Everyone seemed taken by surprise, and we were told to merely stand at attention as he passed along our single line of officers on the way to his car after the burial, but not to salute him. He duly walked slowly along our line with his piercing eyes reviewing everyone. He passed me and after going on past about four others, he stopped and turned back

Grand Admiral Karl Doenitz,
Commander-in-Chief of the
German Navy, was appointed
Führer on the death of Hitler.
He was sentenced to ten years
imprisonment for war crimes in
1946.

to me and asked my nationality. On learning I was British he asked why I was with the German officers and I briefly explained. He nodded and then moved on.

When he reached his car he stopped to say farewell to his small accompanying entourage, and the German officers then broke ranks and swarmed round him. As he looked at this unexpected group, they all took off their caps and made the formal three cheers gesture without uttering a word. He acknowledged this with a wry smile and departed.

Since Doenitz had been convicted as a war criminal to ten years' imprisonment, it would have been illegal under existing German law to have given an obvious accolade to him by cheering. However, many naval officers, including Lord Mountbatten, had not been too happy with the Nuremberg verdict on Doenitz.

The second incident perturbed me much more. I was invited along with my wife, who also spoke German very well by now, by a senior wartime naval officer to a small club in Kiel used exclusively by former senior officers like him. I did not even know of its existence, nor, apparently, did anybody else in my working or social circles. There were about ten senior ex-officers there with a few of their wives.

A convivial evening was in full spate with only German being spoken, and most of our hosts seemed a little the worse for wear. Suddenly, at midnight, one of them staggered to his feet and called '*Das Zimmer*' (the room). He then moved over to a wall hung with a red velvet curtain, which he pulled back to reveal a door, which he unlocked rather unsteadily. He entered the concealed room to be followed by all those present, so Lynn and I followed as nobody seemed to show any dissent.

As I entered the room I was shocked to see all the German men making the Nazi salute to a large photograph of Doenitz, in the uniform of a Grand Admiral, on a table covered with the wartime ensign of the German Navy.

Around the room were prizes of war such as lifebelts bearing the names of British and American ships, a tattered Royal Navy white ensign, and part of a lifeboat still bearing the name of its parent ship.

After some ten minutes we were all ushered back into the main room, where the Germans drunkenly sang wartime songs while we quietly left without any comment. We were utterly appalled at what had taken place and I felt I had no option but to report it to the British consul next day, even though it might put me in a very awkward position in my job.

Apparently nothing was done for a few weeks so as not to connect any reprisal with me, but the club was raided by police and ceased to exist, although I was surprised to see no action was taken against my original host.

Chapter 20

MY TOUR OF DUTY with the German Naval Air Arm ended on a personal high note. I was promoted to the rank of Captain on 31st December 1960 and appointed as Deputy Director (Air) of the Gunnery Division at the Admiralty in London. I was now responsible for the development of air weaponry to meet the requirements of the Fleet Air Arm. This was at a particularly interesting time when firepower in the form of machine-guns, rockets and anti-tank missiles was being given to helicopters operating in the commando assault role, tactical nuclear laydown weapons were envisaged for the Buccaneer strike aircraft, and nuclear depth charges for our anti-submarine attack helicopters.

Whilst I found this work quite fascinating, I was very restless about the lack of flying – which for so long had been a basic ingredient of my life. I suppose I was suffering from withdrawal symptoms, rather like a drug addict in rehabilitation.

However, I did manage to get the odd flight to test fire the conventional weapons we were developing. On one such occasion I was flying a Wessex helicopter fitted with a batch of 3-inch rocket projectiles to be

The Buccaneer 2 strike aircraft for which tactical nuclear laydown weapons were envisaged.

fired from a new type installation. I was over the Larkhill ranges near Farnborough when I fired the first single RP, which I saw correctly leave the launcher horizontally and then, to my horror, rear up vertically into the helicopter's rotor disc. Fortunately it did not hit a rotor blade or that would have been disastrous; Russian roulette of a new kind! It transpired that the rotor downwash acted adversely on the new installation which needed redesign.

During my first year of service in the 'Madhouse', as the Ministry of Defence was generally referred to by Service personnel, the First Sea Lord was Admiral Sir Caspar John. His appointment had been great news for the Fleet Air Arm, because he was the first senior officer with pilot's wings to head up the Royal Navy. I was particularly thrilled to find he was my supreme boss; he had been Captain of the trials aircraft carrier *Pretoria Castle*, on which I had made many landings, so he knew me well. Then, later, he had been Captain of the operational carrier HMS *Ocean*, on which I had made the world's first deck landing of a jet aircraft.

Perhaps these facts influenced my next rapid appointment, in 1962, as Deputy Director of Naval Air Warfare, which was right up my street, with responsibility for drawing up the operational requirements for new naval aircraft and their attendant equipment. Soon I was sent for by the great man, who had just been promoted to Admiral of the Fleet. He made it clear that my priority task was to head up the think tank for the flight deck layout of the projected new aircraft carrier CVA 01, to equip it with the best high performance aircraft – and to be constantly aware that politically the RAF would seek to scupper CVA 01.

I left his presence fully aware that I was being sent into a full-blown inter-service battle for survival, and that I had direct access to him if an update report was required at any time. This may seem unusual, but there were senior officers on the naval staff who were lukewarm in their support for naval air power. At least he knew I was dedicated to it.

CVA 01 was a great challenge, and I had a strong team in the Directorate of Naval Air Warfare (DNAW). The Director was an experienced observer, who gave me virtually complete freedom of action and tremendous personal support, so it was a happy atmosphere to work in and conducive to rapid progress.

The new carrier was to have a displacement of 53,000 tons and be capable of carrying over 70 aircraft. Its innovatory features included a

An artist's impression in 1964 of the Navy's proposed revolutionary design for the CVA 01, its new aircraft carrier.

parallel deck, circulatory taxiing system, totally new design of night lighting, and the brilliantly conceived water spray arrester gear. I enjoyed the work on CVA 01 enormously, as it meant teaming up once more with old colleagues from the Naval Aircraft Department, formerly at RAE Farnborough but later moved to Bedford.

Under the then Conservative government things were looking very rosy for the Fleet Air Arm, with powerful allies in Lord Carrington, First Lord of the Admiralty, and Sir Solly Zuckerman, Chairman of the Defence Research Policy Committee. The RAF meanwhile was vigorously promoting its Island Bases strategy, which argued that the RAF could cover all probable conflict areas by operating its aircraft from strategically placed island bases. However, this received a severe setback when, at an RAF presentation to the Chiefs of Staff, Sir Caspar pointed out that their map of the Arabian Sea area showed the island of Masira had been advantageously displaced by some 200 miles.

In parallel with our work on CVA 01, DNAW was working on the requirements for the aircraft to complement her. The Buccaneer strike aircraft was already in the pipeline when I arrived on the scene, but the fighter and anti-submarine/assault helicopters were still undetermined.

Here again there was a strong lobby from the RAF to have a joint solution, with them favouring the vertical take-off and landing (VTOL) Hawker P.1154 as the fighter and the Boeing-Vertol Chinook as the helicopter. I was certainly not in favour of the P.1154 because I was firmly of the opinion that VTOL aircraft had overwhelming limitations in performance and payload compared with conventional aircraft of equivalent engine power. On the helicopter choice I had an open mind.

My personal choice of fighter was strongly in favour of the McDonnell Phantom II, which had just entered service with the US Navy and had captured a string of speed, climb and altitude records. It was also twin-engined and a two-seater, which the P.1154 was not. I had flown single-engine/single-seat aircraft for all my operational life in the Royal Navy, but now that aircraft were so enormously expensive and complex I felt that we must go twin, which would also give added safety to the equally expensive aircrew. Also twin-engined jets could be recovered on to an aircraft carrier after one engine had failed, unlike their twin piston-engined brethren.

In March 1962 I attended a meeting chaired by Morien Morgan, Controller of Aircraft in the Ministry of Aviation, to hear a presentation by Hawker Aircraft of the P.1154. The RAF was heavily represented as well as various scientific establishments, while Hawker had all their big guns there including Chief Designer Sydney Camm. The presentation was made by John Fozard, and then the RAF said its piece, strongly supporting the adoption of the P.1154 as a Joint Services fighter for both the RAF and RN. I was fighting the Navy's corner and strongly opposed the P.1154. I was rather scathing too about its maximum level flight performance of Mach 1.6 and asked how I was going to justify that to naval pilots when their grandmothers could fly at Mach 2.0 in Concorde. Sydney Camm, who had appeared strangely apathetic up to this point, smacked the table with his fist and roared 'Good point, Winkle'.

Following on from that meeting came a series to further discuss the merits of the P.1154 and Phantom II to meet the requirement for a Joint Services fighter. Meanwhile the First Sea Lord called me to give a presentation on the Phantom II to himself and his senior operational planning staff. Thereafter, with his blessing, I became very heavily involved in the battle to win the Phantom II for the Royal Navy, and found strong support from Sir Solly Zuckerman, who emphasized the limitations of the VTOL concept and stressed the safety factor in having a twin-engine layout. There were, of course, arguments that we should favour a British aircraft from the economic standpoint, but Sir Solly pointed out that we could put Rolls-Royce Spey engines and our British electronics in the Phantom – and we would be less likely to lose as many aircraft and aircrew with the twin layout.

In May I made a four-week visit to the USA, and during that time visited Boeing-Vertol in Philadelphia and flew the prototype Chinook; to Sikorsky at Stratford, Connecticut, to fly the S-61A helicopter, and to McDonnell at St Louis to fly in the two-seat Phantom II. I was impressed with all the aircraft, but particularly with the racy Phantom, and made arrangements to fly it myself on return to England. I also went to China Lake in California to witness some firepower demonstrations, and had my faith in the Sidewinder infra-red passive homing air-to-air guided weapon re-affirmed.

In June 1962 I was given the opportunity to fly the Phantom II at Farnborough; I had made a great effort to keep myself in flying practice since leaving Germany. This aircraft was the McDonnell demonstrator, which was touring Service establishments in Great Britain, and it fully lived up to its reputation of being a superlative aeroplane. I was thrilled with the experience and flew it up to Mach 2.25. I needed no further convincing that this was what the Fleet Air Arm required, but I was going to have to convince a lot more people in the days ahead.

About this time in the year the Russian cosmonaut Yuri Gagarin made a goodwill visit to Great Britain and came to the Ministry of Defence, where I had an opportunity to talk with him through his accompanying interpreter. He struck me as an uncomplicated, amiable man, who rather played down his role in space, describing it as a passenger rather than a piloting experience, and said he preferred his test flying role, which he hoped to return to. This in fact he did after a series of goodwill tours, and was killed in a test flying accident in 1968.

In November I took my Phantom experience a step further by carrying out some carrier landings on the USS *Forrestal* after a visit to it in the company of Vice-Admiral Sir Peter Gretton, who was in effect Sir Caspar John's deputy. The carrier was in the Mediterranean, and on board was Rear-Admiral John Hyland of the US Navy's Carrier Division Four. He was a friend of mine from our Patuxent River days, and he shared my

Preparing to fly the prototype of the tandem-rotor Chinook helicopter in Philadelphia. The Chinook had many advantages over its rival Sikorsky S-61, but Eric Brown was worried about its greater mechanical complexity. No decision had been made when he left his post as Deputy Director, Naval Air Warfare Division at the Admiralty in November 1964.

Landing a McDonnell Phantom II on the USS *Forrestal* in November 1962. Eric Brown was convinced that the Phantom was a worldbeater and the ideal plane for the Fleet Air Arm.

With Vice-Admiral Sir Peter Gretton, who was in effect the First Sea Lord's deputy, on USS *Forrestal*.

enthusiasm for the Phantom II. I left *Forrestal* suitably impressed with the Phantom.

Through 1963 the verbal battles in the P.1154 versus Phantom II struggle continued, and my practical experience on the American fighter meant that I was arguing from a position of strength. Also there were doubts arising about the development time-scale and the costs of the P.1154. In parallel with the fighter requirement skirmishes, there now arose the helicopter requirement meetings. Again, the operations for which the new helicopter would be required were quite different in the RAF and the RN, but even so there was the possibility that a compatible Joint Services helicopter could be found in the tandem-rotor Chinook. It had tremendous lifting capability, and for the Navy's anti-submarine work it offered two operational advantages over its competitor the Sikorsky S-61 – for anti-submarine sonar dunking it did not have to turn into wind to assume the hover in the dunk, and this was important in tracking fast nuclear submarines; with rotors folded more Chinooks could be housed in a carrier's hangar than

S-61s. My only unease about the Chinook was its greater mechanical complexity. Although I was to resolve the fighter situation during my time in DNAW, the helicopter choice was still in the melting pot when I moved on.

At the end of 1963 I went off for a skiing holiday with my family to a remote little village in Austria. After three days the excited village postman brought me a priority telegram – my recall to Whitehall. On my return I was told I was to fly out to the USA for a meeting at the Pentagon, and then report back before returning to the American capital and St Louis for further meetings with McDonnell Aircraft.

I flew out on 31st December and had meetings with US Department of Defense officials and McDonnell, Rolls-Royce and British Embassy representatives before returning on 3rd January 1964. The meetings were mainly to discuss certain modifications that were necessary to the standard Phantom II to make it compatible with the restrictions imposed by the smaller British aircraft carriers, and also to confirm the time-scale for getting the F-4K Phantoms into operational service.

On 23rd January I was off again to Washington, where I was picked up by McDonnell's executive Jetstar for onward passage to St Louis. There we had a technical discussion on the practical solutions to the required British modifications to the Phantom, particularly the mating of the Spey engines to the American F-4 fuselage, which would require widening and the provision of new intake ducts – and all this to be done in the space of one year. However, confidence was the keynote at McDonnell's.

On 8th March I set off once more for the USA, accompanying the Rt Hon Julian Amery, Minister of Aviation, who was to sign a Memorandum of Understanding with the US Government over a deal to provide two Spey-powered YF-4K pre-production aircraft, followed by 20 production aircraft and then later another batch of 39 aircraft. After a stopover at Washington we flew on to St Louis, where I was given a dual check ride in the Phantom II and then another flight on my own to 57,000 feet with a run to Mach 2.5 on the way down. I needed no more convincing that the Phantom was a worldbeater.

On arrival back in Britain I reported to the First Sea Lord and learned that work had started on laying the keel of CVA 01, so I was feeling on top of the world. Sir Caspar was in benevolent mood and said he had decided I needed a change of scene in my next appointment at the end of the year when he would be retiring.

Chapter 21

M Y NEXT APPOINTMENT was certainly a change of scene. I was posted as Naval Attaché in Bonn, Germany, where I would be able to renew old friendships when I took up the post on 5th November 1964. That was an auspicious date in view of the fireworks that were to occur shortly after Sir Caspar departed from Whitehall. The General Election was won by the Labour Party at the end of the year, and storm clouds began forming over the Ministry of Defence. Indeed one of the first acts of the new government was to cancel the entire P.1154 programme.

On arrival in Bonn I reported to the Ambassador, Sir Frank Roberts, who seemed quite impressed by my fluency in the German language, but more so by my modest stature. As he himself was a diminutive man, and both his Army and Air Force Attachés were over six feet in height, I felt this was a strike in my favour.

One of my first consuming interests was to find out if I could get any flying, so I visited my former students in the German Naval Air Arm, some of whom had risen to positions of authority in their Service. They greeted me warmly and we reached an understanding that suited us both once it was approved by higher authority.

Soon after I took up my embassy duties, I was called to attend on Chancellor Adenauer at a Memorial Service in Bonn for Winston Churchill, and this gave me the opportunity to meet many of the main figures in the German Government. This was particularly helpful because preparations were already under way for the State Visit of the Queen and Prince Philip. The visit was to take place from 18th to 28th May, and it was my responsibility to liaise with the German Navy concerning the participation of HM Royal Yacht *Britannia*.

On 6th April the news came through that the Labour government had cancelled the RAF's new supersonic bomber TSR.2, which had already made several satisfactory flights. What appalled me was the vicious follow-up to the cancellation, for all the production jigs were destroyed and the prototype aircraft scrapped or sent to museums. To

With HM The Queen in Hamburg during the 1965 State Visit to Germany.

my mind this was a portent of what might lie ahead for the Services, and I feared for CVA 01, even though it was already under construction.

In May the State Visit began with the arrival of the Royal Party at Cologne airport, before embarking on a comprehensive tour of West Germany. The Royal Yacht, escorted by German destroyers, arrived in Hamburg on 27th May, to await the embarkation of the Queen and Prince Philip next day. They hosted a dinner party that day on board in honour of the German President, after which *Britannia* sailed off to an emotional farewell – a fitting finish to a long and hugely triumphant State Visit.

Next month I had to head for Kiel Week, which has been described as 'like Cowes Regatta Week with knobs on'. From Kiel it was a short trip up to the German Naval Air Station at Schleswig for some flying, and my introduction to the ubiquitous Lockheed Starfighter. On this occasion it was a case of the boot being on the other foot, because I had a check ride with one of my former Sea Hawk students. The Starfighter was virtually a flying missile and totally unsuitable as a naval aircraft. Indeed I had advised the German Navy in 1960 to go for the Blackburn Buccaneer to best carry out its NATO-assigned task, but politics stepped in and took over.

The Starfighter is a 'hot ship' and has to be flown every inch of the way. In bad weather, or with an on-board emergency situation, it is a real handful to cope with. The USAF had recognised this and required pilots assigned to the Starfighter to have at least 1,500 flight hours' experience. The new breed of German military pilots had been trained in the blue skies environment of Texas, then returned to Europe and its fickle

The German F-104G version of the Lockheed Starfighter required great experience to fly; it suffered heavy losses in operational service.

In the cockpit of the Me163B at the German Air Museum, Munich. The Walter rocket motor was found at Farnborough and donated to the Germans.

weather with about 400 hours total flying time. To put such raw pilots into a Starfighter was asking for trouble, especially as the German F-104G version had become a multi-mission aeroplane, weighing 2,000lb more than the standard F-104. Trouble they got in plenty.

The decision to choose the Starfighter was, in my opinion, influenced by the German aircraft manufacturing industry. It had been dormant in the post-war years and now saw a golden opportunity not only to rise phoenix-like from the ashes by building the F-104 under licence, but also to leap straight into the supersonic league in one big bound. In this situation it was almost inevitable that the industry would lobby the Government for the Luftwaffe and Navy to have the same aircraft for financial and logistic reasons, and this resulted in a total requirement of 750 Starfighters for Germany. The price paid for this political intrusion was the loss of 164 Starfighters in operational service with some 50 per cent of their pilots killed.

On 2nd July I was involved in an interesting event, which had all really started in November 1964 when the RAF had handed over to the Germans an Me 163B Komet airframe; but it lacked its rocket motor and no such power plant had apparently survived in Germany. Knowing of my association with the Komet, the Germans asked if I could help them obtain a rocket motor. I vaguely recalled having seen in 1949 the Walter motor from my test aircraft lying in the corner of a hangar at the RAE, together with bits and pieces of V1 and V2 missiles. I contacted

Farnborough, where a search was made and the rocket motor located and generously handed over to the Germans.

Thus, eventually, a complete Me 163B, refurbished in Luftwaffe finish of the war era (minus swastika) was finally unveiled in the German Air Museum in Munich and I was invited to attend the ceremony. It was a nostalgic gathering which included Dr Alexander Lippisch, designer of the Komet, Dr Willy Messerschmitt, Dr Helmuth Walter – who had been responsible for the rocket motor – Rudolf Opitz who made the first flight of the Me 163B, and Wolfgang Späte, the commander of the first operational Komet wing. It was a unique occasion, and I particularly enjoyed talking with the former Messerschmitt chief test pilot, Fritz Wendel, who had made the first flights on the Me 262 with piston engine, with a mix of piston and jet engines, and then with pure jets. He also still held the Absolute World Speed Record for piston-engined aircraft at 469mph, made in an Me 209 (109R) on 26th April 1939.

Interestingly enough, Hanna Reitsch was not present at this function, and indeed had not been invited, for the notoriety of her Hitler's Bunker episode was an acute embarrassment to the Germans at a time when they were feeling their way back to political normality.

Talking to the former Messerschmitt chief test pilot Fritz Wendel at the unveiling of the Me 163B at the German Air Museum, Munich. Wendel had made the first flights in all versions of the Me 262. Behind Eric Brown, half hidden, is Rudolf Opitz who was responsible for much of the flight testing of the Me 163.

Another interesting assignment in 1965 was to attend the 75th anniversary of the handing over of the island of Heligoland, off the mouth of the river Elbe, by Great Britain to Germany in exchange for the island of Zanzibar in the Indian Ocean. The celebrations involved a visit by the Royal Navy's biggest conventional submarine HMS *Opossum*, which had to be berthed in the shallow water Heligoland harbour. This could only be done at high tide, and as the harbour had been much bombed in World War II its bottom was full of lumps of concrete with

With Prince Philip on board the German Navy sail training ship *Gorch Fock* during his private visit to Schleswig-Holstein in June 1966.

The author with Federal German President Lübke and his wife, bidding farewell to the Royal Yacht *Britannia* as it left Hamburg after the State Visit of HM The Queen. In the foreground (right) is Chancellor Ehrhard and (left) HM Ambassador, Sir Frank Roberts.

reinforcing spikes protruding from them. At low tide the submarine hull would rest on the sea bed, so its berthing area had to be inspected by divers and cleared of obstructions. However, *Opossum* proved a great attraction and some very high powered guests, including our Ambassador and the German Chancellor Erhard, were entertained in the confines of the submarine's control room, having to negotiate the narrow vertical ladder in the conning tower – both before and after drinks.

The 1965 State Visit had taken the Royal Party to every county in West Germany, with the exception of the northernmost one of Schleswig-Holstein, which had a particular connection with Prince Philip's family. This omission had not escaped his notice and so it was arranged that he would make a private four-day visit there in June 1966. Our ambassador sent me up to Kiel in mid-June to liaise with the office of the Minister-President of Schleswig-Holstein and with the German Navy. Prince Philip flew himself into Schleswig airfield and set the pace for four days of hectic activity, which included sailing in his yacht *Bloodhound* in Kiel Bay, with a visit to the sail training ship *Gorch Fock*, entertaining the German President Lübke on the visiting Royal Navy destroyer HMS *Naiad*, and being entertained in Kiel's splendid town hall.

In the first ceremony of its kind, Prince Philip presented his personal standard to the Federal German Navy in appreciation of the hospitality he received during his sail on board *Gorch Fock*. I handed this over to Vice-Admiral Zenker, Chief of the German Naval Staff, on 11th July at the German Ministry of Defence.

Prince Philip's visit was in every way a resounding success, but my pleasure of the occasion was dampened soon afterwards by the shattering news that CVA 01 had been cancelled by the Labour government. This created a political uproar, which culminated in the resignations of the First Sea Lord, Admiral Sir David Luce, and the Minister of Defence for the Royal Navy, Mr Christopher Mayhew MP. The alarm bells were now ringing in the Fleet Air Arm, the emasculation of which seemed to be the prime target of the Secretary of State for Defence, Denis Healey.

Almost as if in defiance of this setback, the aircraft carrier HMS *Hermes* paid a five-day visit to Hamburg in early October and aroused enormous interest. Many NATO officers came on board, and in conversation expressed their misgivings about the British Government Defence White Paper. Some saw its implications as extremely serious, and one

Talking to General Trettner, Chief of the German Defence Staff.

American even said 'If you leave a hole the Soviets will fill it, even if they have to learn how to build and operate aircraft carriers on their own'. This was to prove prophetic stuff.

In December I became the doyen of the Naval Attachés Association, which gave me entrée into wider military circles, much to our Ambassador's delight as it helped me pick up titbits of information. One side effect of all this was that I was invited to be an honorary Flotillenadmiral (Commodore) of the Recklinghausen Branch of the German Naval Comrades Association, and this enthusiastic bunch held the induction ceremony in our British Embassy with the Ambassador's blessing. Finally, to be toasted, I had to wear the dress uniform coat of Grand Admiral Prince Frederick of Prussia, which normally resided in Recklinghausen Museum.

My last major assignment in Germany was to attend the State Funeral of former Chancellor Dr Konrad Adenauer, with whom the British had had particularly good relations. This took place in the mighty Cologne Cathedral, where his body had lain in state since his death. After the funeral service on 25th April 1967, the coffin was borne by officers of the German Naval Air Arm to a Fast Patrol Boat of the German Navy in the adjacent River Rhine, for onward passage to its last resting place near his home at Rhöndorf. Two FPBs of the Royal Navy, with myself and my assistant embarked, formed part of the accompanying NATO naval escort. A fundamental chapter in the resurgence of Germany in the post-war years had been closed.

Now I was about to complete my term of duty as Naval Attaché on 27th May and move on to take command of the Royal Naval Air Station, Lossiemouth, situated on the Moray Firth in northern Scotland. In preparation for that task I had first of all to report to Royal Navy Air Station Brawdy in Wales to undergo a flying refresher course in Hawker Hunter aircraft and to re-qualify for my instrument rating. It all seemed so relaxing after the Starfighter.

Chapter 22

LOSSIEMOUTH WAS DESIGNATED A MASTER AIRFIELD, which meant it was open for twenty-four hours a day every day of the year. It had a very long main runway, so long in fact, and with a slight gradient, that its far end from the control tower could only be monitored by closed circuit television. It was also a NATO-designated diversion for nuclear bombers, and was equipped accordingly. Much of this status was due to its exceptionally good local weather factor, influenced by the Gulf Stream which ran from the north-east into the Moray Firth and, just off the coast at Lossie, met the cold water coming from the Caledonian Canal in the south-west. This had the effect of pushing the warm Gulf Stream air upwards and forming a ten-mile diameter hole in the cloud cover. The famous Lossie Hole was no myth, as many anxious aviators could testify.

The air station housed seven training and front line squadrons as well as its own Station Flight of communications aircraft and search and rescue (SAR) helicopters. It was also the home of the RN Observer School and RN School of Photography, but was primarily the Buccaneer Training and Operational Station. The buildings were very modern and housed some 8,000 naval and civilian personnel, a bigger population than the adjacent town of Lossiemouth itself. I took over command of this huge complex on 11th September 1967.

The core aircraft around which Lossie functioned was the Blackburn Buccaneer twin-jet low-level bomber, capable of conventional or nuclear strike. The Mark 1 version with the Gyron Junior engines was decidedly underpowered, and was phased out of service in the mid-1960s in favour of the Spey-engined Mark 2. The north of Scotland was the ideal area for low-level flying with huge expanses of uninhabited mountainous terrain and the inhospitable and vacuous North Sea. Personally, I found this type of flying most exhilarating, and the aircraft very suited to the role.

We had two problems to deal with in our training, and both were caused by our location. Firstly there was the constant danger of bird strikes from the large seagull population that frequented the skies in the vicinity of the fishing port of Lossiemouth. At first these had caused an engine loss rate of one per month until falcons were introduced to counter the menace; we had a falconry of about eight birds and six trained handlers. The falcons were flown about four times a day to clear the seagull flock from the runways where they roosted because the hard surface was up to 4 degrees warmer than the natural terrain. Our second problem was to get sufficient darkness in summer to conduct night flying. With a latitude about the same as Oslo, Lossie had only about one hour of twilight in mid-summer, so we had to detach aircraft to southern airfields to reach our air training quota of night work.

One of my delights at Lossiemouth was to get back into helicopter flying, and we were certainly in helicopter country. There were boating disasters in the Moray Firth, mountain rescues in the Cairngorms, isolated farms cut off in winter by heavy snows, herds of cattle trapped in snow and requiring fodder from the air to survive – and, of course, immediate availability to help aircrew in distress through crash, ditching or ejection.

When a spare machine was available I used it to fly to our somewhat remote bombing and ground attack ranges, and carry out periodic inspections or witness the actual armament training. Occasionally

Low flying in the Blackburn Buccaneer 2 twin-jet bomber over the Scottish Highlands.

unusual demands were made on these aerial workhorses, such as when the aircraft carrier HMS *Eagle* anchored off Lossiemouth in April 1969 to give her ship's company shore leave. Unexpectedly a strong ground swell developed in the evening and prevented the picket boats from ferrying the sailors from shore to ship. They overnighted at the air station, but next day the sea conditions persisted, delaying *Eagle*'s scheduled departure, so the Lossie helicopters had to airlift 600 stranded sailors on to the carrier. This involved 120 short round trips, of which I did 30 to help out. About this time also there began to appear in our area the first North Sea oil rigs, and although they were serviced by their own civil helicopters, I made courtesy calls by helicopter to inform them of the services we could offer in emergencies.

Lossiemouth airfield was built on land requisitioned in the 1930s from the estate of the Laird of Pitgavenie, who was a colourful eccentric character, well advanced in years and well disposed to the Royal Navy. However, Lossiemouth Town Council was not so sure he owned the large grass square in front of the Town Hall, and was in session one day to discuss this when the meeting was disturbed by a loud noise outside. On rushing to the windows they were greeted by the sight of the laird, in kilt as usual, seated on a tractor ploughing a furrow diagonally across the green from one corner to the other. He had made his point – in style.

The Captain's House at Lossie was the former Drainie Manse, and was very popular with visiting admirals, politicians, and official foreign guests. Part of this popularity lay in the fact that the guest bedroom was completely furnished from the former Royal Yacht *Victoria and Albert*, and the fittings and huge bed were of solid silver. This so impressed the Mayor of Cape Town that he insisted that he and his wife be photographed in it, albeit sedately posed.

We had excellent relations with the nearby RAF station at Kinloss, although naturally some inter-service rivalry existed, particularly in the field of sport. The rugby team at RNAS Lossiemouth won the North of Scotland Brin Cup in March 1969, and were invited to have a celebratory party at Kinloss. While this was under way, some of my young officers took the opportunity in the early hours to slide off and paint all the windows of the RAF sleeping quarters matt black, which caused considerable confusion when dawn did not break as was its wont. Naturally some retaliation was expected, but none came and so we maybe relaxed prematurely. Our major Air Day was due to take place in mid-June, and Kinloss always brought in their mobile display the night before to set up next day. On the morning of the big day I was awoken by a petrified Duty Officer, who informed me that a 40ft Douglas Fir was growing out of a concrete base at the intersection of the two main runways. Since visiting aircraft were expected in three hours, the panic button was pressed, and with all hands to the pumps the situation was saved by the skin of our teeth. *Pax nobiscus!*

The year 1969 found the Fleet Air Arm absorbing the sad truth that the Labour government was hell-bent on inflicting irreparable damage on naval aviation, for it had decided to axe yet another fleet carrier after CVA 01. It was now the turn of HMS *Victorious*, which had gone into dock in 1967 for a major refit, during which it suffered a minor fire in the galley. On that flimsy excuse the ship was paid off in 1968, and was earmarked for the shipbreaker's yard.

On the 7th July I was appointed an Aide-de-Camp to HM the Queen, and just after that made a short private visit to Vice-Admiral Gert Jeschonnek, Chief of Staff of the Federal German Navy and an old friend of mine. Indeed we two and our wives had been official guests of the First Sea Lord, Admiral Sir Michael Le Fanu, at the rotating Post Office

Sea Lord, Admiral Sir Michael Le Fanu hosts a dinner at the rotating Post Office Tower, for his German counterpart Vice-Admiral Gert Jeschonnek on 27th November 1968.

Tower restaurant in London on 27th November 1968. Jeschonnek was very impressed with Admiral Le Fanu, who apparently had felt I might well be promoted out of Lossie at the end of 1969. However, I was eventually informed later in the year by Flag Officer Naval Air Command that I was likely to be retired.

This hiatus situation became clearer when I was sent for by the First Sea Lord who told me I had been earmarked to be the next Flag Officer Naval Flying Training (FONFT), but that post was to be abolished by the Minister of Defence as part of his cuts. However, the Navy would seek to have me appointed as Naval Attaché, Washington, in the rank of Rear-Admiral. A month later I was again sent for by Admiral Le Fanu and informed that the Minister had personally vetoed my appointment as he felt it would send the wrong signal to the US Navy at a time when our government was cutting back naval aviation. In the event, a paymaster captain was promoted into the job.

As some light relief from all these shenanigans, I was invited down to lunch at RNAS Yeovilton by the last incumbent FONFT, and decided to fly there in a Sea Vampire 22 trainer – which has side-by-side seating. For the flight south I took Lt Cdr Monty Mellor, an old and bold colleague of long acquaintance and then CO of Station Flight, as pilot and we changed seats for the return flight. As we approached Lossiemouth I was told that a heavy snowstorm was over the airfield and that the short runway was in use due to a strong westerly wind. Cloud base was given as 350ft and visibility 200 yards, with ground-controlled radar approach (GCA) available.

Forced landing of the Whirlwind 7 helicopter in a snow drift in hills south of Banff after the piston engine blew up – only three weeks before the author left the Navy.

The great final send-off from Lossiemouth and the Royal Navy on 12th March 1970.

I opted for a GCA rather than divert to Aberdeen. I was preparing to start my descent when Monty quietly said, 'Don't make a hash of this, sir; remember there's fifty years of flying experience in this cockpit'. This certainly had the effect of relieving any tension there might be.

My swan song at Lossiemouth was an interesting one. In the 1970 New Year Honours List I received the CBE. On 19th February I was flying a Whirlwind helicopter over the hilly area south of Banff to check if any farms were in trouble from the heavy snow that was falling, and carrying a newspaper photographer and a crewman, when with a loud bang the piston engine blew up when we were at 800ft. I immediately went into auto-rotation and looked for any flat terrain within my limited gliding range, but the snow was so deep it obliterated any ground features. However, I noticed a three-stranded wire fence and thought that if I could hook my tail skid to the wire I might make a safe arrested landing, and so it transpired. I had made a Mayday call on the way down, so we were picked up some hours later by road transport.

I left Lossie on 12th March 1970 after a great send-off by my ship's company and the town of Lossiemouth itself, to start my new job in civilian life as the Chief Executive of the recently formed British Helicopter Advisory Board. At least I would still be in the wonderful aviation world.

Aircraft Types Flown

This list includes all the aircraft flown by Eric Brown. It was produced and checked for the *Guinness Book of Records* and is comprised of 'basic' types – not marks or models, e.g. Eric Brown flew fourteen marks of Spitfire, but there is only one entry for Spitfire.

Aeronca Grasshopper
Aerospatiale Alouette
Aerospatiale Ecureuil
Aerospatiale Twin Squirrel
Agusta 109
Aichi Val
Airspeed Ambassador
Airspeed Envoy
Airspeed Horsa
Airspeed Oxford
Arado 96B
Arado 196A
Arado 199
Arado 232B
Arado 234B
Arado 240
Armstrong Whitworth Albemarle
Armstrong Whitworth Whitley
Auster Aiglet
Avro Anson
Avro Athena
Avro Lancaster
Avro Lancastrian
Avro Lincoln
Avro Manchester
Avro Shackleton
Avro Tudor
Avro Tutor
Avro York

B.A. Swallow
B.Ae 125
B.Ae 146
B.Ae Hawk

BAC Lightning
Baynes Carrier Wing
Beagle B.206
Beagle Pup
Beech Baron
Beech Bonanza
Beech Super King Air
Beech Traveller
Beechcraft Expediter
Bell AH-1 Huey
Bell 47
Bell 204
Bell 222
Bell Airacobra
Bell Airacomet
Bell HTL-5
Bell Jet Ranger
Bell King Cobra
Bell Long Ranger
Blackburn Beverley
Blackburn Botha
Blackburn Buccaneer
Blackburn Firebrand
Blackburn Firecrest
Blackburn Roc
Blackburn Shark
Blackburn Skua
Blohm & Voss 138
Blohm & Voss 141B
Blohm & Voss 222 Wiking
Boeing Fortress
Boeing Superfortress
Boeing Vertol Chinook
Boulton Paul Defiant
Boulton Paul P.108

Boulton Paul Sea Balliol
Brantly B-2
Bréguet Alizé
Bréguet Atlantic
Brewster Buffalo
Bristol Beaufighter
Bristol Beaufort
Bristol Blenheim
Bristol Bombay
Bristol Brigand
Bristol Britannia
Bristol Buckingham
Bristol Bulldog
Bristol Freighter
Bristol Sycamore
Britten-Norman Islander
Bücker Bestmann
Bücker Jungmann
Bücker Jungmeister
Bücker Student

Cant Z1007
Caprioni 309
Caprioni 311
Caprioni Ca 135 bis
Cessna 150
Cessna Cardinal
Cessna Skymaster
Cessna Skywagon
Chance-Vought Corsair
Chance-Vought Cutlass
Chilton D.W.1
Chrislea Ace
Comper Swift
Consolidated Catalina
Consolidated Liberator

Consolidated Vultee
  Privateer
Convair 240-5
Curtiss Commando
Curtiss Helldiver
Curtiss Kittyhawk
Curtiss Mohawk
Curtiss Seamew
Curtiss Tomahawk

Dassault Étendard
Dassault Mirage
Dassault Mystère
De Havilland 86B
De Havilland Beaver
De Havilland Chipmunk
De Havilland Comet
De Havilland Devon
De Havilland Don
De Havilland Flamingo
De Havilland Fox Moth
De Havilland Gipsy Moth
De Havilland Heron
De Havilland Hornet Moth
De Havilland Leopard
  Moth
De Havilland Mosquito
De Havilland Otter
De Havilland Puss Moth
De Havilland Rapide
De Havilland Sea Hornet
De Havilland Sea
  Mosquito
De Havilland Sea Vampire
De Havilland Sea Venom
De Havilland Sea Vixen
De Havilland Swallow
De Havilland Tiger Moth
De Havilland Vampire
Dewoitine 520
DFS 230
DFS Kranich
DFS Weihe
Dornier 17
Dornier 18
Dornier 24
Dornier 26

Dornier 27
Dornier 217
Dornier 335
Douglas Boston
Douglas Dakota
Douglas Dauntless
Douglas Devastator
Douglas Invader
Douglas Skymaster
Douglas Skynight
Douglas Skyraider
Druine Turbulent

Elliott Newbury Eon
Embraer Bandeirante
English Electric Canberra
Enstrom F28
Enstrom Shark
Erco Ercoupe

Fairchild Argus
Fairchild Cornell
Fairchild XNQ-1
Fairey IIIF
Fairey Albacore
Fairey Barracuda
Fairey Battle
Fairey Firefly
Fairey Fulmar
Fairey Gannet
Fairey Gordon
Fairey Primer
Fairey Seal
Fairey Spearfish
Fairey Swordfish
Fiat B.R.20
Fiat C.32
Fiat C.42
Fiat G.50
Fieseler Storch
Focke-Wulf 189
Focke-Wulf 190
Focke-Wulf 200
Focke-Wulf 58 Weihe
Focke-Wulf Ta.152
Focke-Wulf Ta.154
Folland 43/37

Fouga Magister
Fournier Milan

General Aircraft Cygnet
General Aircraft Hamilcar
General Aircraft Hotspur
General Aircraft L./56
Gloster E.28/39
Gloster Gauntlet
Gloster Gladiator
Gloster Javelin
Gloster Meteor
Gloster Sea Meteor
Gotha 244
Grumman Ag-Cat
Grumman Albatross
Grumman Avenger
Grumman Bearcat
Grumman Cougar
Grumman Goose
Grumman Guardian
Grumman Hellcat
Grumman Panther
Grumman Tigercat
Grumman Widgeon
Grumman Wildcat

Handley Page Gugnunc
Handley Page Halifax
Handley Page Hastings
Handley Page Hermes
Handley Page Marathon
Handley Page Sparrow
Hawker Fury
Hawker Hart
Hawker Hector
Hawker Henley
Hawker Hunter
Hawker Hurricane
Hawker Nimrod
Hawker Osprey
Hawker P.1040
Hawker P.1052
Hawker P.1127
Hawker Sea Fury
Hawker Sea Hawk
Hawker Siddeley 748

Hawker Siddeley Gnat
Hawker Tempest
Hawker Typhoon
Heinkel 111
Heinkel 115
Heinkel 162
Heinkel 177
Heinkel 219
Henschel 123
Henschel 129
Heston Phoenix
Hiller HTE
Hitachi T.2
Horten IV
Hughes 300
Hughes 500
Hunting Percival Jet
   Provost
Hunting Percival Provost

Ilyushin 2
Ilyushin 4

Jodel Ambassadour
Jodel Club
Jodel Excellence
Jodel Grand Tourisme
Jodel Mascaret
Jodel Mousqetaire
Junkers 52
Junkers 86
Junkers 87
Junkers 88
Junkers 188
Junkers 290
Junkers 352
Junkers 388

Kamov 26
Kawasaki Tony
Klemm 26
Klemm 35D
Klemm L25
Klemm L27

Lavochkin 7
Le Vier Cosmic Wind

Ling Temco Vought
   Crusader
Lockheed Constellation
Lockheed Electra
Lockheed Hercules
Lockheed Hudson
Lockheed Lightning
Lockheed Neptune
Lockheed Shooting Star
Lockheed Starfighter
Lockheed Ventura
Luton Minor

Macchi C.202
Macchi C.205
Martin Baker M.B.5
Martin Baltimore
Martin Marauder
MBB Bo 105
McDonnell Banshee
McDonnell Douglas
   Skyhawk
McDonnell Phantom II
Messerschmitt 108
Messerschmitt 109
Messerschmitt 110
Messerschmitt 163
Messerschmitt 262
Messerschmitt 410
MIG-3
MIG-15
Mil-1
Mil-2
Mil-4
Miles 18
Miles 20
Miles 28
Miles 38
Miles 48
Miles Aerovan
Miles Falcon
Miles Gemini
Miles Hawk
Miles Hobby
Miles Libellula
Miles Magister
Miles Martinet

Miles Master
Miles Mentor
Miles Mohawk
Miles Monarch
Miles Monitor
Miles Sparrowhawk
Mitsubishi Betty
Mitsubishi Dinah
Mitsubishi Zeke
Mooney M20
Morane-Saulnier 406
Morane-Saulnier Paris
Morane-Saulnier Rallye
Muntz Youngman-Baynes

N.S.F.K. S.G.38
Nakajima Frank
Nakajima Oscar
Nipper III
Noorduyn Norseman
Nord 262A
Nord Noralpha
Nord Piingouin
North American Harvard
North American Mitchell
North American Mustang
North American Sabre
North American Savage
North American Super
   Sabre
North American Texan
Northrop 24 Gamma
   Commercial
Northrop Black Widow
Northrop F-5

Orlikan Meta Sokol

Percival Gull
Percival Pembroke
Percival Prentice
Percival Proctor
Percival Q6
Percival Vega Gull
Petlyakov PE-2
Piaggio P.136
Piaggio P.166

Piasecki Retriever
Piel Emeraude
Pilatus Porter
Piper Apache
Piper Aztec
Piper Comanche
Piper Cub
Piper Cub Special 90
Piper Grasshopper
Piper Navajo
Piper Pawnee
Piper Seneca
Piper Supercruiser
Piper Tripacer
Piper Cherokee
Pitts Special
Polikarpov I-15
Polikarpov I-16
Portsmouth Aerocar
　Major

Reggiane 2000
Reggiane 2001
Reid & Sigrist Desford
Republic Seabee
Republic Lancer
Republic Thunderbolt
Republic Thunderjet
Republic Thunderstreak
Robin Royale
Robinson R-22
Rollason Condor
Ryan Fireball

Saab 21
Saab 29
Saab 105
Saab Lansen
Saab Safir
Saunders-Roe P.531
Saunders-Roe Skeeter
Saunders-Roe S.R./A.1
Savoia-Marchetti SM79
Savoia-Marchetti SM82
Savoia-Marchetti SM95
Scheibe Motorspatz
Schmetz Olympia-Meise

Schneider Baby Grunau
Scottish Aviation Bulldog
Scottish Aviation Pioneer
Scottish Aviation Twin
　Pioneer
Short S.31
Short Sealand
Short Skyvan
Short Stirling
Short Sturgeon
SIAI-Marchetti S.F.260
Siebel 204
Sikorsky HRS
Sikorsky R-4B Hoverfly
Sikorsky R-6A Hoverfly II
Sikorsky S-58T
Sikorsky S-61
Sikorsky S-76
Sipa S.903
Slingsby Capstan
Slingsby Kirby Cadet
Slingsby Motor Tutor
Slingsby Prefect
Slingsby Swallow
Slingsby T.21
Slingsby T.31
Socata Diplomate
Stampe et Vertongen
　SV-4
Stearman Caydet
Stinson Junior R
Stinson Reliant
Stinson Sentinel
Sud-Aviation Djinn
Supermarine Attacker
Supermarine S.24/37
Supermarine Scimitar
Supermarine Sea Otter
Supermarine Seafang
Supermarine Seafire
Supermarine Seagull
Supermarine Spiteful
Supermarine Spitfire
Supermarine Walrus
SZD Bocian

Taylorcraft Auster

Taylor J.T.1 Monoplane
Taylor J.T.2 Titch
Thruxton Jackaroo
Tipsy S.2
Tipsy Trainer
Tipsy Type B

Vertol 107
Vickers Valiant
Vickers Vanguard
Vickers VC10
Vickers Viking
Vickers Viscount
Vickers Warwick
Vickers Wellington
Vickers Windsor
Vought-Sikorsky
　Chesapeake
Vought-Sikorsky
　Kingfisher
Vultee Vengeance

Waco CG-3
Waco Hadrian
Westland Aerospatiale
　Gazelle
Westland Aerospatiale
　Lynx
Westland Lysander
Westland Sikorsky S-51
　Dragonfly
Westland Sikorsky S-55
　Whirlwind
Westland Wasp
Westland Welkin
Westland Wessex
Westland Whirlwind
Westland Wyvern
Winter Zaunkönig

Yakovlev-1
Yakovlev-9
Yakovlev-11
Youngman-Baynes
　High Lift

Zlin Akrobat

Phantom Carrier

Captain Brown, while Deputy Director, Naval Air Warfare (1961–4), was
responsible for the design of many of the operational features of the CVA 01.
This article was published in the US Naval Institute Proceedings in 1967.

CVA 01 was the designation given to the new aircraft carrier for the Royal
Navy which was authorized for design studies by the Conservative
Government in July of 1963. This decision had been reached after a series
of the most searching studies into the validity of the concept of the air-
craft carrier as a limited war vehicle. Inevitably, there were arguments
over size, cost effectiveness, vulnerability, and detectability of such a ship.
In 1966, however, the then Labour Government decided to cancel the
CVA 01, largely as a measure to reduce soaring national defence costs.

The CVA 01 was designed with the long-term objective of being able
to handle any aircraft likely to serve with the Fleet Air Arm in the 1970s
and 1980s. Thus, considerable crystal gazing was called for. As a basic
criterion, a take-off weight of 70,000 pounds was set as the upper limit.

The Admiralty's Directorate of Naval Air Warfare (DNAW) was responsible for the carrier's flight deck layout, the feature which essentially gives
any carrier her individuality, and in this respect CVA 01 was going to be
something new. This DNAW Future Planning Section consisted of operational aviators, test pilots, and an aviation engineer. In addition, a Work
Study Group of non-aviators, attached to the Department of the Director
General-Ships, was responsible for incorporating the proposals of the
Planning Section in the overall ship design.

It has always been the obvious ideal to have parallel and separate lanes
for landing, for take-off, and for parking, but somehow over the past 20
years there seems to have grown up a reluctance amongst carrier designers to pursue this ideal. Contentment seems to have set in with the advent
of the partial benefits obtained by the angled deck. This latter idea has
been an eminently successful development, but it has had two major
drawbacks: First, the angled-deck layout isolates, on the port quarter, a
deck area of considerable dimensions which is virtually unusable during

landing operations. Such real estate on a flight deck is much too valuable to be wasted, and the parallel deck design removes this area from the port to the starboard quarter where it can be fully used. Second, during landing in conditions of low cloud or poor visibility, the pilot's first view of the deck occurs very late, so that with the high approach speeds of modern aircraft he has little or no time to make a correction in line. Errors in lining up with the centre line of the angled deck are numerous and often led to accidents or missed approaches, particularly at night.

Interrogation of a cross section of naval pilots confirmed that the first thing a pilot sees on making a carrier approach in bad weather is the ship's wake, which is considerable from such a ship doing 30 knots, and at night is usually brilliantly phosphorescent. However, the wake coincides with the centre line of the ship, but not that of the angled deck, so is of no use as a line-up datum. With a landing lane parallel to the centre line of the ship the wake is a useful line-up reference.

Subsequent examination by the Work Study Group showed that a truly parallel deck was impossible within the 184-foot width limitation of the flight deck. However, the angle required to be put on the parallel deck was cut down to the negligible one of 2¾ degrees (compared to an angle of about 10 degrees in *Forrestal*-class carriers[1]), so that the objective was virtually achieved.

On landing aboard the CVA 01 an aircraft would fold its wings and turn out of the arrester wires to an arming and refuelling park on the starboard side aft. Then, the aircraft would return forward to the catapult launch position. This would mean a counter-clockwise traffic circulation of taxiing aircraft in the parking lane, but the problem was how to define the taxi paths to allow two aircraft to pass safely in opposite directions. The solution was to position the island 34 feet inboard on the starboard side, so that there would be a solid interspace as in highways, with aircraft going aft being on the inboard side and those going forward on the outboard side. Flight deck vehicles, such as tractors, would be parked in tunnels through the island structure at flight deck level.

The 200-foot long and 18-foot wide island shape and position (420 feet from the bow) was the subject of extensive wind-flow tests to ensure an optimum position, which was found to be farther aft than anticipated.

[1] The US Navy's nuclear-powered aircraft carriers with angled decks, steam catapults and mirror landing sight.

Although the ship's after lift was to be of the normal deck-edge variety, British and US experience had convinced us that a forward deck-edge lift took too much of a beating in heavy seas, hence it was decided to replace it with a lift set slightly off the ship's centre line. Of course, three lifts are always better than two, but the penalty in hangar space for a second internal lift was too great in a carrier of the size of CVA 01 with a 660-by-80-foot hangar. The position of the forward lift was such that it could be operated while the starboard catapult was being used with the jet blast deflectors raised.

Although not a flight deck feature, the ship's quarterdeck run-up position is directly connected with flight deck operations. Formerly, an engine change or fault in an aircraft had always necessitated a run-up on the flight deck during a lull in flying operations. Since the repair had usually been made in a quiet corner of the hangar, it meant a major hangar shuffle to get the aircraft on to a lift and all this within a time limited to a gap in flying operations. Once on the flight deck the aircraft had to be tied down and then run-up, much to the annoyance of all for it usually means a prolonged period at full power with the attendant thunderous noise. Finally, if an adjustment was still found necessary, it was back to the hangar and a complete repeat of this upheaval at some future time. All these disadvantages could be removed in the CVA 01 by rolling the aircraft straight out of its quiet corner of the hangar on to an open platform at the stern of the carrier where it can be run up with its tail pointing aft (and usually downwind) and adjustments made *ad infinitum* without interfering with flying operations. This was an extension in idea of the fantail engine run-up stand the author had seen on the USS *Enterprise* (CVAN-65). From a point of view of space, it is unlikely that the above feature could have been incorporated except that it had been proposed to fit a Seadart ship-to-air missile system installation aft, and it and its magazine would only use up half of the available quarterdeck space. The Seadart system, incidentally, was only fitted to give a final self-defence capability against attacking aircraft in the event of any breaking through the outer defence ring provided by the carrier's escorts. Missile systems in the target ship are twice as effective as those on the screen, so this was deemed a sensible, seaman-like precaution. The position of the Seadart system was chosen to give the best all-around field of fire without encroaching on flight deck space.

This after missile position did mean that the flight deck ramp was forward of the quarterdeck and that an aircraft falling short on landing could make a nasty mess on top of the missile system. Extensive research of accident records showed that since the introduction of the mirror landing system, and with the four arresting wires positioned well up the flight deck, we had no case of a stern crash with the aircraft falling short of the flight deck. The airflow in this region was also checked by wind tunnel tests to ensure there was no turbulence to affect approaching aircraft.

This confidence in the survival of the Seadart installation was not the reason for having only one; that factor was a matter of keeping below a limited financial ceiling.

Another innovation planned for the CVA 01 was the arresting gear. The Royal Aircraft Establishment at Bedford had developed an arresting gear working on the water spray principle for emergency use at airfields. This gear had shown itself to possess tremendous entry speed development potential and to be about one-third of the weight and one-half of the cost of any existing arresting gear. The proposal was made to adapt this to shipboard use, where its unusual characteristic of providing a constant arresting wire pull-out distance for any entry speed or landing weight within the gear's operating envelope would simplify and speed up landing operations since the flight deck controllers and handlers could be precisely pre-positioned for assisting the aircraft to turn out of the wires.

Two steam catapults of 250-foot stroke were to be fitted, one on the starboard side of the take-off lane and one on the port side of the landing lane. These were to be the first catapults of this length fitted in a British carrier. Ideally, they should both have been fitted in the take-off lane, but the length of stroke was such that a catapult on the port side of the take-off lane would have encroached severely on accommodation and hangar space in a 53,000-ton ship.

The area on the starboard quarter recovered by use of the parallel deck concept was to be an operating platform for a Sea King SH-3D antisubmarine helicopter or a smaller rescue helicopter.

Besides red or possibly white floodlighting, CVA 01 would have been fitted with the revolutionary new Bedford Lighting Pattern, developed by Bedford, and now being introduced aboard current British carriers. Its main feature is the remarkable reduction in the number of flight deck lights for an increase in attitude reference data.

A new carrier-controlled approach system was to be developed in time for installation in CVA 01, with retrofit planned in other British carriers. Basically, it was to be a much less sophisticated system than the US Navy's SPN-10 as it was felt that the low percentage occurrence of a 200-foot ceiling and half-mile visibility minimum did not justify a high-cost and high-complexity system, especially as such weather conditions usually coincided with a sea state which would in itself restrict flying operations.

Two inertial navigation systems were to be fitted in the CVA 01, as her aircraft would almost certainly use a similar navigation system and so require data from the ship's system as the master reference.

It is perhaps ironical that it was the Royal Navy's intention that CVA 01 would start life as a Phantom carrier, but in an operational sense. The ultra-supersonic F-4K Phantom II all-weather fighter together with the Buccaneer Mk.2 low-level strike aircraft were to comprise her main force on commissioning in 1972–1973. In addition, she was to carry airborne early warning aircraft, SH-3D Sea King ASW helicopters, and utility helicopters.

The actual numbers of aircraft that CVA 01 was to carry cannot be revealed. Two-thirds of the total aircraft complement could be housed in the hangar and two-thirds on the flight deck. The space for the 'extra third' was to be available for a reinforcing squadron of either carrier aircraft or land-based aircraft such as the V/STOL Kestrel (P.1127) strike-fighter.

The essential statistics for the CVA 01 hull design came from the Royal Navy's Director General-Ships. These included a displacement of 53,000 tons with an overall hull length of some 900 feet and an extreme flight deck width of 184 feet.

Design speed for the carrier was 28 knots while 'deep and dirty'. This was to be achieved on three shafts driven by oil-fired steam turbines. Three shafts were chosen because they offer a better margin for battle damage than do two and require less space and manpower than do four shafts.

The complement was to be 3,200 officers and enlisted men, accommodated in fully air-conditioned quarters.

On the premise that every ton displacement would cost £1,000, the basic cost was going to approximate £53 million and probably nearer £60 million. Building time was to be 5½ years.

This, then, was to have been the CVA 01 ... a ship that would have offered many contributions to the advancement of carrier aviation and to British naval strength.

German Aeronautical Scientists

This photograph was taken at Farnborough Court in 1947.
Pictured are some of Germany's most famous aeronautical scientists,
all of whom volunteered to work for the RAE at the end of the War.

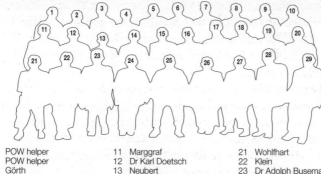

1 POW helper	11 Marggraf	21 Wohlfhart
2 POW helper	12 Dr Karl Doetsch	22 Klein
3 Görth	13 Neubert	23 Dr Adolph Busemann
4 Emte	14 Hilpert	24 Dr Tolmien
5 Jordan	15 Hahnemann	25 Mr Allum (administrator)
6 Sissingh	16 Professor M. Winter	26 E. Schmidt
7 Dr Dietrich Küchemann	17 Professor H. Multhopp	27 Brenner
8 POW helper	18 Havemann	28 Schlichting
9 POW helper	19 Korbacher	29 Eggersglüß
10 POW helper	20 Eggink	

Doetsch and Küchemann were graded as 'German Scientists 1' and soon received permission to recruit one
assistant each (without dependants) from Germany as at that time they were not allowed to supervise anyone
British. That is how after a year Ing. W. Pinsker came to join Doetsch and Dr Johanna Weber joined Küchemann.

Index